# Individual Rights and the Making of the International System

We live today in the first global system of sovereign states in history, encompassing all of the world's polities, peoples, religions and civilizations. Christian Reus-Smit presents a new account of how this system came to be, one in which struggles for individual rights play a central role. The international system expanded from its original European core in five great waves, each involving the fragmentation of one or more empires into a host of successor sovereign states. In the most important, associated with the Westphalian settlement, the independence of Latin America, and post-1945 decolonization, the mobilization of new ideas about individual rights challenged imperial legitimacy, and when empires failed to recognize these new rights, subject peoples sought sovereign independence. Combining theoretical innovation with detailed historical case-studies, this book advances a new understanding of human rights and world politics, with individual rights deeply implicated in the making of the global sovereign order.

CHRISTIAN REUS-SMIT is a Fellow of the Academy of the Social Sciences in Australia and Professor of International Relations at the University of Queensland. Among his previous books, he is author of *American Power and World Order* (2004) and *The Moral Purpose of the State* (1999); co-author of *Special Responsibilities: Global Problems and American Power* (2012); and editor of *The Politics of International Law* (2004).

# Individual Rights and the Making of the International System

CHRISTIAN REUS-SMIT

CAMBRIDGE
UNIVERSITY PRESS

# CAMBRIDGE
## UNIVERSITY PRESS

Shaftesbury Road, Cambridge CB2 8EA, United Kingdom

One Liberty Plaza, 20th Floor, New York, NY 10006, USA

477 Williamstown Road, Port Melbourne, VIC 3207, Australia

314–321, 3rd Floor, Plot 3, Splendor Forum, Jasola District Centre, New Delhi – 110025, India

103 Penang Road, #05–06/07, Visioncrest Commercial, Singapore 238467

Cambridge University Press is part of Cambridge University Press & Assessment, a department of the University of Cambridge.

We share the University's mission to contribute to society through the pursuit of education, learning and research at the highest international levels of excellence.

www.cambridge.org
Information on this title: www.cambridge.org/9780521674485

First published 2013

*A catalogue record for this publication is available from the British Library*

*Library of Congress Cataloging-in-Publication data*
Reus-Smit, Christian, 1961–
Individual rights and the making of the international system / Christian Reus-Smit.
   pages   cm
Includes bibliographical references and index.
ISBN 978-0-521-85777-2 (hardback)
1. Civil rights – History.   2. Human rights – History.   3. Sovereignty – History.
I. Title.
K3240.R485   2013
341.4′809 – dc23      2013012166

ISBN    978-0-521-85777-2    Hardback
ISBN    978-0-521-67448-5    Paperback

*For*

丽俐

*Lili*
*Beautiful and bright by name, beautiful and bright by nature*

# Contents

# Preface

This book is the product of two converging interests. The first is my longstanding interest in the nature and development of international systems, particularly our present global system. Indeed, it is the *global* nature of this system that I have recently found especially intriguing. How did such an utterly unique political order come to be? The second is my interest in the politics of human rights and my frustration with how this politics is conventionally narrated. The overwhelming tendency is to tell a twentieth-century story, as though the rights of individuals had little impact on world politics prior to this. At the very least, events such as the American and French revolutions render these narrations curious. Either the revolutions had nothing to do with world politics, or they had nothing to do with individual rights, both of which seem odd propositions. It was in pursuit of these interests that I happened upon the historical convergences that occupy center stage in the following chapters; namely, the relationship between struggles over individual rights, the fragmentation of empires, and the expansion of the international system.

Understanding these convergences has not been an easy task, and it may well be that this book is but another step in my own reflections on the subject. But to the extent that it is *a* culmination of my struggles, however temporary it might be, I must declare my thanks to the many individuals and institutions who have helped me along the way. My first debt is to my friends and intellectual companions who through our many conversations have helped me wrestle with the issue and fine-tune the argument. I am especially indebted here to Emanuel Adler, Mlada Bukovansky, Peter Christoff, Ian Clark, Tim Dunne, Richard Devetak, Robyn Eckersley, Greg Fry, Paul Keal, Jacinta O'Hagan, Andrew Phillips, Richard Price, Heather Rae, Henry Shue, and Nicholas Wheeler.

From its earliest incarnations I have taken this project on the road, airing its evolving arguments and gathering feedback from all who would listen. I thus wish to thank audiences at the following institutions where I presented seminars and lectures: University of Aberystwyth; Australian National University; University of California, Berkeley; Bielefeld University; University of Bremen; Danish Institute of International Studies, Copenhagen; European University Institute; Goethe University of Frankfurt; Graduate Institute of International and Development Studies, Geneva; London School of Economics; University of Oxford; University of Queensland; School of Oriental and African Studies; Sciences Po, Paris; and University of Sydney.

The research and writing of this book would not have been possible without the generous financial support provided by a variety of institutions. Early work was supported by a three-year Discovery Grant from the Australian Research Council, and by funds provided by the Department of International Relations at the Australian National University. The broad contours of the argument were hammered out in the peace and quiet afforded by the award of a Fernand Braudel Senior Fellowship at the European University Institute (EUI) in the academic year 2008–9. The final preparation of the manuscript took place during my tenure in the Chair in International Relations at the EUI, and I thank the Department of Social and Political Sciences for both its financial support and for providing such a collegial environment in which to discuss and reflect. I am particularly grateful to the late Professor Peter Mair who appointed me to both the Braudel Fellowship and the Chair in IR. He never wavered in his support for my work, and I, like all of those who knew him, mourn his passing deeply.

While at the EUI I was fortunate to teach a doctoral seminar on rights in world politics, and later with Rainer Baubock one on rights in political theory and international relations. These were immensely stimulating classes, and I thank Rainer and participating graduate students for discussions that have greatly influenced my thinking on these issues. These classes were testimony to the fact that research and the teaching of smart, engaged students can be more than complementary; they can be mutually enriching.

During the course of the project, I benefited from the hard work of a number of research assistants, all of whom put their shoulders to the wheel with enthusiasm and skill. My thanks go to Lacy Davey, Gilberto Estrada Harris, Nicole George, Patrick Herron, Lynn Savery, and Andrea Warnecke. Gilberto needs special thanks for translating a number of key documents on Spanish-American independence.

Earlier rehearsals of parts of the argument were published in a number of journals and edited collections, and I thank their publishers for permission to draw on these works. See 'Human rights and the social construction of sovereignty', *Review of International Studies*, 27.4 (2001), 519–38; 'Reading history through constructivist eyes', *Millennium: Journal of International Studies*, 37.2 (2008), 395–414; 'On rights and institutions', in Charles R. Beitz and Robert E. Goodin (eds.), *Global Basic Rights* (Oxford University Press, 2009), pp. 25–48; 'Struggles for individual rights and the expansion of the international system', *International Organization*, 65.2 (2001), 207–42; and 'Human rights in a global ecumene', *International Affairs*, 87.5 (2011), 1205–18. Feedback from the editors and referees of these journals and books played an invaluable role in helping me to sharpen and refine my ideas and central claims, and I thank all of them for their engagement with the project.

Finally, my biggest thanks go to Heather, Lili and Sam, my fellow adventurers in life. In both Canberra and Florence my study has been open to the hustle and bustle of family life; in fact, Lili and Sam have just parried past my desk sword-fighting, followed by our young but horse-like dog, Manuel the giant Weimaraner. They have thus been 'around' this project for its entire gestation, and I would not have had it any other way. Heather's and my conversations about this and other aspects of world politics have been a major influence on my thinking, and without her love and support I might have dropped the whole thing somewhere in the middle of the Reformation. Sam and Lili have also given me lots of love and encouragement, but they have worked their influence through a combination of delightful distraction and surprising engagement with 'Dad's book about human rights'.

Chris Reus-Smit
Villa Mirabello, Fiesole

# Introduction

When we think about the relationship between individual rights and international relations we do so in a particular way. We focus on the system of sovereign states, the world of territorially demarcated political units, forged through often violent struggles for political power. We then ask whether the contemporary human rights regime has had any effect on this system; whether it has impacted, in any significant fashion, upon the internal and external conduct of states. For some the answer is positive. Yes, the rules and norms that comprise the regime have been critical resources in struggles to protect individuals from the predations of states, struggles that have yielded significant political change in regions as diverse as Eastern Europe and Latin America.[1] Others are more skeptical, though. The principles that comprise the human rights regime are noble aspirations, but remain marginal to the cut and thrust of real-world politics. Human rights matter when powerful states say they do.[2] Different as these positions are, they start from a common set of assumptions; that the system of sovereign states is a political formation born of war-fighting, economic competition, and narrowly conceived self-interest, and that the politics of rights is pushing, more or less successfully, against the grain of the system's most basic dynamics and constitutive forces.

This book advances a different perspective. Nowhere do I deny that the contemporary international human rights regime seeks to 'civilize' an international system still marred by egregious human rights violations, or that the system is very much the product of recurring struggles for political power. My central claim is, though, that the importance of individual rights is not confined to the efficacy, or lack thereof, of the contemporary human rights regime. Struggles for the recognition

[1] Thomas Risse, Stephen Ropp, and Kathryn Sikkink (eds.), *The Power of Human Rights* (Cambridge University Press, 1999).
[2] Jack L. Goldsmith and Eric A. Posner, *The Limits of International Law* (Oxford University Press, 2005).

1

and protection of individual rights, I shall argue, have played a significant role in the historical development of the international system
itself. We live in the world's first global system of states: no polities or
peoples lie outside its reach; it is multiregional, encompassing Europe,
Africa, the Asia-Pacific, and the Americas; and it is multicultural. Five
centuries ago the system was very different; its emergent states were
confined to Europe and contained within the cultural bounds of Latin
Christendom. Only after a series of great expansions did the system
globalize, and struggles for individual rights played a key role in this
process.

The system's expansion from its original European kernel to 'blan-
ket the Earth' is, as David Armitage rightly observes, 'one of the most
overlooked effects of globalization'.[3] Few decades have passed since
the system first emerged without a new state celebrating its independence, the most recent being the Republic of South Sudan. Most of
the expansion occurred, however, in five great waves, moments when
empires collapsed producing not a handful of new sovereign states,
but a host. The first accompanied the Peace of Westphalia in 1648,
the second came with the independence of Latin America between
1810 and 1825, the third was a product of the Versailles settlement in
1919, the fourth resulted from post-1945 decolonization; and the fifth
was a consequence of the collapse of the Soviet Union and the former
Yugoslav Federation. Of these, the Westphalian, Latin American, and
post-1945 waves had the greatest impact on the system's globalization.
Not only did they produce most of today's sovereign states, they gave
the system its principal regions: Europe, then the Americas, and in the
twentieth century, Asia, Africa, and the Pacific. Were it not for these
great waves of systemic expansion, much of what preoccupies students
of world politics today simply would not be topics of concern, at least
in their present guise – the world of regions, the clash of civilizations,
the rise of non-Western centers of power, the problem of failed states,
the dilemmas of intervention, to note but a few examples.

The global nature of today's international system is assumed by
most International Relations scholars, and the expansionary processes
that produced it attract only marginal attention. The vast majority
of work in the field assumes the system's existence and focuses on

---

[3] David Armitage, *The Declaration of Independence: A Global History*
(Cambridge, MA: Harvard University Press, 2007), p. 105.

its internal political dynamics. Even when scholars want to understand change, most focus on what Robert Gilpin termed 'systemic'
change – change within an already existing international system.[4] Realists focus on shifts in the distribution of material capabilities, liberals
on international institutional developments and how shifts in domestic regime type affect international political dynamics, constructivists
on the development of norms and changing meaning systems, and so
on. Even those who consider how the present international system
first emerged (what Gilpin called 'systems' change) largely ignore its
globalization. The victory of the sovereign state over preceding heteronomous forms of political organization is told as though it were a
play with one act, the Westphalian moment.

There are, of course, scholars who have examined the system's
expansion, in particular the collapse of empires into sovereign states.
Yet, as Chapter 1 explains, none of their arguments adequately account
for the principal waves of systemic expansion. Realists emphasize great
power rivalry and imperial weakness, but great powers have often been
ambivalent supporters of independence movements in rivals' empires,
fragmentary dynamics have at times emerged in empires at moments
of relative strength, and in some cases colonial peoples in perilously
weak empires only belatedly chose the road to sovereign independence. World-systems theorists emphasize structural changes in the
world economy, claiming that decolonization is more likely under
conditions of economic hegemony and global economic expansion.
Neither of these consistently coincide with waves of systemic expansion, however. Economic hegemony and global economic expansion
correlate with post-1945 decolonization, but not with the independence of Latin America, for example. Scholars of the 'English School'
stress the gradual incorporation of polities into a rule-governed society of sovereign states, with Western powers defining and codifying
that society's membership rules and non-Western peoples coming to
embrace them, and their attendant practices, as their own. Yet this
model fits none of the major waves of expansion, ignoring, among
other things, the intense political struggles that attended these waves.
Sociological institutionalists argue that world society's modernist culture encouraged the spread of states by transmitting the nation-state

---

[4] Robert Gilpin, *War and Change in World Politics* (Cambridge University Press,
1981).

model from imperial powers to their dependencies, and by allowing diffusion of decolonization by example. They fail to explain, however, why subject peoples developed an interest in institutional change in the first place, and as we shall see, the sovereign state model did not 'diffuse' in the simple manner they suggest.

Diverse as these accounts are, they all lack one thing, a coherent account of the demand for sovereignty, of the reasons subject peoples had for escaping empire and embracing the sovereign state as the institutional alternative. Big material and cultural structures are posited, hegemons, empires, and great powers are ascribed interests (often read off the purported imperatives of the structures), and subject peoples are either written out of the story or cast as passive recipients and enactors of world cultural or international societal norms.

This book provides one account of this neglected demand for sovereignty. I begin in Chapter 2 with an argument about the nature of empires as distinctive forms of rule. Empires are hierarchies in which a metropole exercises political control over peripheral polities. Metropolitan control rests in part on material capacities – guns and money – but also on legitimacy, on the degree to which subject peoples accept imperial hierarchy as right, correct, or appropriate. In this sense, empires are what Weber termed systems of imperative control; they rest not merely on coercion and physical force, but also on voluntary submission. The principal challenge of imperative control within empires is sustaining the legitimacy of the prevailing hierarchical order, an order in which social and political powers are distributed unequally between metropolitan and peripheral peoples and polities. While such legitimacy is sustained in part by the discursive practices of imperial elites and their peripheral counterparts, it is also sustained by institutional structures, the norms of which naturalize imperial hierarchy, making the unequal distribution of social and political powers appear both normal and rightful. The empires that concern us here – the Holy Roman, the Spanish, and Europe's great nineteenth- and twentieth-century empires – developed idiosyncratic institutional structures. But these were variations of a generic institutional form. Each empire rested on a regime of unequal entitlements; individual elites and subjects enjoyed different social and political powers, grounded in particular transactions and relationships, and these powers were understood as socially sanctioned entitlements, often codified in law.

In their twilight years the Holy Roman Empire, the Spanish Empire, and Europe's nineteenth- and twentieth-century empires all suffered severe crises of legitimacy. Political systems experience such crises when support among those subject to their rule collapses, forcing elites to engage in either practices of relegitimation or coercion.[5] In each empire, imperial legitimacy eroded as the prevailing regime of unequal entitlements came under challenge. New, distinctly modern ideas about individual rights took root in each context, and as they spread, were interpreted, reconstituted, and embraced as legitimate, subject peoples reimagined themselves as moral and political agents, developed new political interests in the recognition and protection of their rights, challenged established regimes of entitlements, and sought institutional change. In each case, they tried first to reform imperial institutions, but when these systems proved incapable of accommodating their rights claims, subject peoples turned from 'voice' to 'exit'.[6] Without exception it was the sovereign state they turned to as the institutional alternative to empire. This is partly because centralized, territorially bounded political units promised the universal regime of law needed to recognize and protect the new individual rights. It is also because they promised protection from the kind of transnational authorities subject peoples were escaping. But in addition to this, over time the sovereign state came to be seen as the only other game in town. This is not to say, however, that sovereignty norms simply diffused, passively internalized by subject peoples. In each wave of expansion, gaining sovereignty meant fighting not only the empire in question, but in some cases prevailing conceptions of legitimate statehood, and almost always the notion that sovereignty was a privilege of the 'civilized'. Through their struggles, subjects peoples helped transform the norms they embraced.

The traditional entitlements that cemented imperial hierarchy were 'special', in the sense that they arose out of special transactions between individuals or out of special relationships in which they stood.[7] They were also differential; they were allocated to individuals unequally,

[5] Christian Reus-Smit, 'International crises of legitimacy', *International Politics*, 44.2–3 (2007), 166–7.
[6] On this terminology, see Albert O. Hirschman, *Exit, Voice, and Loyalty* (Cambridge MA: Harvard University Press, 1970).
[7] H. L. A. Hart, 'Are there any natural rights?' in Jeremy Waldron (ed.), *Theories of Rights* (Oxford University Press, 1984), p. 84.

on the basis of social role, position, or status. The individual rights that animated struggles for imperial change differed markedly from these older entitlements. They were 'general' not special; individuals had them not because of particular transactions or relationships, but because they were thought to constitute integral moral beings. Furthermore, the new rights were equal not differential; everyone considered an integral moral being held them without distinction. Each of the rights discussed in following chapters had these characteristics, but in different imperial contexts different rights were operative. While problematic in several respects, the classic distinction between negative and positive rights is useful here. In the crisis that befell the Holy Roman Empire, a negative right – the right to liberty of religious conscience – was key. In the Spanish Empire's crisis, a positive right – the right to equal political representation – was critical. And in the crisis of Europe's nineteenth- and twentieth-century empires, a bundle of negative and positive civil and political rights was at work.

These new rights not only varied substantially, in terms of what they were rights 'to', but also regarding their 'zone of application'. In the twentieth century we became accustomed to thinking of individual rights and human rights as synonymous – individuals have certain rights because they are moral beings with certain capacities that need protecting or satisfying, and since all human beings (regardless of class, sex, or race) have these qualities, individual and human rights are taken to be one and the same thing. Yet for most of the political history of individual rights, no such association has existed. Individuals have repeatedly asserted rights on the grounds that they are fully developed moral and political agents while simultaneously denying such status and rights to other human beings. As we shall see, Protestants struggled for liberty of religious conscience while denying the same to Jews, Muslims, atheists, and various heretical sects. Similarly, Creoles (Spanish Americans of European descent) struggled for equal political representation within the Spanish Empire for themselves, Indians, and freed slaves, but not for women or slaves. Only in the last of our three cases, post-1945 decolonization, did the perceived 'zone of application' of rights come to encompass all human beings, irrespective of race, religion, gender, or civilization. At this point, and at this point alone, is it reasonable to speak of the individual rights that concern us as 'human rights'. From this perspective, the last century of human rights politics is but the most recent phase of a longer, more variegated history of individual rights in world politics.

My engagement with this history begins with the long century of religious conflict that culminated in the Westphalian settlement of 1648. A veritable industry of scholarship now surrounds this 'Peace', with scholars divided over both its causes and significance. I cut into the story from a different angle to most, however, leading me to a different understanding of what the settlement 'did'. Chapter 3 reaches back well before 1618 and the start of the Thirty Years' War, back to the first decades of the sixteenth century and the origins of the Protestant Reformation. It is here that we find the ideas that sparked a century of religious conflict, that stymied repeated efforts to resolve these conflicts, and that, in the end, the Peace of Westphalia recognized and accommodated, undercutting the Holy Roman Empire and seeding a nascent system of sovereign states.

Contained within Reformation theology was a conception of individuals as integral moral agents, whose capacities for faith gave them unmediated access to the grace of God, and through this, salvation. For Protestant intellectuals, it was this moral individualism that distinguished Protestantism from Catholicism. And because individuals could gain salvation through faith alone, freedom of religious belief was considered a fundamental entitlement. It was these ideas that fueled the conflicts that engulfed the Holy Roman Empire, challenging as they did the Roman Church's role in mediating the individual's relationship with God, and the empire's status as the guardian of Latin Christendom. More than this, they repeatedly proved key stumbling blocks to the peaceful resolution of these conflicts. Seeking to reunite Latin Christendom, Charles V convened the two Diets of Regensburg (1541 and 1546), but both foundered on the issue of 'justification', on how individuals gained salvation. Was it through faith alone, or did the Catholic Church play a mediating role? The Diet's failure produced a decade of war, temporarily resolved by the Peace of Augsburg (1555). Reuniting Latin Christendom was no longer an option; instead, Augsburg imposed a highly unstable form of statist pluralism, founded on the principle of *cuius regio, euis religio* (whose rule, his religion). While the treaty recognized the fact of religious diversity within the empire (or more correctly, the existence of Catholics and Lutherans), it granted liberty of religious conscience to only a few individuals – the lay princes of the empire. Individuals, more broadly, had no such liberty; they had to embrace the religion of their prince, or leave his territory. Not surprisingly, the settlement soon collapsed, its pluralism challenged by the Counter-Reformation, its statism by persecuted Protestants and Catholics. It would be almost another century before the Treaties of Westphalia brought a lasting settlement to Europe's religious wars. They succeeded where Augsburg failed because they did two things that together addressed the central issue of liberty of religious conscience. They licensed the creation of a host of confessionally independent states, endowing them with the political rights we now associate with sovereignty. They 'compromised' this sovereignty, however, by granting individuals freedom of religious conscience. Protestants living in Catholic states and vice versa were to 'be patiently suffered and tolerated', and princes who changed their religion, or acquired regions of a different religion, could not require their subjects to convert (a right they enjoyed under the Peace of Augsburg).

The second wave of systemic expansion occurred with the collapse of Spain's empire in the Americas (1810 to 1825). As Chapter 4 explains, the collapse was precipitated by Napoleon's usurpation of the Spanish crown in 1808, an event that provoked insurgencies across the empire. On both the Iberian Peninsula and in the Americas, Spanish subjects interpreted the crisis through the lens of traditional Spanish theories of sovereignty. Sovereignty was ordained by God, but it was granted first to the people, who then invested authority in the monarch. With the usurpation, Spain was left without a legitimate monarch, thus returning sovereignty to the people. This begged two crucial questions, though; questions that would divide the empire: Who were the people? And how should they be represented politically? On the first of these, 'Peninsulares' and Spanish Americans disagreed fundamentally. For the former, the empire was one, a single people, a single kingdom. For the latter, the empire comprised several peoples and kingdoms (a claim they justified with reference to the original papal grant of the Indies to the crowns of Castile and Leon). This did not, however, amount to a claim for independence. The reformers, who were at first ascendant, wanted the empire preserved, but only if Spanish Americans were equally represented within reformed political institutions. It was on this issue, however, that Peninsulares and Spanish Americans divided irrevocably. Their divisions came to the fore in the negotiations leading to the 1812 Spanish Constitution, which took place at the insurgent General Cortes (or parliament) convened in Cádiz between

1810 and 1814. The Cortes was dominated by liberals, from both the peninsula and the Americas, and there was broad agreement that it was individuals who merited political representation, not the traditional estates or corporate bodies. They disagreed, however, over who among the many inhabitants of the empire constituted 'individuals' – fully rational moral beings – deserving the right of political representation. For the Spanish Americans, Creoles, Indians, and freed slaves had such a right, but for the Peninsulares, only those of Spanish blood qualified. As we shall see, passionately as the Americans argued, they were repeatedly outvoted by their peninsular counterparts, the net result being the 1812 Constitution that, despite its otherwise liberal characteristics, systematically discriminated against non-Creoles. It was this failure to gain equal political representation within a reformed empire that radicalized the Spanish-American insurgencies, empowering the revolutionaries and turning the reformers from 'voice' to 'exit'.

Our final case is that of post-1945 decolonization, the fourth great wave of systemic expansion. My argument here runs counter to the widespread denial that decolonization had anything to do with human rights,[8] and to the longstanding view that colonial and postcolonial peoples have consistently prioritized social and economic rights, as well as group rights, over the civil and political rights of individuals. This wave differs from the previous two, as not one but several empires imploded simultaneously, replaced by multiple sovereign states. And where particular empires fell into crisis in previous cases, after 1945 the institution of empire itself was under challenge. In the Westphalian and Spanish-American cases, new ideas about individual rights motivated and justified struggles for imperial reform and, in the end, revolutionary change. As we shall see in Chapter 5, similar dynamics were at work in a number of twentieth-century imperial settings. The weight of my argument rests, however, on the role that rights politics played at the international level, in the delegitimation of empire as an institutional form (a critical factor, I shall argue, in the wholesale dismantling of Europe's colonial empires). Central to this delegitimation was the reformulation and reassertion of the collective right of self-determination. After Versailles, this was defined as a right of ethnically defined nations, and non-European peoples were explicitly excluded

---

[8] For a recent example, see Samuel Moyn, *The Last Utopia: Human Rights in History* (Cambridge MA: Harvard University Press, 2010), pp. 84–119.

from its purview. This understanding of self-determination did not survive World War II. The Nazi Holocaust was seen as a logical, if perverse, consequence of the principle that ethnically defined nations had special sovereign rights, and as then formulated, it was a principle unhelpful to the non-European peoples struggling for independence after 1945, almost all of whom were ethnically heterogeneous. After 1945, newly independent postcolonial states, working within the nascent human rights forums of the United Nations, engaged in a two-step process of reconstruction. They first played a central role in negotiating both the Universal Declaration of Human Rights and two international covenants on human rights, consistently prioritizing civil and political over social and economic rights, and supporting stronger implementation mechanisms than their Western counterparts. They then effectively grafted a reformulated right of self-determination to these emergent human rights norms, arguing successfully that self-determination was a necessary precondition for the protection of civil and political rights. Through this process, early postcolonial states not only undercut the moral foundations of empire as a legitimate institutional form, licensing the rapid and wholesale decolonization that would follow, they also played a crucial, though largely unsung, role in the development of the international human rights regime.

In each of these waves of systemic expansion, struggles for the recognition of individual rights were a necessary but insufficient cause. Historical transformations such as these are complex phenomena, the product of multiple, interwoven factors. No single cause is ever sufficient, and rights struggles are no exception. They were, however, necessary causes, in the sense that without them history would have been different, and significantly so. In the Westphalian case, the issue of liberty of religious conscience lay at the heart of the confessional struggles that wracked the Holy Roman Empire for more than a century. It was this issue that stymied attempts to reunite Latin Christendom at the Diets of Regensburg, and that undermined the statist pluralism of the Peace of Augsburg. It was also this issue that shaped the Westphalian settlement, in ways largely ignored in conventional accounts. To resolve the religious wars, the treaties not only created a nascent sovereign order, but also 'compromised' the authority of the emergent states with provisions protecting the individual's right to liberty of religious conscience. Without the struggle for such liberty, the Holy Roman Empire may well have collapsed, but the story and timing would have been different. In the Spanish case, the catalyst for the crisis was the Napoleonic usurpation, but this in itself does not explain the empire's collapse. Despite a century of punishing Bourbon policies in the Americas, prior to the usurpation demands for independence were marginal. Even after the usurpation, prevailing opinion was anti-Napoleonic and pro-empire, albeit with reformed institutions. It was the issue of the individual's right to equal political representation that divided Spanish Americans from Peninsulares, and it was the reformers' failure to gain such representation in Cádiz that radicalized the American insurgency. Had the 1812 Constitution recognized this right, the empire may well have limped on, much as it had for the previous century. In the post-1945 case, the perceived hypocrisy of Europeans embracing civil and political rights at home while denying such rights to their colonial peoples was a key grievance of prominent anticolonial struggles, and the post-1945 delegitimation of empire as an institutional form resulted from the successful grafting, within key United Nations forums, of the right to self-determination on to emergent human rights norms. Take away the politics of individual rights, and the collapse of empire – in its particular manifestations, and as an institutional form – would, in all likelihood, have run a different course.

The argument advanced here, and in following chapters, is about ideas animating and justifying struggles for institutional change. It is no less about interests and power, however. As historical actors encountered, interpreted, and claimed as their own new ideas about individual rights, they developed a repertoire of new interests. These were interests of some importance as well, considered by their claimants to be fundamental entitlements, essential to the most basic issues of human dignity. Added to this, I follow Joseph Raz in defining arguments about individual rights in terms of individuals' interests. An argument is about such rights if a person's 'well-being (his interest) is a sufficient reason for holding some other person(s) to be under a duty'.[9] Or as Jeremy Waldron elaborates, an argument is about individual rights if 'it takes some individual's interests (or the interests of some or all individuals severally) as a sufficient justification for holding others (usually governments) to have a duty to protect or promote that interest'.[10]

[9] Joseph Raz, 'On the nature of rights', *Mind*, 93.370 (1984), 195.
[10] Jeremy Waldron, *The Right to Private Property* (Oxford: Clarendon Press, 1988), p. 87.

Individual rights and social and political power are similarly entwined. In treating empires as systems of imperative control, I am arguing that their persistence as institutionalized configurations of power and authority depends not merely on the mobilization of material resources but also, and crucially, on their continued legitimacy. Furthermore, in holding that imperial hierarchy is cemented by regimes of unequal entitlements, I am arguing that institutionalized entitlements such as these constitute a form of structural power, producing the 'social capacities of structural, or subject, positions in direct relation to one another, and the associated interests that underlie and dispose action'.[11] Finally, in claiming that new ideas about individual rights, and the struggles they animated and rationalized, undermined imperial legitimacy, I am arguing that they were corrosive of existing structures of social power. And in justifying sovereign statehood as the institutional alternative to empire, the very same ideas were constitutive of new structural configurations of power.

This is an ambitious book, contending as it does that struggles for the recognition of individual rights played a significant role in the globalization of the system of sovereign states. Yet its claims are also delimited, in two respects in particular. First, while I develop an argument about the collapse of the Holy Roman Empire, the Spanish Empire, and Europe's nineteenth- and twentieth-century empires, this does not amount to a general theory of imperial decline – my argument relates solely to these imperial complexes. Having said this, however, elements of the argument are suggestive. If it is indeed true that imperial hierarchies are supported by regimes of unequal entitlements, then this may well constitute a common point of weakness, an institutional characteristic vulnerable to the spread and mobilization of new ideas about the moral nature and status of individuals and their fundamental moral and political entitlements. Second, as noted above, this is a book about individual rights, with human rights featuring only in the last of the three cases. My claim is not, therefore, that human rights – understood as the inalienable rights that all human persons are said to possess by simple virtue of their humanity – were implicated in the processes of

[11] Michael Barnett and Raymond Duvall, 'Power in global governance', in Michael Barnett and Raymond Duvall, *Power in Global Governance* (Cambridge University Press, 2005), p. 18.

systemic expansion that predate the twentieth century. Nonetheless, as I will explain in Chapter 2, I consider universal human rights to be but one, particularly recent, manifestation of a broader species of general individual rights, a fact largely ignored in the literature on human rights and world politics. The political principle that all human beings without exception possess certain fundamental rights gains international political salience only after centuries of struggle to expand the zone of application of general individual rights. The proposition, so common in the literature, that human rights became important in world politics only after 1945 is thus true only in the most literal of senses.

Before concluding, a word is needed on the relationship between the argument advanced here and the one I developed more than a decade ago in *The Moral Purpose of the State*. Both books present large, macrohistorical arguments about the development of the present system of sovereign states, and the reader is entitled to ask what connection there is between these accounts. The first thing to note is that any connections are largely accidental, or at the very least were bubbling away at a subconscious level until this volume was well underway. Two connections have gradually become clear, however. The first is usefully explained by conscripting language often applied to the European Union, that of institutional 'broadening' and 'deepening'. *Moral Purpose* set out to explain why different societies of states developed different fundamental institutions; why the ancient Greek city-states privileged a form of interstate arbitration, while modern states have, in general, favored multilateralism and contractual international law. It was thus about institutional deepening, about the differing architectures of institutional norms and practices that states have constructed to facilitate coexistence and cooperation. By contrast, this current work is concerned with institutional broadening, with the globalization of the present system of sovereign states. The second connection relates to one of the limitations of *Moral Purpose*. My analysis there was an exercise in comparative statics; I characterized the constitutional structures of four societies of states and explained how these structures conditioned the development of fundamental institutions. However illuminating this was, there was little if any discussion of where these varied constitutional structures came from; how they evolved through processes of cultural and political negotiation and contestation. While not its primary purpose, *Individual Rights* goes some way to filling this gap. It is not concerned with explaining the origin of constitutional structures, but it does examine how struggles for individual rights challenged and transformed norms that were central to such structures; norms of legitimate statehood, and norms licensing sovereignty at the core and empire in the periphery.

# 1 | *The expansion of the international system*

Systems of sovereign states are rare; a global system of states, even rarer. For most of world history the predominant forms of political organization have been empires, heteronomous systems like that found in medieval Europe, or some combination of the two. Systems of sovereign states emerged in ancient China, Greece, and India, and also Renaissance Italy, but these were isolated affairs, exceptions to the rule. All of them were contained within particular regions, all of them were monocultural, and all of them were vulnerable to encroachment by surrounding political formations. Our present international system is thus unique, the world's first universal, multiregional, multicultural system of sovereign states.

This system first emerged in sixteenth- and seventeenth-century Europe, and then expanded through a series of imperial implosions, each one producing a host of newly independent states. As noted in the Introduction, International Relations scholars have shown surprisingly little interest in this process of expansion, and the accounts that do exist are less than satisfying. This chapter serves several tasks. I begin by defining what I mean by the 'expansion' of the 'international system', and by outlining the waves of expansion that led to the system's globalization. I also deal with a number of potential criticisms: that the system's expansion was as incremental as it was episodic, and that the current global configuration of states is the result of incorporation and aggregation, not the proliferation of sovereign states out of fragmenting empires. Most of the chapter is concerned, however, with outlining and critiquing existing accounts of systemic expansion, opening space for the rights-based argument elaborated in Chapter 2.

## International systems, international societies

A distinction is commonly drawn between international systems, on the one hand, and international societies, on the other. The former are

15

characterized as pure realms of interaction, devoid of social content. An international system, Hedley Bull argued, 'is formed when two or more states have sufficient contact between them, and have sufficient impact on one another's decisions, to cause them to behave – at least in some measure – as parts of a whole'.[1] An international society, in contrast, 'exists when a group of states, conscious of certain common interests and common values, form a society in the sense that they conceive themselves to be bound by a common set of rules in their relations with one another, and share in the working of common institutions'.[2] International systems are thus quasi-physical realms: their constituent states are sufficiently proximate, and encounter one another sufficiently often, that they have to take each other into account. International societies, in contrast, are intersubjective realms where sovereign states are bound together by webs of shared meanings.

For most scholars, the point at which an international system becomes an international society is when sovereign states start basing their relations on mutual recognition. In an international system, a state's sovereignty rests on its material capacities. If a state has the resources to defend its territorial integrity and political independence, it will survive as a sovereign unit. If not, it will be existentially vulnerable. In an international society, a state's sovereignty rests not only, or even primarily, on its relative material power, but on social recognition, on the acknowledgment by other sovereign states that it too has a right to sovereignty. For states to form an international society, Martin Wight argued, 'not only must each claim independence of any political authority for itself, but each must recognize the validity of the same claim by all others'.[3] It is widely assumed that considerable interaction can occur in an international system before mutual recognition emerges. It is also assumed that states will endure high levels of violence and instability before basing their sovereignty on mutual right instead of individual might.[4]

---

[1] Hedley Bull, *The Anarchical Society* (London: Macmillan, 1977), pp. 9–10.
[2] Ibid., p. 13.
[3] Martin Wight, *Systems of States* (Leicester University Press, 1977), p. 23.
[4] See Barry Buzan, 'From international system to international society: structural realism and regime theory meet the English School', *International Organization*, 47.3 (1993), 327–52; and John Gerard Ruggie, 'Territoriality and beyond: problematizing modernity in international relations', *International Organization*, 47.1 (1993), 139–74.

I have become increasingly uncomfortable with this system/society distinction, or at the very least with the way in which we presently think and speak about these concepts and their interrelation. This is partly because it draws those of us who are interested in the social dynamics of international relations into a series of awkward, and ultimately unnecessary, positions and debates. The widespread use of Bull's definition of a society of states has encouraged a view of international societies as settled realms of values, rules, and institutions, and the existence of an international society has hung on whether such a normative order among sovereign states can, at any point in time, be said to exist. Both 'pluralists' and 'solidarists' of the English School work out from this assumption, their disagreements revolving around the nature and relative importance of the norms and values that hold modern international society together.[5] I will return to this issue in the Conclusion, but in brief, so long as we hold on to this view – that society exists when states are 'conscious of certain values', consider themselves 'bound by a common set of rules', and participate in the maintenance of institutions to uphold those rules – we will be forever answering the challenges of skeptics who deny that a society of this kind exists globally, who see contestation over norms not agreement, who want to confine international society to a narrow subset of states (Western, liberal democracies being the favored group at present), and who insist that in the absence of a global society of sovereign states, understood in Bull's terms, we must understand international relations in purely material, systemic terms.

Yet the main reason for my discomfort with the system/society distinction is not conceptual, it is historical. The closer one examines the last six centuries of international history – from the origins of nascent sovereign states in Europe to the present global sovereign order – the harder it is to see a textbook example of an international system, let alone one that transformed with the advent of mutual recognition into an international society. In the sixteenth and seventeenth centuries a group of interacting sovereign states emerged out of the ruins of the Holy Roman Empire, and over time its numbers and territorial reach increased until it spanned the globe. Saying that an international

---

[5] See, for example, the differences between James Mayall's *World Politics: Progress and Its Limits* (Cambridge: Polity Press, 2000) and Nicholas J. Wheeler's *Saving Strangers: Humanitarian Intervention in International Society* (Oxford University Press, 2003).

system, in Bull's terms, has existed for four to five centuries is thus uncontroversial. Yet, if the politics of recognition marks the existence of society among sovereign states, then international society too has existed for the same period. In reality, at no point in the history of the present international system has the politics of recognition been absent. The conflicts that preceded the Peace of Westphalia were, in great part, about the kinds of polities that would be recognized as legitimate, and about the political rights they would be granted. Since then the evolving collectivity of sovereign states has acted like a club, defining and defending particular norms of legitimate statehood, on the basis of which they granted or denied other polities sovereign recognition. Rather than an international system emerging first and then morphing into an international society, as conventional accounts suggest, system and society emerged simultaneously. Or more correctly, in my view, the international system has always had fundamental social dynamics.[6]

I thus refer throughout this book to the expansion of the international system, not international society (as is the practice of scholars of the English School).[7] In making this move, however, and in arguing that the international system is significantly social, I am not suggesting that we should dispense with the concept of international society. Saying that an international system has social dynamics is to say that life within that system – political life in particular – is shaped by more than material things; that it is shaped, in significant measure, by intersubjective meanings (especially about legitimate agency and rightful action), and by the multifaceted practices that produce, maintain, and contest these meanings. This social stuff – ideas, beliefs, and norms, and their generative practices – informs prevailing conceptions of sovereignty, defines which polities are inside or outside the club of states, licenses certain kinds of institutional practices, and conditions the legitimate exercise of social power. For all of these reasons, the 'social' is inevitably a site of contestation and struggle as much as it is of settled understandings. Conflicts over which polities deserve

---

[6] Barry Buzan expresses similar concerns to my own, and reaches a position not dissimilar. See Barry Buzan, *From International to World Society? English School Theory and the Social Structure of Globalization* (Cambridge University Press, 2004), pp. 98–101.

[7] See Hedley Bull and Adam Watson's classic edition *The Expansion of International Society* (Oxford: Clarendon Press, 1984).

sovereign recognition – China and the Ottoman Empire in the past, North Korea and Iran today – are as much the mark of the social as the settled regime of mutual recognition among contemporary European states. This having been said, though, international systems do develop social structures; in particular, relatively stable constitutional norms and attendant reproductive practices that define the terms of legitimate statehood and the parameters of rightful state action.[8] Around these constitutional structures, distinctive kinds of social (or 'international') orders evolve, characterized by particular configurations of systemic membership, politics of recognition and non-recognition, institutions to facilitate coexistence and cooperation, and politics of ethics and morality. 'International society' is an appropriate term, I believe, to describe this kind of social order. It is not a term that describes something counterposed to an 'international system', it describes the social structural formations that coalesce within such systems. And when we refer to 'modern' international society or 'absolutist' international society, we are using these terms as proper nouns to describe social orders with particular cultural content and characteristics. What is distinctive about the present international system is that in its four to five century history it has developed two distinctive social orders, or international societies: the absolutist and the modern (the latter displacing the former).

## International systemic expansion

When the Treaties of Westphalia were concluded, the nascent system of sovereign states was a fraction of its current size, concentrated in Europe, and confined within the cultural bounds of Latin Christendom. If we take membership of the United Nations as the indicator, the international system today comprises 193 recognized sovereign states, it spans multiple regions, and it is as culturally diverse as the human community. It is this global expansion of the international system that concerns me. By 'expansion' I mean, first and foremost, the increase over three to four centuries in the number and geographical spread of the system's constituent states. Historically states have been fully incorporated into the system when they have achieved two things:

[8] I discuss these constitutional structures at length in Christian Reus-Smit, *The Moral Purpose of the State* (Princeton University Press, 1999).

when they have freed themselves from the control of transnational, usually imperial, authorities (*de facto* or empirical sovereignty), and when their sovereignty has been recognized by extant sovereign states (*de jure* or juridical sovereignty). As we shall see, sometimes *de jure* sovereignty has been achieved at the same time as *de facto* sovereignty (Westphalia); sometimes *de facto* sovereignty has preceded *de jure* (the Americas); and at other times *de jure* has preceded *de facto* (by some accounts, post-1945 decolonization).[9]

In the history of the present international system, few decades have passed without the addition of new sovereign states. The process of expansion has been a punctuated one, though, with most states gaining independence in one of five great waves – waves in which one or more empires imploded, producing not a few new states but a host.[10] The first of these occurred with the Westphalian settlement of 1648. To the small group of existing, yet still evolving, states the treaties added the German states, the United Provinces of the Netherlands, and the Swiss Confederacy, ordaining them with what we now interpret as sovereign rights. The second wave came at the beginning of the nineteenth century with the dissolution of the Spanish and Portuguese empires in the Americas. In less than two decades seventeen new states gained sovereign independence, starting with Paraguay in 1811 and ending with Bolivia in 1825. The system was now bi-regional, and the club of European monarchies had to contend with a host of new republics. The third wave followed the Versailles settlement and the creation of the League of Nations in 1919, developments that spawned over twenty new sovereign states. The fourth wave came with post-1945 decolonization. Between 1946 and 1975 the system gained seventy-six new states, and forty-five of these emerged in the decade following the 1960 United Nations Declaration on the Granting of Independence to Colonial Countries and Peoples. It was this

[9] On post-1945 decolonization, see Robert H. Jackson, *Quasi-States: Sovereignty, International Relations, and the Third World* (Cambridge University Press, 1990).

[10] While the system's expansion has been punctuated in this way, the principal waves were not neatly fenced off, hermetically sealed events. Each wave was caused by a crisis in one or more empires, and in this respect they constitute distinct historical phenomena. Yet their boundaries are not always easily delineated. In particular, in many non-Western colonial settings, the roots of the post-1945 wave lie in the early twentieth century, thus overlapping with the largely European processes of the third, post-Versailles wave.

wave that gave the system its African, Asian, and Pacific regions. The fifth, and most recent, wave followed the breakup of the Soviet Union, Yugoslavia, and Czechoslovakia between 1991 and 1993. From these implosions eighteen states gained sovereignty.[11]

Until recently the system of sovereign states has been deeply interconnected with the institution of territorial empire. At the same time that Europeans were struggling to construct sovereign states for themselves at home, they were busy establishing and maintaining empires abroad. As Edward Keene observes, they were quite comfortable 'adopting one kind of relationship, equality and mutual independence, as the norm in their dealings with each other, and another, imperial paramountcy, as normal in their relations with non-Europeans'.[12] Europe's early overseas empires (the Spanish, Portuguese, and Dutch) did, of course, emerge while heteronomy still prevailed in Europe. But the shift to an absolutist society of sovereign states after Westphalia did not lessen Europe's imperial appetite; in many respects it increased it. And the late nineteenth-century advent of modern international society coincided with the most aggressive phase of European expansion, the 'scramble for Africa'. Yet the great waves of expansion considered here saw the disintegration of particular empires, and in the second half of the twentieth century, they undercut the institution of territorial empire itself, severing the link between sovereignty at home and empire abroad.

As noted in the Introduction, I focus here on the three most important waves of systemic expansion: the Westphalian, the Latin American, and the post-1945. While these share crucial things in common – each being an example of imperial fragmentation into successor sovereign states, and each being propelled by struggles over individual rights – they were not chosen because of their formal comparability. Indeed, this is not an exercise in comparative case-study analysis. They were chosen instead for their historical significance. If one is interested in the globalization of the system of sovereign states, these

---

[11] These waves are widely acknowledged in the literature. See, for example, Armitage, *The Declaration of Independence*; Bull and Watson (eds.), *The Expansion of International Society*; Philip G. Roeder, *Where Nation-States Come From: Institutional Change in the Age of Nationalism* (Princeton University Press, 2007); David Strang, 'Global patterns of decolonization, 1500–1987', *International Studies Quarterly*, 35.4 (1991), 429–54; and Adam Watson, *The Evolution of International Society* (London: Routledge, 1992).

[12] Edward Keene, *Beyond the Anarchical Society: Grotius, Colonialism and Order in World Politics* (Cambridge University Press, 2002), p. 6.

are cases of considerable importance. Most of today's sovereign states emerged out of these waves, and these expansions gave the global system all of its regions: Europe, the Americas, Asia, Africa, and the Pacific. The two remaining waves – those following the Versailles settlement of 1918–19, and later the breakup of the Soviet Union and the former Yugoslavia – are less significant in both respects. The first is not entirely neglected, however, as a brief discussion prefaces the analysis of the post-1945 case in Chapter 5. In contrast to the three principal waves, struggles for individual rights were not central in this case: communal forms of nationalism predominated, and the politics of self-determination had a top-down quality, with the great powers defining which peoples constituted 'nations' entitled to sovereign statehood. The politics of this wave, however, and the failings of the self-determination regime established after Versailles, laid the foundations for post-1945 decolonization.

In addition to the increase in the number of sovereign states, the expansion of the international system had a second dimension – the evolution and transmission of the legitimating institutions that sustain sovereignty. As noted above, the political independence of the world's sovereign states does not rest solely on their varied material capacities to defend their political autonomy and territorial integrity. Indeed, as Robert Jackson has observed, many of today's states are profoundly deficient in such capacities.[13] For states granted international recognition, sovereignty is a right, one that rests on intersubjective norms that uphold the sovereign state as a legitimate institutional form and sovereignty as a systemic organizing principle. But as I argue in *Moral Purpose*, sovereignty has never been an independent, freestanding international norm; it has always been conjoined to, and conditioned by, hegemonic ideas about legitimate statehood, or what I term 'the moral purpose of the state'. Over time, as these ideas have changed – from absolutist to modern constitutionalist – so too have the meaning and behavioral implications of sovereignty.[14]

The relationship between these numerical and institutional dimensions of the system's expansion is complex. What matters for us here, however, is that in the struggles for individual rights that drove the key waves of numerical expansion, the legitimating norms that sustain sovereignty were a crucial site of political contestation and over

---

[13] Jackson, *Quasi-States*.    [14] Reus-Smit, *Moral Purpose*, ch. 2.

time these struggles helped transform the norms in question. In the Westphalian wave, the confessional struggles and the Peace of 1648 produced nascent sovereignty norms. In the Latin American wave, the institution of sovereignty was well established in the core of the system, and sovereign statehood stood as an alternative to empire. Yet the republican ideals of the revolutionaries challenged prevailing absolutist norms, and by 1825 the old club of monarchies had to share the stage with a region of new republics. In the post-1945 wave, sovereignty again stood as an institutional alternative to empire, but the liberal constitutionalist ideal of legitimate statehood had now taken root at the core of the system. Sovereignty was not yet a universal organizing principle, however – the universal sovereign order assumed by International Relations scholars was yet to be constructed: sovereignty in the core and empire in the periphery remained the norm. It was the struggles for individual rights waged by subject peoples in particular colonies, and by newly independent postcolonial states in the United Nations, that universalized this principle.

## Two criticisms

At this point it is worth considering two potential criticisms. First, a critic might argue that the international system's expansion was more incremental than episodic, and the entry of each new state had its own story, with its own peculiar mix of causes. As noted earlier, since Westphalia few decades have gone by without the addition of one or more new states, and some of these have been big ones: the United States being a case in point. Yet the striking feature of the system's expansion has been its wave-like quality. Most existing states gained their sovereignty in one of five great bursts, when one or more empires collapsed, producing large numbers of states in a concentrated period of time. Understanding these waves thus goes a long way to understanding international systemic expansion in general. And if, as I suggest, struggles over individual rights helped drive these waves, then their impact on the system's globalization has been significant.

Second, one could argue that it is wrong to characterize the international system's current configuration of sovereign states – its structure of political agency – as the product of 'expansion'; that incorporation and aggregation have been repeated features of the system's development, and that as many, if not more, states have lost their independence, subsumed into larger units, as have gained it. Again, no one could rightly deny that such processes have been important features of the system's development. For example, Mark Greengrass argues that

> there were something like a thousand independent polities in Europe in the fourteenth century. At the beginning of the sixteenth, this had decreased to just below 500. By 1739 it had again fallen to under 350. The changes of the Revolutionary and Napoleonic periods were considerable, particularly in Germany where 294 or so territories with pretensions to be regarded as states shrank to 39 by 1820.[15]

The important thing for us, however, is that it was not sovereign states that were disappearing here. It was a multitude of polities, claiming various forms of authority, with various degrees of autonomy. But with few exceptions these polities lacked the attributes of sovereignty: namely, centralized, exclusive, and territorially demarcated political authority, along with the international entitlements that come with sovereign recognition. Acknowledging the importance of processes of incorporation and aggregation does not, therefore, weaken the claim that a system of sovereign states – a system made up of a very distinctive kind of political unit – emerged in sixteenth- and seventeenth-century Europe and expanded to encompass the globe.

Our critic might respond, though, that genuine sovereign states did disappear in the course of the system's development, that 'state death' is not as rare as some of our theories suggest. Until recently, this has been a largely neglected, though recurrent, phenomenon in international history, one warranting systematic investigation. Yet the numbers remain small in comparison with the increase in sovereign states. Tanisha Fazal, one of the few scholars to investigate the issue, identifies fifty examples of state death between 1816 and 1992, to which we can add the disintegration of Czechoslovakia.[16] If we deduct those states that she counts because they temporarily lost their sovereignty due to Nazi occupation in World War II (such as France, the Netherlands, Norway, etc.), the number drops to thirty-six. In the same period, the

[15] Mark Greengrass (ed.), *Conquest and Coalescence: The Shaping of the State in Early Modern Europe* (London: Edward Arnold, 1991), pp. 1–2.
[16] Tanisha Fazal, 'State death in the international system', *International Organization*, 58.2 (2004), 320. Also see Tanisha Fazal, *State Death* (Princeton University Press, 2007).

great waves of systemic expansion produced 131 new sovereign states, almost four times as many.

## Existing explanations

Critical theorists and constructivists have long chastised the field of International Relations for assuming, instead of explaining, the existence of the system of sovereign states.[17] Mainstream scholars, they argue, have taken the system for granted, focusing on understanding its internal political dynamics, often with a view to remedying its functional deficiencies. Yet when critical theorists and constructivists have themselves sought to explain the system's origins, they have concentrated almost exclusively on the emergence of the principle of sovereignty. Once the social genesis of this principle has been explained (a genesis that is thought to have occurred somewhere between the sixteenth and eighteenth centuries), the system's subsequent development, including its globalization, is largely ignored. Yet despite this general neglect, there are scholars who have sought to explain systemic expansion, albeit indirectly in some cases. Each of their arguments is deficient, however, with none adequately accounting for the five great waves of expansion.

### Geopolitics and imperial incapacity

Realist variables, such as geostrategic competition between great powers and imperial overstretch, pepper the literature on the nineteenth- and twentieth-century decolonization of Europe's empires. While sustained or systematic realist accounts are scarce, two propositions are commonplace. First, it is often asserted that colonies gained independence because they were supported by rival great powers, often a rising hegemon. For instance, Adam Watson (a scholar usually identified with the English School) claims that

---

[17] The two most cited examples are Robert Cox, 'Social forces, states, and world orders: beyond international relations theory', in Robert O. Keohane (ed.), *Neorealism and Its Critics* (New York: Columbia University Press, 1986), pp. 204–54; and John Gerard Ruggie, 'Continuity and transformation in the world polity: toward a neorealist synthesis', *World Politics*, 35.2 (1983), 261–85.

after the Napoleonic Wars Britain actively supported the independence of Latin America: both for economic reasons, in order to open the doors of that continent to what was then the world's most expansive economy, and for strategic reasons, in order to establish new and supposedly democratic states there to balance what were considered in London the reactionary tendencies of the Holy Alliance.[18]

Second, it is often suggested that the declining material capacities of imperial powers were an important factor in decolonization. For instance, Gann and Duignan claim that as early as the end of World War I 'Britain and France stood at the zenith of their imperial might, but at the very moment of success, real power was slipping from their grasp. They were exhausted.'[19]

Few would deny that great powers have at times sought to enhance their power by undermining rivals' empires. Yet this was not a consistent factor in the great waves of systemic expansion. In the Latin American wave, and contrary to Watson's claim, Britain withheld diplomatic and material support for independence movements in the decaying Spanish Empire until these movements had gained *de facto* sovereignty. Similarly, in the post-1945 wave, the United States failed to match its earlier anticolonial rhetoric with sustained practical support for decolonization; indeed, as we shall see in Chapter 5, in debates in the United Nations on the right to self-determination after 1945, Washington consistently sided with the imperial powers. Robert Hager and David Lake make a theoretical case for why great powers might, under certain conditions, seek to undermine rivals' empires, engaging in a strategy of 'competitive decolonization' to shift the balance of power in their favor.[20] But while Hager and Lake claim to offer 'a systematic theory of imperial break-up', they give us no indication of how frequently great powers have practiced competitive decolonization, how important it has been in comparison with other factors, or what role it played in any of the major waves of imperial breakup and international systemic expansion. They do advance nine hypotheses about when rival great powers are more or less likely to engage in such practices, but while some of these predict British and US reticence,

---

[18] Watson, *The Evolution of International Society*, p. 266.

[19] L. H. Gann and Peter Duignan, *Burden of Empire: An Appraisal of Western Colonialism in Africa South of the Sahara* (New York: Praeger, 1967), p. 72.

[20] Robert P. Hager and David A Lake, 'Balancing empires: competitive decolonization in international politics', *Security Studies*, 9.3 (2000), 108–48.

others point in the opposite direction. Even if they did consistently predict this reticence, one would need to look elsewhere for the factors driving waves of systemic expansion.

The proposition that imperial incapacity is the principal cause of decolonization is also problematic. Material weakness has undoubtedly been a factor in the breakdown of particular empires at particular moments in history. But there is no consistent link between imperial weakness and fragmentation. In some cases fragmentary forces have emerged in empires at the height of their material strength; in other cases materially weak empires have seen little demand from colonies for sovereign independence. Three examples illustrate this. First, the violent fragmentation of the Holy Roman Empire, which culminated in the Thirty Years' War, began in the first half of the sixteenth century, at a time when the empire, under Charles V, was at one of its historical highpoints.[21] Second, by the beginning of the eighteenth century the Spanish Empire was in a parlous condition. Heeren, the great nineteenth-century historian, wrote that in Spain 'all the germs of imperial corruption were so fully developed, that it is difficult to explain even the continuance of its political existence'.[22] Seventy years later, with the empire still in a weakened state, Spain's Bourbon monarchs sought to reverse the decline by imposing punishing political and economic reforms in the Americas, sparking often violent resistance. Yet the catchcry of the Comunero Revolution of 1781 was not independence; it was 'Long live the king and death to bad government'. Even in the immediate aftermath of Napoleon's usurpation of the Spanish crown, the turn to independence was not immediate. Third, Europe's imperial powers emerged from the Great Depression and World War II materially crippled. This weakness did not, however, encourage them to loosen their grip on empire. In Britain, for

---

[21] My interpretation differs here from that of Andreas Osiander who attributes the outbreak of the Thirty Years' War to the weakness of the Habsburg emperors. Osiander makes the mistake, however, of treating the Bohemian crisis of 1619 as the origin of the imperial crisis. In reality its roots lie a century earlier when Protestantism unleashes centrifugal forces that the empire, at the height of its strength, was never able to contain. See Andreas Osiander, 'Sovereignty, international relations, and the Westphalian myth', *International Organization*, 55.2 (2001), 253.

[22] A. H. L. Heeren, *A Manual of the History of the Political System of Europe and Its Colonies* (London: Henry G. Bohn, 1846), p. 149.

example, strengthening, not severing, imperial ties was seen as a solution to postwar weakness.[23]

## Structural change in the world economy

World-systems theorists identify two conditions under which the decolonization of empires becomes more likely: economic hegemony and economic expansion. The former exists when one state has '*simultaneously* productive, commercial, and financial superiority *over all other core powers*'.[24] Because economic hegemony is said to reduce great power competition and encourage free trade, imperial powers are free to relax control over their colonies and the hegemon has incentives to promote decolonization. The contrary tendency is thought to characterize 'multicentric' systems, as heightened great power competition encourages greater controls over empire.[25] Expansion in the world economy is also said to encourage decolonization. According to Chase-Dunn and Rubinson,

> when average economic production in the system is expanding, the structure of control is less direct and political domination by core states over peripheral areas is relaxed. During periods when average economic production is contracting and competition among core states is increasing, political domination is increased over older colonies and new areas are brought under the colonial domination of individual core states.[26]

The claim that economic hegemony encourages decolonization appears to be supported by the correlation between post-1945 American hegemony and the wholesale dismantling of Europe's empires. Yet the connection is tenuous at best. For world-systems theorists, under conditions of hegemony, two things encourage decolonization: the hegemon's active anticolonialism, animated by an interest in free trade; and the decline of great power rivalry, which encourages imperial powers to loosen their grip on empire. But as noted above, after 1945 the United States failed to provide sustained or unambiguous support

[23] John Darwin, *Britain and Decolonization: The Retreat from Empire in the Post-war World* (London: Macmillan, 1988), p. 20.
[24] Immanuel Wallerstein, *The Modern World-System*, vol. II (New York: Academic Press, 1980), p. 22.
[25] Christopher Chase-Dunn and Richard Rubinson, 'Toward a structural perspective on the world-system', *Politics and Society*, 7.4 (1979), 453–76.
[26] Ibid., 462–3.

for decolonization. Furthermore, there is little evidence that reduced rivalry among Western great powers encouraged them to weaken their hold on empire. As Hendrik Spruyt demonstrates, imperial elites were in general slow to accept the end of empire, and in some cases fought tenaciously to retain it.[27] If the connection is weak in this case, it is no more apparent in the other waves of expansion. As we have already seen, British support for revolutionaries in Spanish America was piece-meal at best, with London withholding support and recognition until it was clear that the emerging states were robust. There is also no indication that Spanish interest in empire had declined. Indeed, the counterrevolutionary wars waged by Spain after the reinstallation of the Bourbon monarchy in 1814 were intense.

The relationship between cycles of global economic expansion and waves of decolonization is no more compelling. World-systems theo-rists claim that growth in the world economy reduces the incentives for imperial powers to seek economic gains from colonies. Furthermore, 'the resources available to lower classes increase and the coercion of the market decreases leading to a relative downward shift in power. Lib-eration movements are thus more likely and more potent.'[28] As with economic hegemony, a correlation appears to exist between global economic expansion and post-1945 decolonization. This is belied, however, by the imperial powers' continued, even heightened, inter-est in empire after World War II, and by the strength of anticolo-nial movements during the global economic downturn that preceded the war. But even if a correlation can be identified between global economic expansion and post-1945 decolonization, no such corre-lation exists in our other waves of systemic expansion. Concluding his detailed quantitative survey of global decolonization trends since 1520, David Strang argues: 'Periods of economic expansion (upswings in Kondratieff waves) are inconsistently related to decolonization across model specifications.'[29] This mismatch is strikingly apparent in the Spanish-American case, where the struggle for sovereignty took place in near crippling economic circumstances. Instead of economic

---

[27] Hendrik Spruyt, *Ending Empire: Contested Sovereignty and Territorial Partition* (Ithaca, NY: Cornell University Press, 2005).

[28] Terry Boswell, 'Colonial empires and the capitalist world economy: a time-series analysis of colonialization, 1640–1960', *American Sociological Review*, 54.2 (1989), 184.

[29] Strang, 'Global patterns of decolonization', 441.

expansion encouraging a relaxation of imperial control, stagnation fueled ever more desperate strategies of extraction. And instead of feeling emboldened and empowered by a downward flow of resources, struggles for independence occurred in the context of significant economic hardship.

### Incorporation into international society

A third account comes from members of the English School. They begin with the proposition that Europe's sovereign states came to form an international society, understood as a group of states that 'have established by dialogue and consent common rules and institutions for the conduct of their relations, and recognize their common interest in maintaining these arrangements'.[30] From this perspective, the expansion of the international system (or 'society') is conceived as a process of social incorporation, one in which non-European polities were gradually admitted to the rule-governed international order. English School scholars readily admit that this process required 'changes, adjustments, and adaptations' by non-European polities, 'some voluntary some not'.[31] Ultimately, however, they present the expansion of international society as highly rational, even ordered.

During the nineteenth century, the European powers had a practical problem, it is argued: 'the challenge and difficulty of drawing in the non-European countries into their system of international relations in an orderly and humane way, as much as possible within the international legal guidelines which they were themselves evolving to cope with the expanding domain of international law'.[32] To deal with this problem, they codified in international law a 'standard of civilization', a set of rules prescribing the qualities a polity had to demonstrate if it was to gain sovereign recognition. The story English School scholars tell is of how various non-European polities – the American colonies, the Ottoman Empire, China, and Japan – came, eventually, to satisfy these requirements and gain admission to the club of sovereign states. After World War II, colonial peoples gained a categorical right to self-determination, giving them admission to the club without having to

---

[30] Bull and Watson (eds.), *The Expansion of International Society*, p. 1.
[31] Gerrit Gong, 'China's entry into international society', in Bull and Watson (eds.), *The Expansion of International Society*, p. 171.
[32] Ibid.

meet the now defunct standard of civilization. In all cases, however, non-European polities are portrayed as embracing the rules and practice of the expanding international society. In Bull's words, 'While non-European communities in some cases were incorporated in the international system against their will, they have taken their places in international society because they themselves have sought the rights of membership in it, and the protection of its rules, both *vis-à-vis* the dominant European powers and in relation to one another.'[33]

There are two problems with this account. First, it is primarily descriptive not explanatory. This is most problematic when scholars highlight certain developments as important in facilitating particular waves of expansion but fail to explain why these developments occurred. One example is Jackson's discussion of the right to self-determination and post-1945 decolonization. Jackson argues that prior to 1945 a 'positive sovereignty' regime prevailed, in which polities had to demonstrate a range of empirical qualities and capacities (codified in the standard of civilization) before they would be granted sovereignty. After 1945 this was supplanted by a 'negative sovereignty' regime, under which colonies could invoke their categorical 'right to self-determination' to gain sovereign recognition, irrespective of whether they displayed the previously required qualities and capacities.[34] Jackson's account of post-1945 decolonization thus hinges on the construction of the right to self-determination. Yet he provides no explanation for this development. Second, the English School's account (descriptive or otherwise) fits none of the great waves of systemic expansion. In reality, political struggles drove each wave, and in these struggles subject peoples appealed to ideas that challenged dominant interpretations of membership norms. Furthermore, the great waves of expansion were inextricably bound up with revisions to prevailing norms of legitimate statehood. In the first half of the twentieth century, subject peoples challenged the hypocritical pursuit of liberal constitutionalism in the European core and the systematic denial of equal civil and political rights in the non-European periphery. After 1945 newly independent states worked within United Nations forums to graft a reformulated right of self-determination to emergent human rights

---

[33] Hedley Bull, 'The emergence of a universal international society', in Bull and Watson (eds.), *The Expansion of International Society*, p. 124.
[34] Jackson, *Quasi-States*, pp. 32–49.

norms. In doing so, they delegitimated the institution of empire, universalized the organizing principle of sovereignty, and helped construct one of the principal institutions codifying liberal norms of legitimate statehood – the international human rights regime.

### Socialization into world culture

In seeking to explain the universal spread of nation-states, sociological institutionalists have stressed the socializing effects of world society's modernist culture. With its roots in early modern Christendom and capitalism, this culture has globalized, carrying with it rational bureaucratic values; values that license the creation and proliferation of bureaucratic nation-states. From this perspective, 'nation-states are more or less exogenously constructed entities – the many individuals both inside and outside the state who engage in state formation and policy formulation are enactors of scripts more than they are self-directed actors'.[35] According to sociological institutionalists, world culture has encouraged the spread of nation-states through two mechanisms: the 'transmission of the nation-state model from Western powers to their dependencies', and the diffusion of decolonization by example, with early decolonization imitated by later independence movements.[36] Together, these mechanisms are said to explain a notable feature of the history of decolonization: the acceleration of its rate over time, with a dramatic upsurge occurring after 1945. As time marches on, it is argued, more colonial peoples are socialized to believe that the nation-state is *the* desirable model of political organization, and every successful decolonization demonstrates that the path is open.

The first problem with this argument is that it tells us little about the Westphalian wave of expansion: the rational bureaucratic nation-state was an achievement yet to be realized, and nothing akin to decolonization had occurred to be imitated. The situation is more complicated with subsequent waves, however. From the Latin American wave onward, the model of the sovereign state did exist as an institutional

---

[35] John W. Meyer, John Boli, George M. Thomas, and Francisco O. Ramirez, 'World society and the nation-state', *American Journal of Sociology*, 103.1 (1997), 150.

[36] David Strang, 'From dependency to sovereignty: an event history analysis of decolonization, 1870–1987', *American Sociological Review*, 55.6 (1990), 847; and Strang, 'Global patterns of decolonization', 432.

alternative, and after the independence of the Americas, examples of successful decolonization existed to be copied. Yet the sociological institutionalist model of diffusion is too simplistic. Before subject peoples could be receptive to the sovereign state as an institutional alternative, they had to have an interest in institutional change – they had to believe that political change within the framework of empire was no longer possible. Sociological institutionalists suggest that the very existence of the sovereign model, and examples of other states seizing independence, generated this interest. In the Latin American wave, however, the example of the sovereign state was well established, and the independence of Britain's colonies in North America stood as an example to be emulated, but for three decades after 1776 the prevailing mood in the Spanish world favored autonomy within empire, not sovereign independence. The demand for institutional change clearly had other sources. Furthermore, the sovereign state model was more complex than sociological institutionalists assume. Again, in the Latin American wave the prevailing, normatively ascendant form of political organization was dynastic sovereignty at home and empire abroad. In seeking sovereignty over empire, and in seeking to construct republics not monarchies, subject peoples challenged both aspects of this normative complex.

## The missing demand for sovereignty

The limitations of these four explanations can be traced to a common weakness – their failure to provide a coherent account of the demand for sovereignty. None of them explain why subject peoples and polities became dissatisfied with empire as an institutional form and turned to sovereignty as the solution to their political grievances. Nowhere do we find the three elements of a comprehensive account of the demand for sovereignty.

First, all four explanations have an anemic conception of political agency. The world-systems and world culture explanations are purely structural: there are no agents, individual or collective, seeking or opposing the dismantling of empire into sovereign states. The geopolitics and international society approaches are marginally better, including states as political agents engaged in struggles for material power, or states and aspiring polities embroiled in the international politics of membership. But in the former case there are no political agents within empires demanding sovereignty, only meddling external powers. And in the latter case, aspiring polities want admission to the club of states but there is no explanation for the nature and origins of this interest.

Second, their understandings of the structural environment in which expansion took place is either purely material or naively ideational, leaving them without the resources to explain how subject peoples' interests were constituted and reconstituted over time. In the geopolitics and world economy explanations, structure is nothing more than the distribution of material capabilities among great powers or patterns of economic concentration and growth. In the world culture or international society explanations, the operative structures are ideational: in the former case, modern ideas of bureaucratic rationality and progress; in the latter, practically oriented rules of membership. These ideational structures are treated as unproblematically ascendant, as singular normative structures that subject peoples and polities simply internalize.

Finally, none of the above explanations has a developed appreciation of the politics of legitimacy, that realm of human practice that links political agents to ideational structures. Each wave of expansion in the international system involved the simultaneous delegitimation of a particular imperial complex and the legitimation of sovereign statehood as its institutional replacement. In this process, the identities and interests of subject peoples and polities were conditioned by the contending norms of the traditional and modern recognition orders. But these actors brought about political change by innovating to give these norms particular meanings, and by mobilizing them in such a way as to cast empire as an unjust institutional form and sovereignty as a mode of institutional liberation.

# 2 | *Struggles for individual rights*

As the preceding chapter explained, existing accounts of international systemic expansion exhibit a common weakness: a general neglect of the demand for sovereignty, of the reasons subject peoples had for abandoning empire in favor of independent statehood. Material or institutional structures are posited, great power interests are deduced, and subject peoples are either written out of the story or reduced to nothing more than passive recipients and enactors of international rules or normative scripts.

This chapter lays the theoretical foundations of the book, developing an argument about the demand for sovereignty that emphasizes the relationship between struggles for individual rights and imperial crises of legitimacy. After addressing a number of definitional issues concerning the nature of individual rights, I argue that empires should be understood as hierarchies, with their legitimacy historically sustained by regimes of unequal entitlements: institutional frameworks that allocate individuals of different social positions different social powers and entitlements. In the Westphalian, Latin American, and post-1945 waves of expansion, subject peoples embraced local interpretations of new, distinctly modern conceptions of individual rights and challenged the traditional distribution of entitlements that sustained imperial hierarchy. Initially they sought imperial reform, or rights within empire. But in each case a tipping point was reached when the imperial system proved incapable of accommodating the new rights claims, and when subject peoples turned from 'voice' to 'exit'. Each time, it was the sovereign state that subject peoples embraced as the institutional alternative to empire.

The admission of new states into the expanding international system is often characterized as a struggle for recognition; a struggle by aspiring polities for the social acknowledgment of their sovereign rights. But as the final section of this chapter explains, the struggles for recognition that attended the three waves of expansion were dual in nature – struggles by polities for the recognition of sovereign rights were driven by deeper, more fundamental struggles by individuals for the recognition of civil and political rights. More than this, the principal waves of systemic expansion, and their underlying struggles for rights, were part of a broader, macro-level transformation from a traditional to a modern recognition order; a transformation that to this day conditions, among other things, the politics of international legitimacy.

## On individual rights

A right, Henry Shue argues, 'provides a rational basis for a justified demand'.[1] One can gain rights by custom, by contract, by national or international law, or, more controversially, by simply being human. Whatever their source, rights are distinctive kinds of entitlements, ones that license demand-like claims. A 'rights claim ("I *have* a right to that") is more than a reminder or an appeal; it also involves a powerful *demand* for action. And this demand brings into play an array of special social practices that rest on the privileged position of the right-holders.'[2] Because of this, rights claims asserted in trivial contexts sound jarring. Insisting that someone give back my pencil because I have a property right to it is not necessarily wrong, it is just an overreaction. In appropriate contexts, rights are what Ronald Dworkin called normative 'trump cards'.[3] Or as Joel Feinberg put it, 'rights are especially strong objects to "stand upon", a most useful sort of moral furniture'.[4]

We are concerned here with a particular kind of rights: individual rights, the rights of sole persons. These contrast, most obviously, with collective rights; the rights of groups, as groups. Individual rights divide into two broad categories. The first is 'special' rights. These are rights that individuals have because of special transactions or because

[1] Henry Shue, *Basic Rights: Subsistence, Affluence, and US Foreign Policy*, 2nd edn. (Princeton University Press, 1996), p. 13.
[2] Jack Donnelly, *Universal Human Rights in Theory and Practice*, 1st edn. (Ithaca, NY: Cornell University Press, 1989), p. 10.
[3] Ronald Dworkin, *Taking Rights Seriously* (Cambridge, MA: Harvard University Press, 1978), p. 365.
[4] Joel Feinberg, *Rights, Justice, and the Bounds of Liberty* (Princeton University Press, 1980), p. 151.

of special relationships in which they stand.[5] A good example is the rights that stem from a legal contract; a contract to buy a house, for example. Under such a contract, the vendor gains certain rights, as does the purchaser. They only have these rights because of the contract, however. If they were not signatories, they would have none of the rights (or obligations, for that matter). The second category is 'general' rights. Instead of deriving from special transactions or relationships, individuals are thought to have these rights simply because they constitute a particular kind of moral being.[6] The classic example is the idea of human rights. In naturalistic accounts, individuals have such rights because they are human beings; normative agents with the capacity to 'form pictures of what a good life would be' and to 'try to realize these pictures'.[7] Individuals have human rights to protect these capacities, to safeguard their moral 'personhood'.[8]

In the Westphalian, Latin American, and post-1945 waves of systemic expansion, it was general individual rights that were important (henceforth 'individual rights'). Yet these rights varied in two respects. First, they were substantively different in each period. In the Westphalian wave, it was the right to liberty of religious conscience that was crucial; in the Latin American, it was the right to equal political representation; and in the post-1945 wave, it was a compendium of civil and political rights. More importantly, the general individual rights that concern us have varied according to their perceived 'zone of application'.[9] This is the community of individuals who, at a given historical moment, were thought to constitute integral moral beings entitled to these rights. Today we assume that if there are any general individual rights they must be held by all human beings without distinction. But historically this has not been the case. Individuals have repeatedly claimed general rights on the grounds that they constitute fully developed moral beings while denying that other members of the species qualified. Women, unpropertied men, non-Europeans, peoples

---

[5] Hart, 'Are there any natural rights?', p. 84. See also Jeremy Waldron's discussion in *The Right to Private Property*, ch. 4.

[6] Hart, 'Are there any natural rights?', pp. 87–8. For Hart, this quality of being a particular kind of moral being was reflected in background equal rights of all humans to be free.

[7] James Griffin, *On Human Rights* (Oxford University Press, 2008), p. 32.

[8] Ibid., pp. 33–7.

[9] Axel Honneth, *The Struggle for Recognition: The Moral Grammar of Social Conflicts* (Cambridge, MA: MIT Press, 1995), p. 113.

of color, slaves, and indigenous peoples all found themselves outside the zone. In the Westphalian wave, champions of the right to liberty of religious conscience believed that only individuals of particular Christian denominations qualified: Muslims, Jews and heretics were excluded. In the Latin American wave, advocates of Americans' right to equal political representation believed that male Creoles, Indians, and freed slaves counted, but not women or slaves. Only in the last of the three waves did the perceived zone of application come to encompass all human beings, regardless of race, religion, gender, color, or civilization. Here we can reasonably speak of individual rights as 'human rights', but not in the earlier waves.

Individual rights are usefully understood as power mediators, as normative principles that materially weak actors can invoke to alter the power relationship between themselves and materially preponderant actors or institutions (empires, sovereign states, etc.). John Locke pointed to this function of rights when he described the natural right to freedom as a 'fence against tyranny'.[10] More recently, Shue has argued that a 'fundamental purpose of acknowledging any basic right at all is to prevent, or to eliminate, insofar as possible, the degree of vulnerability that leaves people at the mercy of others'.[11] In John Vincent's words, individual rights are 'a weapon of the weak against the strong'.[12] If this is the case, we should expect individual rights to come to the fore within, and help to generate, highly contentious politics.[13] Because individual rights are invoked to alter power relations, they challenge existing social hierarchies – hierarchies in which privileged actors are often deeply invested. The politics of rights is thus almost invariably the politics of struggle.

## Empires, legitimacy, and individual rights

Each of the great waves of international systemic expansion involved a fundamental institutional transition; a transition from one way of

[10] John Locke, *Two Treatises of Government* (Cambridge University Press, 1988), p. 279.
[11] Shue, *Basic Rights*, pp. 29–30.
[12] R. J. Vincent, *Human Rights and International Relations* (Cambridge University Press, 1986), p. 17.
[13] In using the term 'contentious politics' I seek to locate the politics of individual rights within a wider array of political forms that are disruptive of established social and political practices. For a good introduction to such politics, see Charles Tilly and Sidney Tarrow, *Contentious Politics* (Boulder, CO: Paradigm, 2006).

organizing political authority to another, a transition from empire to
the sovereign state. In what follows I develop a distinctive argument
about these transitions. Central to this argument is the politics of
legitimacy. I define empires as hierarchical forms of rule, that rest on
regimes of unequal entitlements that undergird their legitimacy, and
that in each of our three cases were delegitimated by new, politically
mobilized ideas about individual rights.

## Empires as systems of imperative control

In his classic work on the subject, Michael Doyle defines an empire as
a 'system of interaction between two political entities, one of which,
the dominant metropole, exerts political control over the internal and
external policy – effective sovereignty – of the other, the subordinate
periphery'.[14] Metropolitan control, Doyle argues, has five dimensions:
domain, scope, range, weight, and duration.[15] Among these, range is
particularly important, as it encompasses the principal means of imperial control. Doyle identifies three such means: persuasion, coercion,
and physical force. Of the four existing explanations canvassed in
Chapter 1, only those emphasizing geopolitics and imperial incapacity, on the one hand, and structural change in the world economy, on
the other, have anything to say about the means of imperial control,
and these imply that imperial rule rests primarily, if not exclusively, on
coercion and physical force. But as Doyle observes, 'persuasion' was
always a central means of imperial control, delivering relatively cheap
compliance as 'crucial collaborators' internalized metropolitan values
and came to see imperial policy as 'both "civilized" and "correct"'.[16]

The centrality of persuasion points to the nature of empires as systems of imperative control. Imperative control, Max Weber argued, 'is
the probability that a command with a specific content will be obeyed
by a given group of persons'.[17] Weber was particularly interested in the
exercise of imperative control within 'compulsory associations', corporate groups in which established order 'has, within a given sphere
of activity, been successfully imposed on every individual who con-
forms with certain specific criteria'.[18] The quintessential example of

[14] Michael Doyle, *Empires* (Ithaca, NY: Cornell University Press, 1986), p. 45.
[15] Ibid., p. 35.    [16] Ibid., p. 45.
[17] Max Weber, *The Theory of Social and Economic Organization* (New York: Free Press, 1947), p. 152.
[18] Ibid., p. 151.

such an association was, for Weber, the sovereign state. The concept is no less applicable, however, to empires, the authority of which is also compulsory. The key thing is that imperative control, whether exercised within compulsory associations or elsewhere, can never rest on coercion or physical force alone; it requires 'a certain minimum of voluntary submission; thus an interest (based on ulterior motives or genuine acceptance) in obedience'.[19] This interest can rest on a variety of factors, including custom, affectual ties, purely material concerns, or ideal motives. Weber is clear, however, that none of these is sufficient. Successful and sustained imperative control rests on one additional thing, the belief on the part of those subject to such control in the established order's legitimacy.[20]

## Traditional entitlements and imperial legitimacy

Empires are hierarchies; their defining features are the asymmetrical distribution of power between the metropolitan state and peripheral polities, and the unequal distribution of social powers between metropolitan 'citizens' and peripheral 'subjects'. Hierarchy exists, David Lake argues, when one actor has authority – or rightful or legitimate rule – over another.[21] Hierarchical relationships are not all the same, though; they vary in how comprehensive they are. 'When there are relatively few actions that the ruler can legitimately regulate, hierarchy is low. Conversely, when there are relatively many actions that a ruler can legitimately command, hierarchy is high.'[22] By this measure, empires lie at the extreme end of any continuum. For example, according to Lake: 'When security and economic hierarchies exist between two polities the relationship captures what is commonly known as either informal empire or, at an extreme, empire.'[23]

[19] Ibid., p. 324.      [20] Ibid., p. 325.
[21] David Lake, *Hierarchy in International Relations* (Ithaca, NY: Cornell University Press, 2009), p. 51. Not all scholars see hierarchy as necessarily an authoritative relationship. For instance, John Ikenberry argues that extreme forms of hierarchy can rest on coercion and physical force, not legitimacy. Empires, he contends, fall into this extreme category, and can be compared with more liberal forms of hierarchy, of which American hegemony is considered a prime example. See John G. Ikenberry, *Liberal Leviathan: The Origins, Crisis, and Transformation of the American World Order* (Princeton University Press, 2009), pp. 66–75.
[22] Lake, *Hierarchy in International Relations*, p. 45.      [23] Ibid., p. 57.

Like other systems of imperative control, empires require legitimation, and their principal challenge in such systems is sustaining the
legitimacy of imperial hierarchy. Historically, two things have contributed to this. First, the legitimacy of imperial hierarchy has been sustained by institutional structures, the social and legal norms of which
exert a form of structural power, generating unequal subject positions
and allocating them with differential capacities and entitlements.[24]
These institutional structures serve to naturalize hierarchy, making the
unequal distribution of social powers and the resulting social order
appear both normal and rightful. Second, the legitimacy of imperial
hierarchy, and its attendant institutional structures, have been rationalized by the legitimation practices of metropolitan elites and their local
collaborators. Generally this has involved discourses of civilizational
superiority and inferiority, differences that have been used to justify
the unequal distribution of social powers and imperial tutelage.[25]

The empires that concern us here – the Holy Roman, the Spanish, and Europe's nineteenth- and twentieth-century empires – were
all different, of course. They rose and fell at different points in time,
and had different cultural and historical origins. Because of this, they
developed their own distinctive institutional structures to sustain imperial legitimacy. These were instantiations, however, of a generic institutional form. Each empire rested on a regime of unequal entitlements. The social powers of individual elites and subjects, and the
relation between them, were defined in terms of socially recognized
entitlements.[26] While often articulated in the language of 'rights', these
were not the individual rights that would, in time, animate struggles for
institutional change. To begin with, they were 'special' entitlements,
arising out of particular transactions between individuals or out of the

---

[24] Michael Barnett and Raymond Duvall, 'Power in international politics',
*International Organization*, 59.1 (2005), 53.
[25] See Michael Adas, *Machines as the Measure of Men: Science, Technology, and
Ideologies of Western Domination* (Ithaca, NY: Cornell University Press,
1989); and Carlos A. Forment, *Democracy in Latin America 1760–1900*, vol. I
(University of Chicago Press, 2003).
[26] Nexon and Wright argue that empires are characterized by heterogeneous
contracting between the metropole and its multiple peripheries. I am
suggesting here, however, that in addition to these specific metropole–
periphery contracts, empires are structured by deeper, empire-wide, social
contracts embedded in regimes of unequal entitlements. See Daniel H. Nexon
and Thomas Wright, 'What's at stake in the American empire debate',
*American Political Science Review*, 101.2 (2007), 253–71.

distinctive social relationships in which they stood. Second, they were 'differential', in the sense that they were allocated unequally to individuals on the basis of social role, position, and status. This is clearly apparent in the feudal structure of the Holy Roman Empire,[27] as it is in the differential entitlements of Peninsulares, Creoles, Indians, 'free colored castes', and slaves in the Spanish Empire.[28] Even in the British Empire, where all 'British subjects' were notionally equal, the superiority of imperial legislation, the restriction of the franchise to sectors of metropolitan society, and institutionalized discrimination against the employment of colonial subjects in the imperial bureaucracy established a clear hierarchy of social and political entitlements.[29]

The stability of these empires depended on the continued legitimacy of their regimes of unequal entitlements, as these regimes fulfilled three functions in structuring imperial social and political relations. They helped, first of all, to constitute the different subject positions that made up the imperial social hierarchy. Whether one was a peasant farmer or an imperial viceroy, one's social role was both reflected in, and constituted by, the entitlements one could legitimately invoke. Added to this, entitlements and interests were inextricably entwined. Traditional entitlements were the product of longstanding historical bargains, however amorphous, asymmetrical, or incremental these were. Moreover, actors came to see their traditional entitlements as fundamental prerogatives they had powerful interests in defending. Lastly, traditional entitlement regimes institutionalized the unequal distribution of legitimate social powers within an empire. Given these three functions, the delegitimation of these regimes was particularly threatening to imperial imperative control.

## Imperial crises of legitimacy and the revolutions in rights

In their latter histories, the Holy Roman Empire, the Spanish Empire, and Europe's nineteenth- and twentieth-century empires all suffered crises of legitimacy. A political institution commands legitimacy when

[27] See Friedrich Heer, *The Holy Roman Empire* (London: Weidenfeld & Nicolson, 1968).

[28] François-Xavier Guerra, 'The Spanish-American tradition of representation and its European roots', *Journal of Latin American Studies*, 26.1 (1994), 1–35.

[29] Arthur Berriedale Keith, *The Constitution, Administration, and Laws of the Empire* (London: W. Collins & Sons, 1924), pp. 16–27.

those subject to its rule consider it rightful, when they see it as 'desirable, proper, appropriate within some socially constructed system of norms'.[30] Elsewhere I have argued that an institution suffers a crisis of legitimacy when a decline in such perceptions reaches a critical turning point. Because legitimacy is but one source of social power, this critical turning point is not necessarily, or immediately, marked by a precipitous decline in political capacity. Such decline can be averted through either of two forms of adaptation. An institution can reconstitute the social basis of its legitimacy, or it can draw on material resources (guns and money) to compensate for eroding legitimacy. A crisis of legitimacy can thus be defined as that critical turning point when decline in an institution's legitimacy forces either adaptation (through relegitimation or material inducement) or institutional disempowerment.[31] The principal indicators of such crises are, first, heightened dissent and social unrest, and second, institutional elites seeking to reestablish control through dialogue and/or coercion. The Holy Roman Empire experienced such a crisis in the century preceding the outbreak of the Thirty Years' War, the Spanish Empire after the Napoleonic usurpation in 1808, and Europe's remaining colonial empires from the late nineteenth century onward.

In each case imperial legitimacy eroded as the regime of unequal entitlements that sustained imperial hierarchy came under challenge. While each story differs, new distinctly modern ideas about individual rights emerged, or took root, in each context. As explained above, these were general rights, said to be held by individuals not because of particular transactions or relationships, but because they were thought to constitute integral moral beings. These rights varied substantively from one case to another, and in terms of their zones of application; the latter gradually expanding over the *longue durée*. In each imperial context, however, the articulation and mobilization of new ideas about individual rights had a revolutionary effect.

They helped, in the first instance, to ferment imperial crises of legitimacy. As new ideas about rights spread and were interpreted, reconstituted, and embraced, subject peoples reimagined themselves as moral and political agents. In doing so, they acquired new political interests

[30] Mark C. Suchman, 'Managing legitimacy: strategic and institutional approaches', *Academy of Management Review*, 20.3 (1995), 574.
[31] Reus-Smit, 'International crises of legitimacy', 167.

in the recognition and protection of their new rights. And in pursuit of these interests, they challenged prevailing regimes of entitlements and sought institutional reform. Because, in each case, the spread of these ideas was a transimperial phenomenon, they undermined the structural capacity of metropoles to divide and rule their peripheries, overcoming 'peripheral segmentation' by providing subject peoples with a common sense of entitlement and grievance.[32] Second, ideas about individual rights, and the arguments they informed, provided justificatory resources in struggles over legitimate political authority. Anticolonial elites used them to mobilize subject peoples and as a moral basis on which to critique established imperial norms and practices. As ideas about individual rights took root in metropolitan societies, they were used to highlight the hypocrisy of the imperial order. And when human rights norms received international codification, newly independent postcolonial states grafted on to them a reconstituted norm of self-determination. Finally, new ideas about individual rights served as deal-breakers, principles that had to be recognized if attempts to resolve imperial crises of legitimacy were to succeed. Time and again, however, attempts to reestablish imperial legitimacy through negotiated settlements foundered because they failed to recognize new rights claims. As we shall see, this was the case at the Diets of Regensburg in 1541 and 1546, and at the General Cortes of Cádiz in 1812.

In all three crises of empire, new ideas about general individual rights performed each of these functions. Yet there is a significant difference between the Westphalian and Latin American cases, on the one hand, and the post-1945 case, on the other. In the first two, crises of legitimacy occurred within single empires, and the broader institution of empire was questioned only at the margins.[33] In the latter, multiple empires fell into crisis, and the institution of empire itself was challenged directly. This has two implications. First, while strong claims can be made that new ideas about individual rights fermented imperial crises of legitimacy and served as deal-breakers in the first two waves, these are harder to sustain with the post-1945 wave: too many empires spanned too many diverse societies for generalization.

---

[32] Nexon and Wright, 'What's at stake in the American empire debate', 262–3.

[33] See Sankar Muthu, *Enlightenment against Empire* (Princeton University Press, 2003).

My claim regarding this last wave is thus more qualified. Ideas about individual rights did not ferment all twentieth-century anticolonial struggles, or constitute the principal sticking points in attempts to reestablish imperial legitimacy. They did, however, in key struggles, such as those in British and French sub-Saharan Africa and British South Asia. Such ideas were also at work in Egypt, but this was not the norm in the Middle East, where Arab and Islamic cultural politics were important.[34] Second, as noted above, the emergent human rights institutions of the United Nations enabled newly independent post-colonial states to challenge the legitimacy of the institution of empire in general. Ideas about individual rights were thus particularly important here as justificatory resources in debates over legitimate political authority. The upshot of all of this is that the balance between the roles played by ideas of rights varied across the three waves of expansion, with the diversity of imperial contexts, and new institutional opportunity structures, privileging their justificatory role in the post-1945 case.

A critic might argue at this point that it is anachronistic to see the politics of individual rights (particularly general rights) at work in all three waves of systemic expansion – that such rights, properly speaking, became important only after the American and French revolutions. This is to ignore, however, the long history of debates about natural rights, and specifically, the centrality of rights thinking in the seventeenth-century writings of Grotius, Hobbes, and then Locke. Even if this were not the case, however, the criticism mistakenly treats the prevalence of explicit rights terminology as the marker of rights-based political claims, arguments, and struggles. But this would be like saying that arguments are only about democracy if they use the term explicitly; an utterly nonsensical position. What matters is the form arguments take, not the terminology employed. As noted in the Introduction, I follow Raz and Waldron in holding that an argument is about individual rights if 'it takes some individual's interest (or the interests of some or all individuals severally) as a sufficient justification for holding others (usually governments) to have a duty to protect

---

[34] See John Breuilly, *Nationalism and the State* (Manchester University Press, 1993), pp. 152–4; and Hugh Seton-Watson, *Nations and States: An Inquiry into the Origins of Nations and the Politics of Nationalism* (London: Methuen, 1977), pp. 260–71.

or promote that interest'.[35] Further, an argument is about 'general' individual rights if the interest in question is important – and hence counts as a sufficient justification for others incurring obligations – because it is said to be essential to the individual's integrity as a moral being. By this measure, the Reformation argument that individuals had a fundamental interest in liberty of religious conscience, and that this justified the imposition of duties on others (princes, emperors, and popes), was about individual rights.

## The demand for sovereignty

Individual rights are institutionally referential. To begin with, they are *institutionally ambitious*. In social orders where individual rights and rights claims are culturally novel – where there is, as yet, no established framework of social norms that give such rights social meaning and purchase – arguments for the recognition and protection of individual rights are institutionally constitutive in ambition. That is, when individuals seek support or protection by invoking their rights they are, among other things, seeking to construct a set of intersubjective understandings that acknowledge the normative force of such rights. Second, individual rights are *institutionally presumptive*. In social orders where rights and rights claims are culturally acknowledged (if not protected), existing rules, norms, and principles give rights meaning and rights claims veracity. Rights gain political force when they are socially recognized, and it is within the intersubjective framework of institutional norms that social recognition is embedded. Invoking a legal right appeals to a legal institution that gives that right meaning and force; invoking a social right appeals to norms and understandings that make that right intelligible and persuasive; and invoking one's international human rights today appeals to the international human rights regime for institutional legitimacy and political purchase. Finally, individual rights are *institutionally dependent*. The protection and satisfaction of rights requires an enabling or executing institutional architecture. Without this individual rights might exist – metaphysically, at the level of social understandings, or within laws cast aside by tyranny – but they will be inherently weak. Even so-called negative

---

[35] Waldron, *The Right to Private Property*, p. 87. See also Raz, 'On the nature of rights', 195.

rights, which supposedly require other actors to do nothing more than refrain from obstructing or harming rights-holders, in reality require institutions for their protection.

The institutionally referential nature of individual rights is nicely illustrated with reference to the right to physical security, or what Hobbes called 'the right to self-preservation'. To what extent can we conceive of such a right as not institutionally referential? For classical social contract theorists, like Hobbes and Locke, this was a natural right, an entitlement individuals had prior to the establishment of civil or political society, an entitlement readily apparent to all humans endowed with 'right reason'. This would appear to be a situation in which the right to physical security is not institutionally referential in either our second or third sense (though it may be in the first): it exists without reference to social norms (as reasoning through the content of natural law is not the same as reasoning with intersubjective meanings), and it exists without enabling institutions. It is clear, though, that Hobbes, Locke, and others believed that a natural right to physical security was radically insufficient, that rights which existed outside the realm of the social compact – outside the realm of formal or informal intersubjective understandings – and without supporting or executing institutions were rights that would be forever assailed. This led Hobbes to his oft-quoted conclusion that 'the natural state of men, before they entered into society, was a mere war, and that not simply, but a war of all men against all men'.[36] Locke's conclusion was similar: while individuals possess rights in the state of nature, they are impossible to enjoy as they are 'constantly exposed to the invasion of others'.[37] Individuals can only escape this condition of vulnerability by contracting to establish political society and a sovereign authority, in doing so converting their natural rights into civil rights. The key thing is, though, that the social contract gives rights institutional referents in both the second and third senses – it establishes an executing institution in the form of the sovereign, and a set of intersubjective understandings, or norms, among right-holders.

At this point in the argument, I am primarily concerned with the third respect in which rights are institutionally referential: their

---

[36] Thomas Hobbes, *Leviathan* (Cambridge University Press, 1991), ch. 17, p. 120.

[37] Locke, *Two Treatises of Government*, p. 337.

dependence on an enabling or executing institutional framework. The struggles for individual rights that were implicated in the Westphalian, Latin American, and post-1945 waves of expansion were all centrally concerned with the formal institutional architecture that would uphold these rights. Because the formal institutions of imperial states legally sanctioned traditional regimes of unequal entitlements, institutional change was imperative if new rights claims were to be recognized and protected. As we shall see, in each imperial crisis subject peoples first sought to reform imperial institutions, or, as Lake puts it, to renegotiate the social contract on which imperial hierarchy rested.[38] Yet each time a tipping point was reached in which rights claimants lost faith in the capacity of 'voice' to yield meaningful imperial institutional reform and decided to 'exit' instead.[39] In the first crisis, this point was reached after the failure of the Diet of Regensburg in 1546, in the second during the constitutional negotiations at the General Cortes of Cádiz in 1812, and in the third in 1918 in British India and 1945 in key colonies in sub-Saharan Africa. In each case, the institutional alternative subject peoples exited to was the sovereign state.

My argument here is an empirical one – Reformation Protestants, American subjects of the Spanish Empire, and twentieth-century colonial peoples did in fact turn from empire to the sovereign state. But why this institutional form and not some other? Three mutually reinforcing factors seem to have been at work. First, integral to each struggle was a universalizing yet bounding political imperative. Each of the general rights pursued by subject peoples required a political space, and matching institutional architecture, that was universalist, if not universal. If, for example, all those recognized as integral moral beings have a right to liberty of religious conscience, then the recognition and protection of this right requires a political space that encompasses all said individuals, and an institutional architecture, conterminous with that space, that recognizes that right and has some prospect of providing for its authoritative defense. This universalizing imperative was matched, however, by an equally strong imperative to build fences. In

---

[38] Lake, *Hierarchy in International Relations*, pp. 28–9.
[39] Albert Hirschman defines 'voice' as 'an attempt at changing the practices, policies, and output of the firm from which one buys or of the organization to which one belongs'. 'Exit', by contrast, occurs when 'customers stop buying the firm's products or some members leave the organization'. See Hirschman, *Exit, Voice, and Loyalty*, pp. 4, 30.

all three waves of expansion, those claiming new rights had a deep distrust of transnational institutional formations, a distrust born of their experience with empires as suboptimal rights providers. Together these factors pushed toward the sovereign state. 'Westphalian' sovereignty promised the desired freedom from external authorities, and 'domestic' sovereignty a universalist regime of law.

Second, and as noted in Chapter 1, in all but the Westphalian wave a process of dynamic modeling was at work. The nascent sovereign states that emerged out of Westphalia were products of endogenous political struggles, institutional by-products of the curtailing of transnational authorities and the transfer of political powers to local princes. But, as sociological institutionalists observe, as the number of sovereign states increased, and the institutions sustaining sovereignty took root, the sovereign state came to be seen as *the* institutional alternative to empire. It is wrong, however, to describe this as a simple process of diffusion. While the organizing principle of sovereignty existed at the core of the system from the seventeenth century onward, it was conjoined to ideas of legitimate statehood that changed dramatically over the ensuing three centuries. Furthermore, until the latter half of the twentieth century, sovereignty was not a universal organizing principle – sovereignty at home and empire abroad was the norm. Subject peoples did internalize sovereignty as the institutional alternative to empire, but their political struggles helped transform the norms on which sovereignty rested, challenging prevailing conceptions of legitimate statehood and pushing for the universalization of sovereignty as an organizing principle.

Lastly, if the above two factors help explain the turn to sovereignty, they do not explain why particular states, in particular locales, with particular boundaries, emerged with the collapse of particular empires. Here Philip Roeder's observation that empires have tended to fragment along preexisting administrative lines is useful. The Holy Roman Empire splintered into its principalities, the Spanish Empire broke up into its viceroyalties (or lesser administrative units), and Europe's African and Asian empires divided into their colonies.[40] But while preexisting institutional structures undoubtedly provided opportunities and resources for revolt, they do not, in and of themselves, explain

---

[40] Roeder, *Where Nation-States Come From*. Note that in the case of the Spanish Empire, Gran Colombia, a former viceroyalty, eventually fragmented into a number of smaller sovereign states.

why the demand for institutional change emerged in 'segmented states' in the first place. For this, I suggest here, we need the advent of new ideas about individual rights, the crises of legitimacy they engendered, and the institutional failure of empires to accommodate the new rights claims.

### The causal role of rights struggles

In advancing the above argument, I am making a set of causal claims about the role that ideas about individual rights, and the struggles they animated, played in three great waves of systemic expansion. By transforming actors' identities and interests, and by providing justificatory resources in debates over legitimate political authority, their influence was constitutive – they worked their effects through inspiration, motivation, and justification. This makes them no less causal, however: their articulation, circulation, and mobilization had real consequences. Indeed, in social science parlance, they can be seen as necessary but insufficient causes of the fragmentation of particular empires into sovereign states. They were 'insufficient' because history is complex, and a multitude of factors were implicated in each wave of expansion; in fact, each had its own peculiar cocktail of causes. They were 'necessary', however, because in their absence history would have been different. The issue of liberty of religious conscience lay at the heart of the confessional conflicts that wracked the Holy Roman Empire, and dealing with the issue was the centerpiece of the Westphalian settlement, significantly affecting the nascent sovereign order it helped produce. Similarly, the issue of the individual's right to equal political representation was the central Spanish-American concern in attempts to negotiate a reformed post-Napoleonic Spanish Empire, and the refusal of the Peninsulares to grant such representation turned the Americans from reform to revolution. Had the Cortes of Cádiz granted Spanish Americans the representation they sought, the radical case would have been greatly weakened, and the empire may well have limped on, much as it had for over a century. Finally, the perceived hypocrisy of Europeans embracing civil and political rights at home while denying the same to their non-European colonial peoples was a key grievance of prominent twentieth-century independence movements, and the post-1945 delegitimation of empire as an institutional form resulted in the successful grafting, within key

United Nations forums, of the right to self-determination on to emergent human rights norms. Take away the politics of individual rights, and the collapse of empire – in its particular manifestations, and as an institutional form – would, in all likelihood, have run a different course.

## The question of nationalism

Of the five great waves of systemic expansion, only the Westphalian occurred before the eighteenth-century rise of nationalism as a salient political force.[41] It is well to ask, therefore, what role I attribute to nationalism in the remaining waves. I follow Ernest Gellner in defining nationalism as 'a political principle that holds that the political and national units should be congruent', and a nationalist movement as one designed to bring about or preserve such congruence.[42] I follow others, however, in distinguishing between civic and ethnic forms of nationalism.[43] In the former, the 'nation' deserving its own political unit is imagined as a collectivity of free and equal individuals; in the latter, as a cultural community bound together by bonds of language, religion, race, etc. As we shall see in Chapter 5, only in the post-Versailles wave did ethnic nationalism predominate, characterizing both the European nationalist movements and the international criteria for self-determination. In the Latin American wave, and in key anticolonial struggles of the post-1945 wave, varieties of civic nationalism predominated. This was in part a consequence of the cultural conditions of revolt. For the Creole elite in the Americas, not only did the denial of individual rights fuel their grievances, but their Spanish ancestry and the need to mobilize Indians and freed slaves meant that

[41] On this dating of the rise of nationalism, see Benedict Anderson, *Imagined Communities*, 2nd edn. (London: Verso, 1991); Ernest Gellner, *Nations and Nationalism* (Oxford: Blackwell, 1983); Eric J. Hobsbawm, *Nations and Nationalism since 1780* (Cambridge University Press, 1970); and Seton-Watson, *Nations and States*. A notable exception is Liah Greenfeld, *Nationalism: Five Roads to Modernity* (Cambridge, MA: Harvard University Press, 1992).

[42] Gellner, *Nations and Nationalism*, p. 2.

[43] In an earlier version of this argument, I contrasted 'aggregative' and 'communal' forms of nationalism. I was persuaded, however, that all forms of nationalism have a communal dimension. See Christian Reus-Smit, 'Struggles of individual rights and the expansion of the international system', *International Organization*, 65.2 (2011), 223–4.

an ethnic conception of nation was not an option. A similar situation existed in most of Europe's African, Asian, and Pacific colonies, where, as generally observed, cultural heterogeneity was the norm.

What matters for us, however, is that in the Latin American and post-1945 waves of expansion, struggles for individual rights and nationalism were deeply entwined – indeed, the former helped constitute the latter (and in the subsequent histories of most postcolonial states, the latter would in turn shape the former). In each, the metropole's denial of equal rights was a catalyst for mobilization. But as Craig Calhoun observes, one can only be a free and equal rights-bearing individual within a community of recognition and reciprocity, in which the recognition of your rights is matched by your recognition of others'.[44] In the reform phase of colonial campaigns for equal rights, this community was the imperial populace, with subject peoples seeking recognition of their rights as 'full citizens of empire'.[45] But when these campaigns failed, a new community had to be imagined, and this was the 'nation', the bounds of which were generally determined not by the extent of cultural affinities, but by the territorial limits of colonial administrations. In the Latin American wave, therefore, and in key anticolonial movements of the post-1945 wave, struggles for individual rights had a collectivizing dynamic, the result of which was emergent civic nationalisms. Civic conceptions of nation as a collectivity of free and equal individuals informed almost all of the early republican constitutions of the newly independent Latin American states,[46] as they did the constitutions of states such as India. True Indian nationalism, Nehru argued, was 'something quite apart from... [the] religious and communal varieties of nationalism and strictly speaking... the only form which can be called nationalism in the modern sense of the word'.[47]

---

[44] Craig Calhoun, 'Nationalism and cultures of democracy', *Public Culture*, 19.1 (2007), 154.

[45] This was the terminology employed by Nigerian elites after World War I. See Bonny Ibhawoh, *Imperialism and Human Rights* (Albany: State University of New York Press, 2007), p. 142.

[46] See Anderson, *Imagined Communities*, p. 51; Roberto Gargarella, 'The constitution of inequality: constitutionalism in the Americas, 1776–1860', *International Journal of Constitutional Law*, 3.1 (2005), 1–23; and Hilda Sabato, 'On political citizenship in nineteenth century Latin America', *American Historical Review*, 106.4 (2001), 1290–315.

[47] Jawaharlal Nehru, *Glimpses of World History* (Bombay: Asia Publishing House, 1961), pp. 1129–30.

Very often these senses of nationalism, and conceptions of nation, remained inchoate at the time of independence. As José Carlos Chiaramonte observes, in Latin America, for example, ideas of nationality and nation were not the root cause of independence, 'they were the result of a long drawn out process sparked off by it'.[48]

A critic might respond that even if ethnic nationalism did not lie behind the waves of systemic expansion, and civic nationalisms were, in the cases in question, products of processes generated by struggles over individual rights, other collective forms of identification must surely have been involved in the breakup of empires into sovereign states. Political communities and religious groupings already existed when new ideas about individual rights took root, and the very process of asserting and defending the individual rights of a subject people constituted them as a group with an identity and set of entitlements. Nothing I say here denies any of this. What I do deny, however, is that we can understand the imperial crises in question in terms of the claims and struggles of preexisting social or cultural groupings, understood as coherent collectivities with interests not reducible to the interests of their members. Groups existed prior to struggles over rights, but these struggles produced new collectivities. In the Westphalian case, reformation theology, and its propagation throughout Europe, constituted 'Protestants' and 'Catholics' as distinctive confessional groupings. And in the Latin American case, post-usurpation struggles over the individual's right to equal political representation helped to galvanize a sense among Spanish Americans that they were a people apart; that they were a distinctive political community, with distinctive interests, that was different from peninsular Spaniards, on the one hand, and more than the Creole elite, on the other (they were a community that encompassed Indians and freed slaves as well). Furthermore, to the extent that these larger transnational groupings later fragmented into postimperial sovereign communities, these latter communities were not the same as the groups that existed prior to the imperial crisis. Even where the territorial boundaries of new states coincided neatly with the administrative boundaries of former colonies, as was often the case, the communities contained within these boundaries were not the same;

[48] José Carlos Chiaramonte, 'The principle of consent in Latin and Anglo-American independence', *Journal of Latin American Studies*, 36.3 (2004), 565.

they had been transformed by ideational changes that reconstituted the individual and patterns of social recognition, and by processes of struggle and mobilization.

## Rights by other means

The argument advanced here contrasts with two others that also draw a link between the politics of individual rights and the development of the system of sovereign states. The first stresses the role that 'rights for revenue' bargains played in the development of European states, and the second stresses the constitutive power of ideas.

Charles Tilly provides the most succinct statement of the revenue for rights thesis. He sets out to explain the formation of 'nation-states' in Europe; in particular, the different forms these states have taken.[49] His starting point is the war-fighting imperatives of nascent rulers – 'war makes states', as he famously put it. In the late medieval period, warfare was endemic. But the monarchs, princes, and lords who fought to secure and enhance their political power and territorial control faced two challenges: first, they had to fund their war-fighting activities (which became ever more costly as the nature and technology of European warfare changed); and second, the regions they suppressed had to be administered, adding to the logistical and financial costs of rule.[50] The difficulty of meeting these challenges almost always produced fiscal crises for emergent rulers, compelling them to establish new modes of economic extraction. And not surprisingly, local populations often responded hostilely to these new impositions.[51] To gain stable access to capital, rulers were thus forced to 'bargain' with local interests, with bargaining understood broadly to include 'pleading with parliaments, buying off city officials with tax exemptions, confirming guild privileges in return for loans or fees, regularizing the assessment and collection of taxes against the guarantee of their more willing payment, and so on'.[52] The nature and extent of such bargaining varied from one region to another, with Tilly highlighting differences between 'coercion-intensive', 'capital-intensive', and 'capitalized-coercive' regions. But a common feature of all such bargaining was the exchange of revenue for rights. In Tilly's words, they

[49] Charles Tilly, *Coercion, Capital, and European States: AD 990–1992* (Oxford: Blackwell, 1992), p. 5.
[50] Ibid., p. 20.     [51] Ibid., p. 98.     [52] Ibid., p. 101.

created or confirmed individual and collective claims on the state, individual and collective rights vis-à-vis the state, and obligations of the state to its citizens. It also created rights – recognized enforceable claims – of states with respect to their citizens. The core of what we now call 'citizenship', indeed, consists of multiple bargains hammered out by rulers and ruled in the course of their struggles over the means of state action, especially the making of war.[53]

This line of reasoning is also articulated by new institutionalist economic historians, such as Douglass North. Unlike Tilly, their objective is to explain why some regions, and some states within them, have been sites of economic growth and dynamism. Despite this different purpose, however, they too advance a version of the revenue for rights thesis. North's starting point is the same as Tilly's – the endemic warfare that characterized tenth- to sixteenth-century Europe. From the fourteenth century onward, changes in the technology and organization of war escalated its cost, and the plague's decimation of Europe's population made it harder for rulers to raise the additional revenue.[54] All of this led again to the fiscal crisis of the emergent state: 'Declining revenues and increasing fiscal costs posed an ever worsening dilemma for European princes. Custom and tradition set limits on the extractions they could obtain from lesser lords, and a king who stepped across the boundary of accepted custom faced the possibility of revolt.'[55] According to North, rulers could respond by either confiscating the monies, borrowing them, or trading revenue for rights. As the first two options were unsustainable in the medium to longer term, most European monarchs engaged in some version of the latter practice. Crucial here was the granting of property rights in return for taxes.

In order to prevent loss of revenue (from evasions) rulers granted rights to alienate land or to allow inheritance, thereby establishing more secure and efficient property rights. Towns were granted trading privileges in return for annual payments; alien merchants were granted legal rights and exemptions from guild restrictions in return for revenue. Guilds received exclusive rights of monopoly in return for payments to the Crown.[56]

---

[53] Ibid., p. 102.
[54] Douglass C. North, *Understanding the Process of Economic Change* (Princeton University Press, 2005), p. 131.
[55] Ibid., p. 141.    [56] Ibid.

Just as importantly, rulers were often compelled to establish representative bodies, such as Parliaments, Cortes, and States General, that had some say over taxation rates and practices. The relative strength of rulers and subjects in these revenue for rights bargains determined the eventual institutional character of particular European states, and this was in turn critical in determining their capacity for economic dynamism and growth.[57]

The second argument that draws a connection between individual rights and the development of the state system stresses the constitutive power of ideas. In a series of landmark articles, John Ruggie sets out to explain the European transition from medieval heteronomy to modern sovereignty, a transition from a system of rule 'in which authority was both personalized and parcelized within and across territorial formations' to one that saw the 'consolidation of all parcelized and personalized authority into one public realm'.[58] This shift, he contends, was the product of three interrelated factors: the change in material environments associated with the plague-induced collapse of the European economy in the second half of the fourteenth century; the new strategic opportunities opened up by this changed material context; and a revolution in social epistemes, 'the mental equipment that people drew upon in imagining and symbolizing forms of political community'.[59] It is the last of these that Ruggie considers most important, setting him apart from rationalist historical sociologists and economic historians. At the heart of this epistemic revolution, and of crucial importance for the advent of modern sovereignty, was a shift in prevailing conceptions of property rights. In medieval Europe, such rights were non-exclusive and conditional; a landed property, for example, could be subject to multiple titles, and property entitlements came with social obligations. This was reflected in, and entwined with, the medieval system of authority, which comprised multiple centers of personalized power with non-exclusive, overlapping jurisdictions.[60] In modern Europe, in contrast, property rights came to be conceived as exclusive and unconditional, as the rights of individuals 'to exclude others from

---

[57] Ibid., pp. 142–5. Also see Douglass C. North and Robert P. Thomas, *The Rise of the Western World* (Cambridge University Press, 1973).

[58] Ruggie, 'Territoriality and beyond', 150–1. Also see his 'Continuity and transformation'.

[59] Ruggie, 'Territoriality and beyond', 157.

[60] Ruggie, 'Continuity and transformation', 274.

the possession of an object'.[61] Again, Ruggie draws a link between this new understanding of property rights and modern conceptions of authority, particularly sovereign authority: 'the rediscovery of the concept of absolute and exclusive private property from Roman law no doubt aided in formulating the concept of absolute and exclusive sovereignty.'[62] In both the medieval and modern worlds, therefore, Ruggie sees not only an analogous relationship between conceptions of property rights and understandings of legitimate authority, but also a constitutive relation between the two: how Europeans have understood property rights has shaped how they have understood and justified forms of social and political authority. With modernity, the idea that individuals have exclusive, unconditional property rights 'made possible' the idea that monarchs have absolute, territorially exclusive sovereign rights.

Both of these arguments about individual rights and the development of the system of sovereign states differ markedly from the one advanced in this book. To begin with, they are concerned with a different category of individual rights from those that interest me here: special rights, not general rights. The property rights and rights to representation emphasized by Tilly and North were special because they were the products of particular bargains; special transactions between rulers and subjects. More specifically, they were special rights *in rem*, meaning that although they were the product of specific bargains between rulers and subjects, all members of society were obliged to observe them.[63] The rights emphasized by Ruggie are harder to categorize, as bargain-like special transactions play no role in his account. In the end, though, he too appears to be talking about special rights *in rem*. While the modern conception of individual property rights displaced the medieval conception 'via mechanisms of social empowerment and delegitimation' (though Ruggie has little say about this),[64] individuals gained such rights in practice through specific transactions: there might have been a revolution in what constituted a property right, but these were not rights that everyone had; one had to be propertied to have property rights. As in the revenue for rights argument, these are special property rights *in rem*, as all of society's members have an obligation to observe them.

---

[61] Ibid., 275.   [62] Ruggie, 'Territoriality and beyond', 157.
[63] Waldron, *The Right to Private Property*, pp. 106–9.
[64] Ruggie, 'Territoriality and beyond', 169.

Second, Tilly, North, and Ruggie are interested in different aspects of the international system's development than those that most interest me. While they are centrally concerned with intra-European processes of sovereign state formation, my focus is the expansion of the system of sovereign states from its original European kernel to encompass the globe. Our projects do intersect, of course, as my account of the Westphalian wave of expansion is very much concerned with intra-European state formation. Beyond this, however, I am interested in a dimension of the system's development they largely ignore – the collapse of territorial empires, and the resulting proliferation (in the latter two cases) of non-European sovereign states. On this, Tilly, North, and Ruggie have little to say. Ruggie and North neglect extra-European state formation altogether, and while Tilly notes that the forces at play in European state formation were absent in the non-European world (resulting, among other things, in the distinctive position of the military in many postcolonial states), he provides no account of the factors that were at work.[65]

These differences aside, one might still ask whether the revenue for rights and epistemic constitution theses could be fruitfully applied to the problem of systemic expansion. Tilly's and North's arguments undoubtedly capture significant aspects of European state formation, but only with distortion could the politics of the principal waves of expansion be squeezed into their explanatory models. For them, existing social orders were undermined by material forces, the key agents were nascent rulers and propertied classes animated by material interests, and individual rights entered the equation as political outcomes not motivating interests. As Chapters 3 to 5 explain, however, ideational factors played a critical role in the imperial crises that characterized the principal waves of expansion; subject peoples, mobilized in defense of individual rights, were key agents of change; and rights were not simply outcomes of bargains: they worked at the level of motives and justifications. Ruggie also sheds important light on the rise of the sovereign order, but in focusing on the analogous relationship between exclusive property rights and absolutist sovereignty,

---

[65] Tilly, *Coercion, Capital, and European States*, pp. 205–11. See also, Charles Tilly, 'War-making and state-making as organized crime' in Peter B. Evans, Dietrich Rueschemeyer, and Theda Skocpol (eds.), *Bringing the State Back In* (Cambridge University Press, 1985), pp. 185–6.

and on how the former cognitively enabled the latter, he neglects altogether the additional role that individual rights played in concrete political struggles; how new conceptions of individual rights came to inform subjects' fundamental understandings of themselves as moral and political agents with distinctive civil and political entitlements, how this undercut the legitimacy of imperial orders, and how this fueled the demand for sovereignty.

## Revolutions in recognition

To this point my emphasis has been on the nature of empires as hierarchies, on the role that regimes of unequal entitlements played in sustaining the legitimacy of these hierarchies, on the crises of imperial legitimacy engendered by the mobilization of new ideas about individual rights, and on the eventual fragmentation of empires into sovereign states as subject peoples turned from voice to exit. There is, however, a second way to tell the story; one in which the same dynamics are at play, but they are seen through the lens of the politics of recognition. There has, of course, been much written about the recognition of new states and the expansion of international society, often from the standpoint of international law. Yet the politics of recognition is almost always conceived as a third image or systemic phenomenon, in which aspirant polities struggle with existing sovereigns for *de jure* recognition and admission to the club of states. But as we have seen, the struggles for recognition that drove our three great waves of expansion were far more complex, with struggles by individuals for the recognition of their general rights preceding, and establishing the conditions for, struggles by polities for the recognition of sovereign rights. More than this, when these waves are viewed over the *longue durée*, they reveal a large-scale historical shift from a traditional to a modern recognition order.

Recognition is central to accounts of international relations that emphasize the social dimensions of the international system. For English School theorists and constructivists alike, mutual recognition of sovereign rights is a fundamental marker of society between states: until such recognition exists, relations between states are said to be purely systemic. Earlier I challenged this distinction between system and society, arguing in part that there has never been a 'really existing' international system devoid of the social politics of recognition.

My concern here is different, though. As noted above, international recognition has been studied to date as if it were a third image phenomenon, the politics of which occurs among existing and aspiring states in the 'external' political space between them. Sometimes the focus is bilateral, with authors concentrating on the conditions under which individual states extend recognition to particular polities.[66] At other times the focus is collective, addressing the recognition practices of the society of states.[67] In all cases, however, the model is the same: the actors are sovereign states and the political elites of aspiring polities, and struggles for recognition take place within the institutional and material structures of the international system (or society). Because aspirant polities are not yet fully incorporated within that system, the third image nature of these approaches is imperfect. What is missing, however, is any sense that struggles for recognition occurring at this systemic level might be connected to, even driven by, social forces operating 'below' or 'outside' the international realm (narrowly conceived).

These approaches to international recognition are problematic in two respects. First, they have no account of the demand for sovereignty (discussed above). Rationalists are often criticized for bracketing interest formation, for focusing solely on the strategic pursuit of already constituted preferences. But this is also true of most approaches to the international politics of sovereign recognition: the interests of aspirant polities in sovereignty is taken as given, as is the interest of established states in policing membership of the club of states. Yet as we have seen, these interests have social and political origins, and a comprehensive understanding of the politics of international recognition must come to terms with these. Second, and related to this, standard approaches to international recognition are rarefied, disembedded from deeper social processes. The international realm, the world of sovereign states engaged in 'external' interactions, is treated as

---

[66] M. J. Peterson, 'Political use of recognition: the influence of the international system', *World Politics*, 34.3 (1982), 324–52; Beverley Crawford, 'Explaining defection from international cooperation: Germany's unilateral recognition of Croatia', *World Politics*, 48.4 (1996), 482–521; and Eric Ringmar, *Identity, Interests and Action: A Cultural Explanation of Sweden's Intervention in the Thirty Years War* (Cambridge University Press, 2002).

[67] Hedley Bull and Adam Watson, 'Introduction', in Bull and Watson (eds.), *The Expansion of International Society*, pp. 1–9; John Dugard, *Recognition and the United Nations* (Cambridge: Grotius, 1987); and Gong, 'China's entry into international society', pp. 171–84.

self-generating, as produced and reproduced through international practices and engagements. For recognition theorists, these interactions are social, involving struggles over identity and legitimacy within frameworks of intersubjective norms and attendant practices. But they are international nonetheless, with social processes within the 'domestic' black box largely ignored.

There are, of course, struggles for recognition that take place largely at the systemic level, where no grave analytical injustices occur if one neglects domestic social processes. Historically, the French struggle for recognition as a great power at the Congress of Vienna might be one example, and a contemporary case might be the present Taiwanese struggle for recognition as a sovereign state. The great waves of expansion considered here were major recognition events, however; each resulted in substantial transformations in the membership of the club of states. Indeed, they are of interest because they were *the* recognition struggles that ultimately produced the global system. In each case, though, the politics of recognition extended well beyond the international realm. Each had an important international dimension: the Westphalian treaties were acts of *de jure* international recognition; after Latin American states had secured their *de facto* independence, they still had to secure *de jure* recognition by the established powers; and the post-1945 struggle by colonial peoples for the right to self-determination was in significant part an international process. Yet all of these 'international' struggles were grounded in, and generated by, struggles for recognition occurring within imperial societies, struggles by subject peoples for the recognition of their individual rights.

Constructivists generally shy away from ascribing to individuals any basic interests. If individuals' interests are informed by their social identities, and these identities are constituted by prevailing social norms, then interests are, by definition, culturally and historically contingent. Yet the constructivist account of identity formation does imply a basic human need (and in turn primary interest). When Alexander Wendt defines social identities as 'sets of meanings that an actor attributes to itself *while taking into account the perspective of others*, that is, a social object', he is pointing to the dependent relationship between actors' sense of self and social recognition.[68] At a most fundamental level, the

---

[68] Alexander Wendt, 'Collective identity formation and the international state', *American Political Science Review*, 88.2 (1992), 385.

individual self cannot develop without the recognition of others, as it is through recognition that individuals gain, first, an understanding of what it is that makes them unique and distinctive as human subjects, and second, a sense that, as distinctive subjects, they are valued. In Axel Honneth's words, 'one cannot conceive of oneself as a unique and irreplaceable person until one's own manner of self-realization is recognized by all interaction partners to be a positive contribution to the community.'[69]

The individual's need for social recognition is a potent source of political struggle. Because the development of an individual's social identity is so dependent on the recognition of others, denial or withdrawal of recognition – 'disrespect' – threatens basic self-understandings and esteem.[70] But while disrespect almost always generates emotional responses of anger and humiliation, not all forms of disrespect are politically consequential or transformative. For an individual's experience of disrespect to produce political struggle it must be generalizable; it must be a form of disrespect that applies to a wider class or category of individuals who, through communication, can experience it, and identify with it, in common. When disrespect is generalizable, it can motivate the collective action essential to political struggle. Recognition theorists commonly distinguish between three forms of recognition, only two of which are amenable to generalization. The first is emotional recognition, the form that occurs in loving interpersonal relationships, in which individuals 'mutually confirm each other with regard to the concrete nature of their needs and thereby recognize each other as needy creatures'.[71] The second is legal recognition, the recognition an individual gains as an acknowledged member of a community, possessing certain socially sanctioned entitlements or rights. The third is achievement recognition, through which an individual's qualities, capacities, and achievements 'are judged inter-subjectively according to the degree to which they can help realize culturally defined values'.[72] Only the disrespect that comes from the denial or withdrawal of legal or achievement recognition is politically consequential, as such disrespect is generalizable: it involves 'a prac-tical process in which individual experiences of disrespect are read

[69] Honneth, *The Struggle for Recognition*, pp. 89–90.     [70] Ibid., p. 131.
[71] Ibid., p. 95.     [72] Ibid., p. 122.

as typical for an entire group, and in such a way they can motivate collective demands for expanded relations of recognition'.[73]

We are primarily concerned here with forms of legal recognition. Broadly conceived, this refers 'to the situation in which self and other respect each other as legal subjects for the sole reason that they are both aware of the social norms by which rights and duties are distributed in their community'.[74] Defined in this way, legal recognition encompasses respect for a wide range of socially sanctioned rights and entitlements: from the special entitlements, rooted in an individual's social position and status, that I have argued characterize empires (and are often seen as a feature of traditional societies), to the general rights, grounded in an individual's quality as a moral being, that helped ferment imperial crises of legitimacy (and are generally attributed to the long rise of modernity). It is important to note here that in cultural and institutional contexts in which special rights or entitlements predominate, legal and achievement recognition are deeply entwined: legal recognition is 'completely fused with the social role accorded to one within the context of a generally unequal distribution of rights and burdens'.[75] Only in contexts where general rights provide the basic grammar of moral entitlement are legal and achievement recognition segmented, with the recognition of, and respect for, an individual's basic rights quarantined, at least in principle, from considerations of social role and status.

The individual's need for legal recognition is politically consequential not only because it is generalizable, but because of its implications for political institutions. I argued above that general individual rights are institutionally dependent, that they require an enabling or executing institutional architecture that formally recognizes such rights and provides some authoritative mechanisms for their defense. Yet this is also true of more traditional special rights or entitlements: they too rest on institutional norms and enforcement mechanisms. The important thing here is that general and special rights require different kinds of institutional architectures: feudal orders, in which special rights predominate, demand and sustain very different political and legal institutions than orders in which the recognition of universal rights is central. This is why the advent and mobilization of new ideas about

---

[73] Ibid., p. 162.    [74] Ibid., p. 109.    [75] Ibid.

general individual rights in social systems ordered by regimes of special rights is institutionally destabilizing; because recognition of the new rights claims requires fundamental institutional change. In essence, this is the story in each of our great waves of systemic expansion: new ideas about individual rights challenged the regimes of unequal entitlements that sustained imperial hierarchy, sparking institutional change eventually in the direction of the sovereign state.

Recognition, like security, may well be a universal human need, but what counts as valued recognition is neither common to all humans, in all contexts, at all points in time, nor idiosyncratic. The kind of agent one requires recognition as, with the qualities, needs, and entitlements one wants acknowledged, is conditioned by the intersubjective structures, and attendant social practices, of the social order in which one lives. These structures and practices are always variegated and multilayered, working at micro and macro levels. At the most micro level, individuals' recognition needs are shaped by the norms and practices of close interpersonal relationships, like those within families. Such norms license social roles, like mother and father, and privilege repertoires of social achievement, with professional or commercial achievement valued in some families, intellectual or cultural achievement in others, and artisanal achievement in still others. All of this takes place, however, within the macronormative structures of the prevailing social order, and it is these order-wide systems of meaning that define the terms of legal recognition: shaping individual's recognition expectations, patterns of social acknowledgment, and practices of disrespect.

Honneth calls these macrostructures 'recognition orders', and distinguishes between the present 'capitalist recognition order' and the 'traditional' order that preceded it.[76] In the traditional recognition order the norms shaping legal recognition sanctioned the differential allocation of rights and entitlements to individuals according to their social roles and statuses: the 'conventional ethical life of such a community constitutes a normative horizon in which the multiplicity of individual rights and duties remains tied to differently valued tasks within a system of social cooperation. Legal recognition is thus still

---

[76] Axel Honneth, 'Redistribution as recognition: a response to Nancy Fraser', in Nancy Fraser and Axel Honneth, *Redistribution or Recognition?* (London: Verso, 2003), p. 137.

situated hierarchically, in terms of the esteem that each individual enjoys as a bearer of a role...'[77] In the modern capitalist recognition order, in contrast, rights are distributed to individuals equally, on the grounds that they all constitute rational moral agents. In such a world, Honneth argues, 'individual rights have become detached from concrete role expectations because they must, from that point on, be ascribed in principle to every human individual as a free being'.[78]

Recognition theorists have little say about the transition from the traditional recognition order of feudal Europe to the modern, capitalist recognition order. The implication is, though, that it was one of simple displacement; the latter supplanting the former *in toto* in a discrete period of change. The argument advanced here about the expansion of the international system suggests a different account of this transition. Recall that I have defined empires as hierarchies sustained by regimes of unequal entitlements, and argued that our three great waves of systemic expansion were driven, in significant part, by struggles over general individual rights. Note also that the process of expansion, punctuated as it was, took the best part of five centuries, in which the institution of the sovereign state gradually displaced that of empire, but where both the institution of empire, and its concrete manifestations, not only persisted but were considered, outside particular struggles for imperial reform and sovereign independence, as entirely legitimate forms of rule. If this is correct, then the transition from the traditional recognition order to the modern was a gradual one, with traditional and modern principles and practices of recognition coexisting in a condition of revolutionary tension until the latter finally displaced the former in second half of the twentieth century. My contention here is that so long as empire constituted an integral and legitimate element of the organization of political rule globally, traditional regimes of recognition can be said to have persisted, and robustly so.

Honneth and others are right to argue that a modern recognition order now exists globally. This is partly because the delegitimation of the institution of empire, and the fragmentation of Europe's last great colonial empires into successor sovereign states, removed large zones of political rule formerly sustained by regimes of unequal entitlements. It is also because, in a process connected to the delegitimation of

---

[77] Honneth, *The Struggle for Recognition*, p. 111.   [78] Ibid., p. 110.

empire (see Chapter 5), an architecture of international norms has been constructed, enshrined most prominently in the international human rights regime, in which individuals are recognized as rights bearers not because of their social role or status but because they are human, understood as a particular kind of moral being. But while such an order can be said to exist, as a set of predominant international recognition norms and attendant practices, it is neither totalizing nor constitutive of all recognition practices globally. The macro-level norms of the recognition order coexist, often in a contradictory relationship, with more traditional norms working at other levels: from local, regional, or transnational cultural norms, embedded in class, caste, religious, or national forms of identification, to the micro-level familial norms discussed above. Thus, while modern recognition norms now predominate, struggles over legal recognition continue at multiple levels of the global system.

## Conclusion

In his classic work *The Anarchical Society*, Bull denied that ideas about individual rights had much impact on international relations. This was inevitable, he argued, because international society rests on the mutual recognition of sovereign rights, and recognition of the rights of individuals risks eroding these order-sustaining rights of states: 'In this system, in which rights and duties applied directly to states and nations, the notion of human rights and duties has survived but it has gone underground. Far from providing the basis from which ideas of international justice or morality are derived, it has become potentially subversive of international society itself . . . '[79] Three and a half decades after Bull wrote this, it is harder to claim that human rights have gone underground, ever present features of contemporary world politics that they are today. Bull was right, however, that international recognition of human rights would affect the recognition of sovereign rights. The establishment of the International Criminal Court, and the Tribunals for the former Yugoslavia and for Rwanda, have compromised the categorical rights of states to do what they will within their territories. And new ideas about the 'responsibility to protect', the salience of

[79] Bull, *The Anarchical Society*, p. 83.

which is still in question, threaten to undermine the cardinal principle of non-intervention.

But while a considerable literature now focuses on these corrosive effects of human rights on the constitutive norms of international society, the argument advanced above comes at the issue from the opposite direction: struggles over individual rights played a significant role in the development of Bull's global society of states (or international system, as I prefer to call it). Empire looms large in this story: out of the long century of conflict that befell the Holy Roman Empire emerged a nascent system of sovereign states in Europe, this system entwined other regions of the globe through the great colonial empires, and it was out of the crises and collapse of these empires, and of the institution of empire itself, that the global system of sovereign states emerged. Empires are hierarchies, the legitimacy of which is sustained by regimes of unequal entitlements that constitute different subject positions and institutionalize the unequal distribution of legitimate social powers. In the cases of the Holy Roman Empire, the Spanish Empire, and Europe's remaining twentieth-century empires, the mobilization of new ideas about individual rights undermined the legitimacy of these regimes, and when empires proved incapable of accommodating the new rights claims, subject peoples turned to the sovereign state as an institutional alternative. Each case had its own peculiar characteristics and dynamics, however; different rights were involved, the crises played out in different imperial and international contexts, the first two crises occurring in single empires, the last across the remaining empires in general, and earlier crises cast shadows over subsequent ones. The next three chapters explore these complexities, differences, and interconnections.

# 3 | *The Westphalian settlement*

The seventeenth century was momentous in two respects: the Thirty Years' War and the Peace of Westphalia (1648) played a crucial role in the development of the European system of sovereign states, and ideas about the rights of individuals began to animate political movements and inform political philosophy. Two of the most important phenomena conditioning present-day political thought and practice – phenomena many consider antithetical, or at least uneasily reconciled – thus emerged, incomplete and historically contingent, from the same cauldron of political struggle.

Yet if the existing literature is anything to go by, the relationship between these developments is so remote as to barely rate a mention. Those interested in the seventeenth-century rise of the sovereign state credit everything from war-fighting to the rediscovery of single-point perspective, but ideas about individual rights, and the politics they engender, are largely ignored (appearing only in the 'revenue for rights' arguments discussed in the previous chapter). Even those who focus on the minority rights provisions of the Treaties of Westphalia leave aside the question of how rights politics may have shaped the Westphalian settlement itself: the states it created as well as the scope of sovereign authority. Rights, in all of this, are seen as consequences not causes. When it comes to those interested in the early history of rights in world politics, the reverse tendency is apparent. The story of how ideas about individual rights evolved is told with little if any mention of how this was related to, or implicated in, the development of the system of sovereign states.

This chapter takes up this neglected relationship between sixteenth-century and seventeenth-century rights politics and the emergent system of sovereign states. More than this, as anticipated in previous chapters, it contends that the two were inextricably linked, with ideas about the right to liberty of religious conscience informing the political struggles that would determine (a) which polities gained sovereign

68

recognition, and (b) the powers these polities could legitimately exercise. Reformation theology generated new ideas about moral individualism and the imperative of liberty of religious conscience. These ideas lay at the heart of the century of conflicts that wracked the Holy Roman Empire and led, in their most tragic phase, to the Thirty Years' War. The Westphalian settlement resolved these conflicts by not merely reaffirming the 'Augsburg principle' of *cuis regio, eius religio* (as is often thought) but qualifying it with formal recognition of the individual's right to liberty of religious conscience. In doing so, it created a nascent system of emergent sovereign states, and 'compromised' sovereignty in a distinctive way.

The discussion is divided into four parts. I begin by examining the impact of Westphalia on the development of the international system, intervening in debates about its status as a unique point of origin. I then critically review the existing literature, making good my claims about the general neglect of rights and systemic development. In the third part I turn to the empirical heart of the chapter, explaining how ideas about liberty of religious conscience were implicated in the 130 years of conflicts that culminated in the Thirty Years' War. The fourth part examines the nature of the Westphalian settlement, focusing in particular on its simultaneous recognition of the political authority of princes and of the rights of individuals to freedom of belief and worship.

## Origins and expansion

For a long time it was taken as axiomatic that the Peace of Westphalia marked the birth of the system of sovereign states. In Kalevi Holsti's words, it 'organized Europe on the principle of particularism. It represented a new diplomatic arrangement – an order created by states, for states – and replaced most of the legal vestiges of hierarchy, at the pinnacle of which were the Pope and the Holy Roman Empire'.[1] This view has been challenged recently by a diverse group of scholars, all questioning the magnitude and import of the Westphalian transition. Stephen Krasner, the most well known of these critics, denies that Westphalia produced states with unqualified sovereignty, or that

[1] Kalevi J. Holsti, *Peace and War: Armed Conflicts and International Order 1648–1989* (Cambridge University Press, 1991), p. 25.

it dissolved entirely the transnational authorities of the papacy and the Holy Roman Emperor. The Treaties of Westphalia 'compromised' sovereignty, they did not consolidate it.[2] Such views have not gone uncontested, though, with a range of scholars stepping forward to defend Westphalia's status as a moment of great transition. Its critical contribution, Daniel Philpott argues, was to establish 'the state as the legitimate European polity – the first face of authority'.[3]

My own position is set out in *The Moral Purpose of the State*. I argue there that the Westphalian settlement did constitute an important step in the development of the European system of sovereign states. Philpott is correct that the treaties established states as the legitimate European polities, forever weakening the political legitimacy and authority of the papacy and the empire. Two qualifications are need here, though. First, the Treaties of Westphalia defined the scope of sovereign rule but not its territorial extension. They codified the substantive areas over which princes could legitimately exercise political authority, most notably in the area of religion. But the idea that sovereign rights were bounded by clearly demarcated territorial borders was not a Westphalian achievement. To the contrary, the treaties reaffirmed a characteristic feature of European heteronomy, the distribution of feudal rights in the form of fiefs. And because such rights had come to be seen as personal patrimony, dynastic ties, the bonds of lineage, and the extent of the family tree were as important in defining the reach of sovereign authority as territorial boundaries. Only after the War of Spanish Succession (1701–13) and the Peace of Utrecht (1713) was the fusion of sovereignty and territoriality complete.[4]

Second, while Westphalia played a key role in the development of a sovereign order in Europe, it was not the modern sovereign order we have inherited. The Westphalian settlement helped create an absolutist society of sovereign states, an international society with a constitutional structure markedly different from that which evolved after 1848. Constitutional structures are the complexes of international norms that define what constitutes a legitimate actor, as well as the parameters of

[2] Stephen D. Krasner, *Sovereignty: Organized Hypocrisy* (Princeton University Press, 1999).

[3] Daniel Philpott, *Revolutions in Sovereignty* (Princeton University Press, 2001), p. 30.

[4] Reus-Smit, *Moral Purpose*, ch. 5.

rightful political action.[5] For some scholars, it is sufficient to observe that the constitutional structure that evolved after 1648 ordained the sovereign state as the legitimate actor. But the post-Westphalian constitution did more than this; it upheld a particular conception of the moral purpose of the state, a conception that licensed dynastic monarchies as the legitimate form of sovereign state. Moreover, the absolutist conception of the moral purpose of the state defined the bounds of rightful state action in distinctive ways, not least in the realm of institutional design and practice.[6] It was not until well into the nineteenth century that the post-Westphalian constitutional structure was supplanted by a distinctly modern set of constitutive norms.

In *Moral Purpose* I thus argued that Westphalia was a key moment in the last great configurative transformation in the international system; the constitutional structure it helped forge entailed a shift in the organizing principle that determined how political units stood in relation to one another, a shift from heteronomy to sovereignty. But as argued above, Westphalia was but one step, albeit an important one, in this transformation, and the international society it helped bring forth comprised dynastic monarchies, not modern constitutional states. What does this mean, though, for treating Westphalia as a key moment in the expansion of the international system? How does one speak of a system 'expanding' that is only partially formed? And how can one say that the Westphalian settlement constituted the first great wave of systemic expansion – that it brought into being a host of new sovereign states – when the sovereignty of those states was incomplete, their territoriality yet to be constituted?

Answers to such questions will always be judgments open to contestation. My answer is this, though. As explained in Chapter 1, I mean two things by the 'expansion' of the international system: the increase, over three and a half centuries, in the number and geographical spread of the system's constituent states; and the evolution and transmission of the legitimating institutions that sustain sovereignty. None of this depends on the notion that the international system emerged fully formed at a distinct moment in time (as Athena sprang from Zeus's head, a mature goddess, armed to the hilt) and expanded thereafter.

---

[5] Philpott, *Revolutions in Sovereignty*, ch. 2; and Reus-Smit, *Moral Purpose*, ch. 2.

[6] Reus-Smit, *Moral Purpose*, ch. 2.

International systems, like all social systems, evolve over long periods
of time, gradually taking form out of preceding systemic formations.
At certain points in this process a system's constituent political units
become legible, assuming characteristics that come, with time, to be
seen as definitive. For those of us interested in systemic expansion,
the task is to make judgments about the relative significance of these
points; to decide when the system and its units are sufficiently legible to say that they exist, even in nascent form. Westphalia, I believe,
constitutes just such a point. The treaties were a major act of *de jure*
recognition: they ordained certain polities as legitimate centers of political rule, and granted them rights that constituted them as sovereign
(even if the process was far from complete). The Westphalian settlement was thus implicated, in a non-trivial way, in both the numerical
expansion of the system and the development of the norms sustaining
the sovereign order.

The settlement consisted of three treaties, though it is commonplace to consider only the second two: the Spain–United Provinces
of the Netherlands Treaty of 15 May 1648; the Sweden–Holy Roman
Empire Treaty of 24 October 1648 (the 'Treaty of Osnabrück'); and the
France–Holy Roman Empire Treaty of 24 October 1648 (the 'Treaty
of Münster'). Together, these treaties brought into being a host of new
sovereign states, all carved out of the German and Spanish sectors of
the empire, and all of them at a significant cost to the political influence of the papacy. The treaty between Spain and the Netherlands
recognized the United Provinces as a 'free state', and the Treaty of
Osnabrück and the Treaty of Münster gave autonomy to the German
principalities, both Protestant and Catholic. Much of the literature
simply refers to 'the German states' as a collectivity, as the task of
enumerating and distinguishing them is immensely complex. (In the
history of the Holy Roman Empire there were over 300 entities that
have been described as 'states'.) However, the principal beneficiaries
of the treaties – the German polities that gained recognizable sovereign
powers – were Habsburg Austria, Bavaria, Saxony, Brandenburg-
Prussia, the Palatinate, and Württemberg.

## States without rights, rights without states

As noted above, the story of the Westphalian settlement and its contribution to the development of a system of sovereign states is generally

told with little if any reference to the politics of rights. And histories of the evolution of human rights barely mention parallel developments in the international political system. From both directions, these phenomena are discussed as though they were separate developments, as though the construction of the sovereign order was in some way isolated from rights-based ideas about legitimate state power.

The limitations of the literature on the development of the international system is usefully illustrated with reference to three oft-cited works. These are illuminating because each represents a different theoretical approach, and each comes close to a consideration of individual rights but stops short.

The first is Krasner's *Sovereignty: Organized Hypocrisy*. Sovereignty never had a golden age in which states commanded absolute authority within their borders and denied all authority beyond, he argues. In practice it has been repeatedly compromised. Voluntarily, states have qualified their sovereign rights through conventions and contracts. And involuntarily, they have seen their rights compromised by coercion and imposition. The net effect, he concludes, is that sovereignty should be seen as a form of 'organized hypocrisy' – it is defined by widely understood social norms, but compromised routinely. He illustrates this argument with a number of case-studies, the first of which is minority rights. The first part of his discussion examines the role of such rights in the international settlements of the sixteenth and seventeenth centuries, including, most notably, the Peace of Westphalia. He argues that the minority rights provisions of the treaties 'were essentially [self-imposed] invitations to compromise the autonomy of signatory states'.[7] On the surface, therefore, it would seem that Krasner attributes some significance to rights in the Westphalian settlement. This is deceptive, though. In his schema, rights are consequences, and at best only secondary causes. In seeking to explain the minority rights provisions of the treaties, Krasner cites two causes: the recognition by European rulers that religious strife would remain a potent source of instability, and 'principled' beliefs about the illegitimacy of coerced beliefs. Of these two factors, however, it is the first that he considers primary, the second only reinforcing: 'Practical experience was *reinforced* by a long-standing Christian view that true religious beliefs could not be coerced' (emphasis added).[8] Nowhere does Krasner

---

[7] Krasner, *Sovereignty*, p. 84.     [8] Ibid., p. 78.

recognize ideas – particularly those concerning rights – as sources of the disorders that led to the Thirty Years' War and, in turn, the Westphalian settlement. In fact, he goes so far as to downplay the role that conflict over religion (and hence conflict over ideas) played in these disorders: 'No conflict in Europe was more costly than the Thirty Years' War, which was *exacerbated* by religious conflict' (emphasis added).[9]

Like Krasner, Hendrik Spruyt questions the conventional account of sovereignty. His central observation is that the shift from medieval heteronomy to modern sovereignty was not a unilinear process. Instead of the old feudal structures giving way to the sovereign order in a single move, feudalism was displaced initially by a range of political forms, most notably city-leagues, city-states, and nascent sovereign states. Only later, in a second move, did the sovereign state displace the other two forms. Spruyt's goal is to explain why this multiplicity of political forms at first emerged, and then why the sovereign state eventually triumphed.[10] The initial catalyst for political change, he argues, was the dramatic growth in European trade from the eleventh century onward. This growth prompted widespread political realignments, realignments that took different forms in different places. These were 'essentially permutations and combinations of bargains based on material interests and shared belief systems'.[11] With the Peace of the Westphalia, sovereign states emerged as the dominant political form, largely as a consequence of their superior capacity to rationalize their economies and mobilize resources internally, establish effective relations externally, and exclude other political forms that did not fit the new territorial order. To explain this transition, Spruyt adopts a rationalist (or methodological individualist) approach, but he stretches this to encompass the causal power of ideas and beliefs. Material power and interests cannot alone tell us why actors choose one institutional form over another: 'Beliefs and norms inform one's preferences. Hence, in order to ascertain the actual preferences of an actor, that individual's belief system must be examined.'[12] This is an important step beyond Krasner's treatment of ideational factors, such as those concerning rights, as consequences or secondary forces. For Spruyt, such factors are primary causes. Yet curiously he manages to tell the story

[9]  Ibid.
[10]  Hendrik Spruyt, *The Sovereign State and Its Competitors* (Princeton University Press, 1994), p. 18.
[11]  Ibid., p. 26.     [12]  Ibid., pp. 26–7.

of the sovereign state's non-linear ascendancy without reference to the politics of rights. As we shall see, fueling the religious conflicts that the Peace of Westphalia settled were a set of ideas about the individual's status as an integral moral agent, ideas that over time put a premium on rights to liberty of conscience. Yet nowhere are such ideas mentioned in Spruyt's account.

The proposition that ideas, beliefs, and norms played an important role in the development of the sovereign order is taken a step further by Philpott. As we saw earlier, he sees Westphalia as a watershed in the evolution of the international system, 'as clean as historical faults come'.[13] The treaties, and the conflicts from which they were born, instituted the 'constitution' of modern international society, that foundational body of norms that governs 'Who are the legitimate polities? What are the rules for becoming one of these polities? And, what are the basic prerogatives of these polities?'[14] This constitution established the sovereign state as the legitimate form of political organization in Europe: 'It revised all three faces of authority, and established constitutional authority in the form of the sovereign states system.'[15] Philpott attributes this 'revolution in sovereignty' to the causal power of ideas, to their role in, first, constituting individuals' identities and, second, motivating such individuals to pressure their leaders to pursue sovereignty as a political end. The ideas in question were those of the Protestant Reformation:

> The Reformation created religious pluralism, which led to the crisis that was eventually resolved through Westphalia's toleration, the abjuration of international enforcement of religion. The Reformation also yielded the idea that the authority of kings and princes could be separated from the temporal powers of the universal Church. Both of these prongs of Protestantism – toleration and separation of powers – led to the system of sovereign states at Westphalia, a solution of pluralism to a crisis of pluralism.[16]

In advancing this thesis, Philpott moves us well beyond Spruyt's notion of beliefs shaping actors' preferences. Protestant ideas are working at the deep level of identity constitution, a step before they shape institutional preferences. Moreover, in the end these ideas give international society a constitutional structure, a normative framework that exerts causal power in structuring international relations. Ideas thus work at

---

[13] Philpott, *Revolutions in Sovereignty*, p. 77.
[14] Ibid., p. 12. Original in italics.    [15] Ibid., p. 32.    [16] Ibid., pp. 147–8.

the level of both agency and structure. Yet Philpott's analysis is limited in two respects. First, like Spruyt, he pays insufficient attention to the moral individualism that attended the Reformation, and the link between this and demands for liberty of conscience. Second, when he looks at the constitutive impact of Reformation ideas, he looks only at their impact on the collapse of transnational authority and the consolidation of princely power. We see this in his understanding of 'Westphalia's toleration' as 'the abjuration of international enforcement of religion'.[17] But the Westphalian settlement was more than this – the politics of rights, revolving around issues of freedom of belief and worship, was responsible not only for the erosion of papal and imperial authority, but also for the minority rights provisions that compromised the sovereignty of emerging states.

If the literature on the origins of the Westphalian system neglects the politics of individual rights, the literature on the history of human rights offers little in the way of a corrective. Most accounts of human rights and world politics begin with the twentieth-century construction of the international human rights regime, occasionally referring to earlier movements against slavery, for women's suffrage, and for worker's rights.[18] Studies in the history of ideas often cast back to the time of the Greek and Roman Stoics, and then deal with the likes of Grotius, Hobbes, and Locke as part of a genealogy of rights thinking. Yet these works evince little interest in how evolving ideas about individual rights were implicated in the processes of social and political change. One of the earliest and best works on human rights and international relations, John Vincent's work of that title, begins with this kind of disembedded history of ideas, his excuse being 'that our task here is to provide a backdrop to the discussion of human rights in contemporary international politics, rather than to follow a historical path wherever it might take us'.[19] Only in the second half of the book does he consider the relation between rights and international politics, and this is almost exclusively a post-1945 story. A number of scholars have written deeper, more expansive histories of human

[17] Ibid.

[18] See, for example, Paul Gorden Lauren, *The Evolution of International Human Rights: Visions Seen*, 3rd edn. (Philadelphia: University of Pennsylvania Press, 2011); and David Forsythe, *Human Rights in International Relations*, 3rd edn. (Cambridge University Press, 2012).

[19] Vincent, *Human Rights and International Relations*, p. 17.

rights, in which they have sought to locate ideational developments within broader processes of social and political change. Yet even the finest of these studies have curiously little to say about the impact of ideas on the development of the international system,[20] and even those who address explicitly the connection between Reformation theology, developments in the philosophy of rights, and things like the Westphalian settlement, do so in but a few pages.[21]

## The crisis of Latin Christendom

Contrary to these general tendencies in the literature, the politics of individual rights and the seventeenth-century development of the international system were deeply interconnected. At the beginning of the sixteenth century, Europe's political order was heteronomous: it comprised multiple centers of authority, the jurisdictions of which were non-territorial and non-exclusive, overlapping in complex and often contradictory ways.[22] Within this order, the hierarchical institutions of the Holy Roman Empire provided the closest thing to a transnational, if partial and non-exclusive, political architecture. This political edifice, and the wider heteronomous order in which it was embedded, was held together by a framework of traditional rights and entitlements. The Emperor, the Pope, the princes of the empire, local lords, churchmen, knights, and even serfs routinely, and legitimately, invoked these rights to satisfy their interests, express their social identities, and affirm their positions within the hierarchical order. These were special rights, though: different individuals had different entitlements because they occupied different social positions, with different social statuses.

The ideas of the Reformation directly challenged this regime of unequal entitlements, containing within them a distinctive conception

---

[20] David Boucher, *The Limits of Ethics in International Relations: Natural Law, Natural Rights, and Human Rights in Transition* (Oxford University Press, 2009).

[21] Micheline Ishay, *The History of Human Rights: From Ancient Times to the Globalization Era*, 2nd edn. (Berkeley: University of California Press, 2008).

[22] See Perry Anderson, *Lineages of the Absolutist State* (London: Verso, 1974); Ruggie, 'Territoriality and beyond', 150–1; Saskia Sassen, *Territory, Authority, Rights: From Medieval to Global Assemblages* (Princeton University Press, 2006); Joseph Strayer, *On the Medieval Origins of the Modern State* (Princeton University Press, 1970); and Gianfranco Poggi, *The Development of the Modern State* (Stanford University Press, 1978).

of the individual as an integral moral being with a fundamental right
to freedom of religious conscience. This not only undercut social hierarchy by asserting, at one crucial level, the moral equivalence of all
individuals, it also undercut the authority of the Catholic Church, with
its purported role in mediating the relation between the individual and
God, and undermined the Holy Roman Empire's principal rationale:
its status as the guardian of Catholic Christendom. Over the course
of the sixteenth century, various attempts were made to resolve this
crisis of legitimacy, the most notable being the Diets of Regensburg
(1542 and 1546) and the Peace of Augsburg (1555). Their failure led
ultimately to the Thirty Years' War and, in time, the Westphalian settlement. As we shall see, the settlement provided a durable resolution to
the underlying confessional conflicts, reaffirming the principle of *cuis
regio, eius religio* but qualifying it with recognition of the individual's
right to liberty of religious conscience. In doing so, it licensed the creation of a host of confessionally independent states, but compromised
their emergent sovereign rights.

## Heteronomy, empire, and special rights

Earlier I argued that Westphalia played a key role in the development of an international system with a distinctive constitutional structure, one that licensed the organization of European political life into
absolutist sovereign states. Yet the heteronomous order of medieval
Europe also had a distinctive constitutional structure. The concept
of constitutional structures is usually employed to understand systems of sovereign states, but it is equally applicable to other kinds
of 'international' orders. Broadly defined, constitutional structures are
ensembles of intersubjective norms and principles that license a particular systemic configuration of political authority (by privileging a
given organizing principle), define what constitutes legitimate political
agency (with reference to hegemonic ideas about the moral purpose of
the state, broadly understood), and sanction certain kinds of fundamental institutional practices (shaped by underlying norms of procedural justice).[23] Normally, we consider orders in which sovereignty is
the organizing principle, where it is the moral purpose of centralized,

---

[23] This is an adaptation of the definition provided in Reus-Smit, *Moral Purpose*,
p. 30.

territorially demarcated political units that concerns us, and in which norms of procedural justice shape interstate institutions, conventionally understood. Yet in the case of medieval Europe, heteronomy was the organizing principle, and it was the transnational political institutions of the Holy Roman Empire that were the principal, though not exclusive, referent of conceptions of the moral purpose of the 'state'.

Heteronomy found concrete expression in Europe's complex configuration of multiple, overlapping centers of authority and their variegated jurisdictions. This configuration had four key components. The first was its *cultural domain*. The physical boundaries of the heteronomous order were constantly shifting, and the very nature of heteronomy meant that these boundaries were never clearly demarcated territorially. If the order had any boundaries, they were cultural not physical, and these cultural boundaries were defined by the reach of Latin Christendom. Where this cultural formation butted up against the Islamic world, the Byzantine world, and the New World of the Americas was where the boundaries of the heteronomous order lay. The second element was the *quasi-state institutions* of the Holy Roman Empire. I describe these as 'state' institutions to differentiate them from the ecclesiastical institutions of the Roman Catholic Church, as both were 'political'. But they were only 'quasi-state' because the empire never developed the kind of institutional capacities that we associate with the state. Political institutions they were, however, and the combination of hierarchy and non-exclusive jurisdictions that characterized the relationship between the Emperor, the Princes, and the Estates provided the rudimentary political architecture of the heteronomous order.

The third element was the *ecclesiastical institutions* of the Catholic Church. These institutions, which tied the papacy to regional bishoprics and local priests and monasteries, exerted profound political influence, influence wielded through the exercise of canon law, the Church's control of land, and disciplinary practices such as the Inquisition. The institutions of the empire and the Catholic Church were not only both political, but deeply entwined.[24] The most pronounced

---

[24] It is important to note here that our present distinction between the 'political' and the 'religious' had not emerged at this time. See Elizabeth Shakman Hurd, *The Politics of Secularism in International Relations* (Princeton University Press, 2008); Talal Asad, *Formations of the Secular: Christianity, Islam, Modernity* (Stanford University Press, 2003).

manifestations of this were the empire's dependence on the papacy for its legitimacy, the papacy's dependence on the empire for its security, and the central role that the ecclesiastical princes played in the formal governance structures of the empire, positions they enjoyed by virtue of their occupancy of key German bishoprics. The fourth and final element was the *social structure of feudalism*. This structure had different regional expressions, but its central feature was the binding of princes, lords, knights, and peasants in a hierarchical relationship of mutual exchange and dependence, a relationship that shaped the distribution of military power and the nature of agricultural production and trade, a relationship bound together by an amalgam of Germanic and Roman institutions, principally those of *Gefolgschaft* (the bond of loyalty between a warrior chief and his retinue), *Commendatio* (when inferiors entrust themselves to the protection of a superior in return for duties of submission), *Benificium* (rights to land, people and agricultural products so as to supply the needs of the individual and community), and *Immunitas* (the exempting of an individual or collectivity 'from the fiscal, military, and judicial powers normally exercised by the holder of a public office over the territory including them').[25]

As noted above, this complex configuration of authorities and jurisdictions was held together by a distinctive regime of unequal entitlements. In debates, pronouncements, and treatises of the time, the term 'right' was used to describe these entitlements. But these were special not general rights; they were held by an individual, or category of individuals, by virtue of their occupancy of particular positions within the heteronomous order. There was no notion that rights were universal, possessed by individuals equally, or that the universal rights of individuals could form the basis of legitimate authority. Rights were grounded variously in custom, contract, law, or interpretations of religious orthodoxy. Rights were at times traced to particular contracts or treaties, at times to readings of God's will (revealed by scripture and/or religious tradition), at times to both. As in all rights cultures, they served to stabilize and mediate power relations. To have a right was to have a legitimate power, and the existence of that right stabilized that power over time. One of the most notable examples was the 'ancient' right that the electoral princes enjoyed to elect the Holy Roman Emperor. Once established, this right forever limited the Emperor's power in relation to the princes, and enhanced their power with the papacy,

[25] Poggi, *Development of the Modern State*, pp. 19–20.

diluting the Pope's capacity to name the Emperor. Not surprisingly, rights became key focal points for political struggle within the heteronomous order. To claim or challenge a right successfully was to bolster one's power or undermine another's.

The moral purpose of the heteronomous order – its legitimating rationale – was intimately connected to its cultural domain. In addition to being a community tied together by belief, history, and ritual, Latin Christendom was an ideal. It was an 'imagined community' of faith, sanctioned by God. It was an ideal that brought an element of unity to an otherwise fractious order while simultaneously animating conflictual engagement with the Islamic, Byzantine, and New worlds, the most extreme example being the Crusades. The Holy Roman Empire was cast as the guardian of this community; the Emperor, Christ's vicar on earth. The empire was seen as the last bulwark against the coming of the antichrist. In Friedrich Heer's words, the 'idea that while the Holy Roman Empire still existed . . . the end of the world and the Last Judgment would be postponed was the great theme of medieval theologians of the Holy Roman Empire and of its poets and literary champions at critical moments in its history'.[26] Powerful as these ideas were, the amalgam of an idealized Latin Christendom and a guardian empire was inherently unstable. Most notably, it was open to any number of arguments about the relationship between secular and ecclesiastical authority, an opening emperors and popes were more than willing to exploit in their perpetual struggle for supremacy. Pope Leo III's crowning of Charles the Great in 800 was a symbolic highpoint of consensus, but conflict would be the norm, typified by Pope Gregory VII's and Emperor Henry IV's eleventh-century struggle, a struggle in which they both claimed paramount authority over secular and ecclesiastical issues. These struggles for supremacy were bounded, however; the ideological contest was elastic but not limitless. The ideals of Latin Christendom, imperial Rome, and the Petrine Doctrine were the cloth from which imperial and papal political legitimacy could be cut, and from which political institutions gained moral purpose.

## Protestantism, the individual, and legitimate political authority

The heteronomous order was vulnerable to numerous centrifugal forces, and by the end of the fifteenth century these had become

---

[26] Heer, *The Holy Roman Empire*, p. 3.

particularly pronounced. A series of bargains, including most notably Emperor Charles IV's Golden Bull of 1356, enhanced the power and independence of the electoral princes in the Holy Roman Empire. The thirty-year Papal Schism (from 1378) undermined the popes' authority and encouraged calls for conciliar decision-making within the Roman Catholic Church. Repeated squabbles between emperors and popes over paramount authority weakened the prestige of both. Europe's commercial revolution of the fourteenth and fifteenth centuries increased the importance and power of trading cities, prompting various strategies of independence, including the creation of the great city-leagues. And increasingly powerful monarchies had emerged in France, England, Sweden, and Spain, all of which had designs on the empire and the Church. It was the rise of Protestantism in the early sixteenth century, however, that would eventually bring an end to the heteronomous order and its replacement with a system of sovereign states.

At this point in the argument my claim is essentially the same as Philpott's – 'no Reformation, no Westphalia'.[27] While the Reformation comprised a variety of reform movements, Philpott argues that four ideas – or 'Solas' – united them: *Sola Fide*, salvation through faith alone; *Sola Gratia*, only through grace is a believer saved; *Sola Scriptura*, revealed truth comes from scripture alone; and *Sola Deo Gloria*, only God commands glory.[28] The logical consequence of these ideas was to deny the temporal as well as the spiritual authority of the Roman Catholic Church. Temporally, the reformers argued that civil power ought to have authority over spiritual power, and, spiritually, they denied that the Church was a universal institution, insisting that the true church was a community of believers and that forms of worship need not be the same everywhere. Addressed to Emperor Charles V in 1530, the Augsburg Confession stated:

The Church is the congregation of saints [and true believers], in which the Gospel is rightly taught and the Sacraments are rightly administered. And to the true unity of the Church it is enough to agree concerning the doctrine of the Gospel and the administration of the Sacraments. Nor is it necessary that human traditions, that is rites and ceremonies, instituted by men, should be everywhere alike.[29]

---

[27] Philpott, *Revolutions in Sovereignty*, p. 108.      [28] Ibid., p. 105.
[29] Augsburg Confession, Article VII, 1530. At www.reformed.org/documents/index.html (accessed 13 June 2012).

These arguments not only undermined the political power of the Roman Catholic Church, they bolstered the authority of the state. The reformers called for the separation of civil and church powers, powers that 'must not be confounded'.[30] They were Erastians, however, and argued that civil power has a responsibility to support church authority. Philpott concludes, therefore, that these core Protestant ideas led directly to sovereignty: 'sovereignty, in substance if not in name, comes directly out of the very propositions of Protestant theology, in all of its variants.'[31]

In a recent book, Daniel Nexon has also emphasized the central role played by the Reformation in the development of a system of sovereign states in Europe. But unlike Philpott, Nexon downplays the importance of Protestant ideas, stressing instead the impact of religious mobilization on the stability of composite states such as the Holy Roman Empire. 'The most important political ramifications of the Protestant Reformations did not stem from any sui generis features of religious contention; they resulted from the intersection of heterogeneous religious movements with ongoing patterns of collective mobilization.'[32] Rejecting approaches that 'spend too much time in the realm of the spirit', Nexon focuses on the 'composite' nature of bodies such as the Holy Roman Empire; on their internally fragmentary nature, their low penetration capacity, and their reliance on dynastic forms of legitimation to sustain rule in the face of centrifugal forces. Religious contention, he argues, was particularly damaging to such states, setting off processes that eroded the institutional barriers that had previously localized opposition, undermined the capacity of rulers to communicate coherent, singular identities that legitimated their policies, gave intermediaries new opportunities for autonomy, accentuated cross-pressures on rulers, and permitted the internationalization of domestic disputes.[33] The importance of the Reformation lies, therefore, not in the revolutionary content or implications of its ideas, but in the way in which religious mobilization altered modalities of resistance and undermined the institutional structures and practices that sustained the Holy Roman Empire as a composite state.

---

[30] Ibid., Article XXVIII.     [31] Philpott, *Revolutions in Sovereignty*, p. 109.
[32] Daniel Nexon, *The Struggle for Power in Early Modern Europe: Religious Conflict, Dynastic Empires, and International Change* (Princeton University Press, 2009), p. 3.
[33] Ibid., pp. 3–4.

This argument sheds important light on why the Reformation was so damaging to the political institutions of Latin Christendom, and much of what Nexon contends is compatible with the thesis advanced here. In moving away from the content of Reformation ideas, however, and in shifting the focus to religious mobilizations and institutional vulnerabilities, Nexon loses sight of what the Reformation, and the long century of conflict it generated, were about. In fact, the doctrinal roots of the Reformation conflicts virtually disappear from his account, replaced by an emphasis on movements, grievance linkage, and the shifting dynamics of resistance and rule. Important as these things are, this emphasis not only leaves the origins of the conflicts unexplained, it neglects the persistent doctrinal divisions that repeatedly stymied conflict resolution. Furthermore, by downplaying the theological roots of the conflicts, and by neglecting their stubborn centrality in failed peace initiatives (particularly those at Regensburg and Augsburg), Nexon sheds little light on why the Treaties of Westphalia constitute a peace settlement, and why they helped generate a particular kind of nascent sovereign order.

In seeking to understand these phenomena, I thus follow Philpott in stressing the nature of Reformation ideas, and how these ideas animated political struggles. What Philpott misses, however, is the foundational idea that underlay Protestant thought, an idea (and associated principles) that would deeply affect the provisions of the Westphalian settlement. Beneath the *Solas* lay a distinctive conception of the individual; the individual as an integral moral agent, whose capacity for faith gave them direct access to the grace of God, and through this, salvation. 'Grace in itself, and still more in its close bond with the Word, is a gift offered to an individual, not to a thing, not even to a group of persons collectively, in the same way as we speak of a particular person to whom the words are addressed, by whose needs they are shaped.'[34] In the minds of Luther, Calvin, and other Protestant intellectuals, it was this moral individualism that differentiated Protestantism from Roman Catholicism. 'The religion of faith came to be contrasted with the religion of works, as a personal, interior religion, engaging the deepest level of the soul, to a religion of social attitudes, liable to degenerate into pure conformity.'[35] Protecting the individual's

---

[34]  Louis Bouyer, *The Spirit and Forms of Protestantism* (London: Harvill Press, 1956), p. 99.
[35]  Ibid., p. 98.

capacity for an autonomous, unmediated relationship with God was one of the animating principles of the reform movement, informing at the most fundamental level its critique of the Roman Church.

With this move, early Protestant thinkers laid a keystone in the construction of modern, ultimately liberal, notions of individualism. They were still some distance from the fully fledged political individualism that would emerge in the writings of Grotius, Hobbes, and later Locke. But in early Protestant thinking we see an ideal of the individual as an integral moral agent, equipped with a capacity for the highest form of human attainment – salvation through the faithful receipt of God's grace – that was not dependent upon the constitutive processes and hierarchies of community and its social institutions. And while early Protestant intellectuals never articulated a theory of individual rights *per se*, they established an idea of an individual who has capacities that are universal, inalienable, and worthy of non-obstruction, even protection, an idea that they bequeathed to the great seventeenth-century rights theorists, all of whom were Protestants. But while they saw the individual's capacity for moral agency as independent of community, their individualism was not atomistic. The individual was spiritually, though not socially, constituted. Protestant individualism was 'not merely unthinkable apart from its relation to the object (grace, or the Word), but it is entirely directed towards, even determined by, the intrinsic properties of this object'.[36]

Luther, Calvin, and others believed that God had created two kingdoms: the kingdom of God, and the kingdom of the world. The first was the kingdom of all true Christians, a kingdom ruled by Christ himself. The true believers who made up this kingdom had no need of the legal or coercive powers of the state. 'For what were the use of them', Luther wrote, 'since Christians have in their hearts the Holy Spirit, who instructs them and causes them to wrong no one, to love everyone, willingly and cheerfully to suffer injustice and even death for every one.'[37] The kingdom of the world comprised all non-Christians, those whose lack of faith left them open to all sorts of wickedness and evil. For this world God created the civil power of the state. God 'has created for the non-Christians a different government outside the

---

[36] Ibid., pp. 98–9.
[37] Martin Luther, 'Secular authority: to what extent should it be obeyed', in John Dillenberger (ed.), *Martin Luther: Selections from His Writings* (New York: Anchor Books, 1961), p. 369.

Christian estate and God's kingdom, and has subjected them to the sword, so that, even though they would do so, they cannot practice their wickedness, and that, if they do, they may not do it without fear nor in peace and prosperity'.[38] Although Christians had their own kingdom, and faith gave them the capacity to self-regulate, Luther believed that they also lived in the kingdom of the world and that they were obligated to observe the dictates of the civil power. True Christians would always be a minority, he held, and for their own protection, and out of Christian obligation to help all others, they were bound as tightly by civil rule as non-Christians. 'Because the sword is of great benefit and necessary to the whole world, to preserve peace, to punish sin and to prevent evil, he submits most willingly to the rule of the sword, pays tax, honors those in authority, serves, helps, and does all he can to further the government, that it may be held in honor and fear.'[39] As we have seen, early Protestant thinkers not only believed in the separation of temporal and spiritual authorities, but argued for the supremacy of the former. In Luther's words, 'Forasmuch as the temporal power has been ordained by God for the punishment of the bad and the protection of the good, therefore we must let it do its duty throughout the whole Christian body, without respect of persons, whether it strikes popes, bishops, priests, monks, nuns, or whoever it may be.'[40]

The conception of civil power advanced by Luther and others was absolutist. In general, subjects had no right of resistance. For Luther, subjects might legitimately rebel against a madman, but not against a tyrant, as it was God's role to punish the latter, the subject's to suffer in obedience. But like Grotius and Hobbes, Luther granted princes only so much authority as was needed to ensure social order. The domain of civil authority was the domain of external goods, and the prince's role was to protect his subjects' life and property. 'Worldly government', Luther argued, 'has laws which extend no farther than to life and property and what is external upon earth.'[41] What lay outside this domain of civil authority was as important as what lay within. In particular, civil powers had no right to control belief. 'For over the soul God can and will let no one rule but Himself. Therefore, where

[38] Ibid., p. 370.      [39] Ibid., p. 373.
[40] Martin Luther, 'Address to the nobility of the German nation' (1520). At www.fordham.edu/halsall/mod/luther-nobility.asp (accessed 13 June 2012).
[41] Luther, 'Secular authority', pp. 382–3.

temporal power presumes to prescribe laws for the soul, it encroaches upon God's government and only misleads and destroys souls.'[42] Luther's reasoning here was threefold. First, as anticipated above, he held that the realm of the soul and belief was God's realm, and since he had already advocated an absolute separation of the kingdom of God from the kingdom of the world, civil authority trespassed against God if it tried to dictate belief. Second, Luther believed that prescribing belief was a pointless exercise. 'For no matter how much they fret and fume, they cannot do more than make the people obey them by word and deed; the heart they cannot constrain, though they wear themselves out trying.'[43] Third, all that compelling belief does is encourage 'lies and false confessions', 'dreadful alien sins' that 'fall back upon him who compels them'.[44]

What we see here in early Protestant thinking is the individual's right to liberty of conscience, although not couched in the language of rights. In Luther's words, 'belief and unbelief is a matter of every one's conscience, and since this is no lessening of secular power [because that power extends only to external goods], the latter should be content to attend to its own affairs and permit men to believe one thing or another, as they are able and willing, and constrain no one by force. For faith is free work, to which no one can be forced.'[45] Luther had already laid the foundation for this right with his idea of moral individualism, of the autonomous moral agent whose capacity for faith gave them unmediated access to God's grace. It was but a logical step to see the individual's ability to exercise that faith as a fundamental, inalienable entitlement, an entitlement that licensed the individual to disobey civil commands to believe against their conscience. In the face of such commands, Luther recommended the individual declare:

Dear Lord, I owe you obedience with life and goods; command me within the limits of your power on earth, and I will obey. But if you command me to believe, and to put away books. I will not obey; for in this case you are a tyrant and overreach yourself, and command where you have neither right nor power, etc.[46]

Luther was adamant, however, that the right to disobey was not the same as the right to resist. Refusing to believe as one is commanded

[42] Ibid., p. 383.    [43] Ibid., p. 385.    [44] Ibid.
[45] Ibid.    [46] Ibid., p. 389.

by a civil authority is disobedience and a right; rebelling against that authority because of persecution for disobedience is resistance and is forbidden. 'Outrage is not to be resisted, but endured, yet they [the subjects] should not sanction it, nor serve or obey or follow by moving foot or finger.'[47] This was because punishing tyrants was God's role, and suffering for one's faith was evidence of how blessed an individual was.

The purity of these beliefs was, however, complicated by their practical expression. The Protestant rebellions that engulfed the German states, the United Provinces, and France were not only acts of resistance but acts committed in the name of belief. From the rebels' point of view, though, these were not rebellions against legitimate civil powers, but against civil powers that had been colonized by the Roman Church, contradicting the prescribed separation of temporal and spiritual authorities. Second, the ideal of the church as nothing more than a community of true believers in which the gospel is properly taught and the sacraments rightly administered was inherently unstable. The very notion of the gospel being properly taught and the sacraments rightly administered contained within it the seeds of authoritarianism, an authoritarianism increasingly apparent in Luther's later thinking and in the principal tenets of Calvinism. Furthermore, as the conflict between Protestants and Catholics escalated in the latter half of the sixteenth century, Protestants placed more and more weight on the civil power's responsibility to support the authority of the true church, a move that led directly to the creation of the Protestant state churches that survive today. Through all of this, the Protestant ideal of the individual's liberty of conscience remained intact, but it was increasingly encroached on by the contradictions of a century of resistance, rebellion, and political consolidation.

*Ideas in movement*

Showing that Protestant intellectuals held these ideas is one thing; showing that they animated the Reformation movements is another. The translation of philosophical ideas into the realm of political struggle is never straightforward. The ideas of great thinkers are always

---

[47] Ibid.

open to interpretation, and struggles over meaning characterize the internal constitution of political movements as much as the battles between them. Movements are also shaped by local and regional contexts, and these contexts affect how ideas are selected, framed, and mobilized. This having been said, though, the philosophical ideas of Luther, Calvin, and others did animate the Reformation movements, and they did so in distinctive, highly consequential ways. The remainder of this section examines how key Protestant ideas found political expression in the region most central to the Westphalian settlement: the German states.

Before proceeding, however, a word is needed on those mechanisms of diffusion that were common to all regions affected by the European Reformation. First, the Reformation was, before anything else, a movement of disaffected clerics. Luther, Calvin, Zwingli, and others formulated its principal doctrines and an ever expanding network of evangelical preachers spread these to wider populations. In a world in which literacy was still the preserve of the political, commercial, and ecclesiastical elites, it was charismatic, highly mobile individuals, preaching to the masses in the vernacular, that gave Reformation philosophy popular salience. Second, in addition to the medium of the pulpit, Reformation ideas diffused through the spread of pamphlets, woodcuts, and satirical pictures, media that carried both the positive case for change while ridiculing the most despised aspects of the Roman Church. Third, cities and towns were critical to the spread of the Reformation. Often this is attributed to the affinity between the sensibilities of the emerging bourgeoisie and Protestant discipline and austerity. But the importance of urban centers lay, most critically, in the ease of communication and mobilization they allowed. The sixteenth and seventeenth centuries were eras of attenuated communication, where a papal or imperial edict could take weeks if not months to reach its intended audience. In this context, cities and towns were the only arenas of rapid social communication. Finally, despite many attempts to cast the Reformation as the project of a particular class or social order, in reality it appealed to a broad cross-section of European society. It found converts among the greater and lesser nobility, among the commercial elite and artisans of the cities, and among the increasingly disaffected knights and peasants. Not all of these groups were engaged or mobilized in all contexts, but nor did any clear pattern of class affinity emerge.

The German states of the Holy Roman Empire lay at the heart of the Reformation. It was there that Protestant ideas received their first formulation, sparked the first reform movements, and then spread out to the rest of Europe, setting in train the century of conflicts that would eventually produce the Westphalian settlement. The period 1517 to 1552 marked the opening phase of German Reformation, encompassing the failed reconciliation attempts at the Diets of Regensburg (1541 and 1546) and ending in the attempted settlement of the Peace of Augsburg (1555).

We have already dealt at some length with Luther's ideas, focusing on his conception of the individual as an autonomous moral agent whose capacity for belief furnished direct access to the Grace of God. To what extent, however, did these ideas survive the process of political mobilization? At one level, the reformist pamphlets that proliferated at this time emphasized a secondary, or derivative, set of ideas. 'The negative aspects, in particular the assaults on traditional practices, were thus stressed. The insufficiency of human "works" and rites; the false claims made by the priesthood and papacy; the exaggerated powers attributed to masses or indulgences; the superfluous detail demanded in auricular confession; pamphlets addressed all these kinds of topics.'[48] Reformist pictorial imagery operated at a cruder level again. It conveyed

personal admiration for the person, or more properly the image, of Luther; exploitation of the slogans and emblems of popular insult and parody to denounce the old Church; the drawing of sharp antitheses between 'true' and 'false' religion, to the extent of representing the papacy as the antichrist of the apocalypse; and only later the somewhat laborious portrayal of dogma through diagram and allegory.[49]

When it came to the ideas mobilized by preachers, however, a greater fealty to the primary ideas of the Reformation was apparent. As already noted, preaching was a crucial catalyst for popular reform movements, and studies of German preachers' sermons reveal a measure of consistency in their message.

---

[48] Euan Cameron, *The European Reformation* (Oxford: Clarendon Press, 1991), p. 229.
[49] Ibid.

The preachers presented the basic common denominator of the early Reformation message in a series of fundamental themes. The primacy of the Bible, the supreme importance of belief in Christ for the forgiveness of sins, the Church as the communion of all who believe, and the sufferings of the Church in the context of the last days, were all expounded in broadly similar fashion.[50]

Each of these ideas presupposed the moral individualism propounded by Luther. The Bible was primary because it placed the individual in an unmediated relationship with the word of God. Belief was supremely important because it gave the individual direct access to God's grace. And the church was a community of believers because belief was the mark of a true Christian, and there was no room in the Protestant understanding of a Christian's relationship with God for a mediating institution such as the Roman Catholic Church. Without the idea that individuals were moral agents whose capacity for faith gave them a path to salvation, each of these ideas propagated by the reform preachers would have lacked foundation.

The political revolution generated by the preachers and propagandists was profound. In 1521 there were eighty-five 'Free and Imperial Cities' in the Holy Roman Empire, most of which were in the German states. Bernd Moeller estimates that during the sixteenth century more than fifty of these officially recognized the Reformation. Roughly half became Protestant, others allowed both Protestant and Catholic congregations to coexist, and a small group of remaining states had Protestant revolutions that were later suppressed.[51] In cities where the Reformation was most comprehensive, the process of reform moved through two broad phases: the destruction of the old order, and the establishment of 'reform churches'. In the first phase, the authority, status, and prerogatives of the Roman Catholic Church were challenged, aspects of Catholic worship were abolished (especially the mass), and the material assets of the Roman Church were seized or destroyed.[52] In the second phase, Protestant 'confessions' or 'statements of belief' were adopted, reformed standards of worship were introduced, and new church structures were established.[53] For most cities that experienced the Reformation, movement through these phases was rapid,

[50] Ibid., p. 309.
[51] Bernd Moeller, *Imperial Cities and the Reformation: Three Essays* (Philadelphia: Fortress Press, 1972), p. 41.
[52] Cameron, *The European Reformation*, p. 246.    [53] Ibid., pp. 267–72.

with the highpoint of urban reform in the German cities occurring in the 1520s to early 1530s.

The impact of reformist activism on the princely states of the empire was no less significant. In contrast to the urban councilors and magistrates, the German princes were generally closer, legally and politically, to the Emperor than they were to the people. This made them more concerned about imperial retribution and less responsive to demands from the street. As a consequence, reform was slower in the princely states than in the towns.[54] In the end, however, it was the conversion of significant sectors of the German high nobility to Protestantism that brought the Reformation to the heart of the empire. By the middle of the sixteenth century, all three of the lay electors of the empire were Protestants, and the territories of 'reformed' princes stretched from the Baltic to the borders of Switzerland.[55] The insecurities this produced within the empire were profound. As repeated efforts at conciliation within the empire failed, Catholic and Protestant princes divided into defensive leagues, the most famous of which were the Catholic League of Dessau (1524) and the Protestant League of Schmalkalden (1530).

The ideational roots of conflict among the German states were most apparent in the failure of the various conciliation efforts that preceded the Peace of Augsburg in 1555. Between 1540 and 1546 Charles V convened a series of 'colloquies' in the hope of reunifying Latin Christendom through dialogue. The most important of these were the 1541 and 1546 Diets of Regensburg. The central issue of concern at these meetings was the doctrine of 'justification', or the way in which sinners established their righteousness before God. Luther described justification as 'the doctrine by which the church stands or falls', and Calvin defined it as the 'hinge' of the Reformation. As we have seen, according to the Protestant principle of *Sola Fide*, individuals could attain salvation through faith alone. For Catholics, however, righteousness was also dependent upon doing good works and performing the sacraments, the last of which gave the Roman Church a mediating role in the process of justification. Negotiations at the 1541 Diet of Regensburg focused on what has come to be called 'The Book of Regensburg', a compromise document of twenty-three Articles designed to foster conciliation between the parties. The Article on justification was vigorously contested, but in end an agreement was reached. This was

[54] Ibid.    [55] Ibid., pp. 271–2.

short-lived, however, as subsequently neither Luther nor the papacy would endorse the terms.

The second Diet of Regensburg, convened five years later, was the Emperor's last significant attempt at reunification through conciliation. Its circumstances were not favorable, though. Tensions were high between the Emperor and the Schmalkalden League, and the Diet was competing with the Pope's Council of Trent (convened in December 1545). Having boycotted the Council, Protestant attendance at the Diet was strong. But because the Catholics saw a Church Council as the only body that could legitimately decide questions of faith, their commitment to the Diet was weak. Under such circumstances, the prospect of agreement was remote, and participants would not even renew the previous Diet's precarious agreement on justification. Soon after the Diet closed war broke out between the Emperor and the League, resulting eventually in the defeat of Protestant forces at the Battle of Mühlberg in April 1547. Angered by the Pope's transfer of the Council from Trent to Bologna, and despairing of the prospects of reunification through dialogue, Charles sought unity through imperial decree. In 1548 he issued the Interim of Augsburg, or *interreligio imperialis*. Catholic in spirit, the Interim tried to paper over the principal theological divisions, providing only the broadest formulations on key issues such as justification. Its status as an imperial edict, however, doomed it from the start, and its artful compromises on critical issues such as justification satisfied neither Catholics nor Protestants.[56]

War was the Interim's immediate consequence. Allied with France, the Prince Elector Maurice of Saxony and Wilhelm of Hesse invaded Augsburg and the Tyrol, forcing the Emperor and his brother (and successor) Ferdinand I to flee Innsbrück. Unable to pursue the war, Charles sued for peace at Passau in July 1552. The religious divisions animating the conflict were not settled, however, until the Diet of Augsburg in 1555. The Peace of Augsburg is famous for instituting the principle of *cuius regio, eius religio* – whose rule, his religion. The time for the reunification of Latin Christendom had passed, and the best that could be achieved was a religious pluralism drawn on the political map of the day. The Peace upheld two core principles. First, that the Emperor and the Catholic Electors and Princes shall do

---

[56] Donald Nugent, *Ecumenism in the Age of Reformation: The Colloquy of Poissy* (Cambridge MA: Harvard University Press, 1974), p. 9.

no 'violence or harm to any estate of the empire on account of the Augsburg Confession' (Article 15), and the Protestant estates 'shall let all the Estates and Princes who cling to the old religion live in absolute peace and in the enjoyment of all their estates, rights and privileges' (Article 16). Second, that subjects whose religion conflicted with that of their Prince shall be free to move to another region, 'hindered neither in the sale of their estates after due payment of local taxes nor injured in their honour' (Article 24).

The Peace is noteworthy in two respects. The idea that Princes should define the religion within their regions is often presented as a political solution to the problem of irreconcilable division, and this it was. But it was also an idea with theological roots. As we have seen, Luther held that the civil power was superior to the religious power, partly because of the need to sustain order, but also to combat heretical and blasphemous practices. For both of these reasons, Luther came to the conclusion that each state should have a single religion. But he reached this conclusion not out of concern for the peace and stability of the empire, but for reasons of theology and domestic political order. The second noteworthy feature of the Peace was its inherent instability. There was an inextricable link between the idea of justification by faith alone and the individual's liberty of conscience – if salvation came from belief, then freedom to believe was essential to salvation. Yet the Peace of Augsburg gave only a tiny minority of the German population such liberty, the lay princes of the empire (as the ecclesiastical princes were forbidden to change their confession). Key Protestant princes – the electors of Brandenburg and the Palatinate – had proposed that the subjects of each state should be free to choose between the Lutheran and Catholic faiths, but this 'apparently very liberal suggestion' was scuttled by mutual fears that Protestant princes would persecute their Catholic subjects and vice versa.[57] The Augsburg solution of *cuius regio, eius religio*, combined with the individual's stated right of exit, pasted over the central confessional controversy of the Reformation – the issue of justification – and its statism clashed with the moral individualism that animated Lutheran reformism and its attendant conflicts.

[57] Joseph Lecler, *Toleration and the Reformation*, vol. I (New York: Association Press, 1960), p. 257.

While the Peace took more than half a century to collapse into the Thirty Years' War, its precarious nature was apparent all too soon. The pluralism of the settlement was challenged almost immediately by the Counter-Reformation, a movement that combined a militant religious and political campaign to roll back Protestantism across Europe with an equally energetic campaign to reform the Roman Church itself. The institutional focal point of the Counter-Reformation was the repeatedly disrupted Council of Trent, convened by Pope Paul III in 1545, Pope Julius III in 1551, and Pope Pius IV in 1562. Boycotted by leading Protestants after they were denied a vote, and dominated by Italian bishops, the Council resulted in the uncompromising rejection of everything Protestant and the categorical rearticulation of the principal articles of Catholic religious doctrine and discipline, including traditional Catholic ideas on justification. The Counter-Reformation's most vigorous protagonists were the Society of Jesus (or Jesuits), formally recognized by Rome in 1540 and established as the most politically significant Catholic order by the time of the Augsburg settlement.

The Society was a militant force, equipped with 'heavenly' armour and 'spiritual' weapons for the conquest of souls lost to Protestantism or paganism. The Society, emphatic in the obedience which it owed to its General and the Pope, was the Church's international force and played a dominant part in extending Catholic rule, in instructing Catholic youth, in attracting the attention and devotion of kings and nobles, as active in the European battlefield of the Catholic faith as in the missions of North Africa, Asia and America.[58]

The uncompromising doctrinal reassertion of the Council of Trent, combined with the highly disciplined teaching and preaching of the Jesuits, stalled, and in places reversed, the spread of the reform churches. Poland reverted to Catholicism, and Catholic bishops and secular princes within the empire embarked on vigorous, often violent, campaigns against heretics. But if the purpose of the Counter-Reformation was the uncompromising reunification of Latin Christendom, it failed utterly, further entrenching a pluralism born of division. The pluralism it produced, however, was not the ordered pluralism envisaged at Augsburg (a pluralism of Catholic and Lutheran princes

---

[58] V. H. H. Green, *Renaissance and Reformation* (London: Edward Arnold, 1969), p. 179.

satisfied with confessional unity within their realms); it was a constantly shifting pluralism of continued religious struggle, a struggle in
which princes upheld their right to define the religion within their territories with zealotry and intolerance, and in which religious activists
sought to change the confessional orientations of princes and subjects.

Within this struggle, the reform churches found themselves at a distinct disadvantage. Faced with an increasingly unified Catholic opposition, they were ever more deeply divided – Lutherans against Calvinists, and both against radical sects such as the Anabaptists. The one
moderating force in all of this was the conciliatory stance of successive
emperors. Though resolutely Catholic in faith, and never wavering in
their commitment to the reunification of Latin Christendom, Emperors
Charles V (1530–6), Ferdinand I (1556–64), Maximilian II (1564–76),
Rudolf II (1576–1612), and Matthias (1612–19) were all influenced
by the Erasmian belief that the path to reunification lay through compromise instead of confrontation. While conciliatory initiatives such as
Charles V's colloquies were repeatedly tempered by authoritarian acts
like his Interim of Augsburg, these emperors were generally more liberal in their application of the principle of *cuius regio, eius religio* than
their subject princes. Most notably, within the territories they controlled personally, Maximilian II, Rudolf II, and Matthias all granted
Protestants the right to worship instead of exile.[59]

It was the rise of the far more militant Emperor Ferdinand II that
transformed this precarious situation into the Thirty Years' War. In
the last years of Matthias's reign, Ferdinand of Styria was installed
as King of Bohemia, one of the strongholds of Protestantism in the
empire. Deeply influenced by the Jesuits, Ferdinand was determined
to remove the religious liberties previously granted to the Bohemians
under Rudolf II's 1609 'Letter of Majesty'. Angered by Ferdinand's
attacks on their freedoms, the Protestants rebelled in 1618, and in
August 1619, two days before Ferdinand's election as emperor, they
deposed him as king and enthroned the Calvinist Frederick of the
Palatinate.[60] With the aid of papal subsidies and Spanish military assistance, Ferdinand crushed the Bohemian rebellion at the famous battle
of White Mountain, deposed Frederick, and went on to conquer the

---

[59] Lecler, *Toleration and the Reformation*, pp. 261–86.
[60] E. A. Beller, 'The Thirty Years War', in J. P. Cooper (ed.), *The New
Cambridge Modern History*, vol. IV: *The Decline of Spain and the Thirty
Years War 1609–48/59* (Cambridge University Press, 1970), pp. 311–12.

Palatinate in 1622. Catholic military successes in the German states threatened the Lutheran states of the Baltic, encouraging Christian IV of Denmark to strike a military alliance in 1625 with England and France (both of which feared Habsburg hegemony), and the Dutch Republic (which was once again at war with Spain). After a series of humiliating defeats, however, Denmark withdrew from the war in 1629. In the same year Ferdinand decreed the Edict of Restitution, returning to Catholic control all church lands that had become Protestant after 1552. These events sparked a new Protestant offensive, with Sweden and the German states of Saxony and Brandenburg joining forces to invade the Rhineland and enter Bavaria. The tide of the war turned again, however, in 1632 after Gustavus Adolphus, the Swedish king, was killed in the Battle of Lützen. In 1634, imperial, Bavarian, and Spanish forces combined to defeat the Protestant states, prompting a succession of German states to withdraw from the war. Concerned by Sweden's flagging war effort, Cardinal Richelieu swung French forces into the war in 1635, aiming to counter the threat of Habsburg hegemony. Though defeated initially, the French recovered and, with Swedish, English, and Dutch assistance, inflicted devastating losses on the Austrian and Spanish Habsburgs between 1637 and 1648, ultimately forcing Emperor Ferdinand III to accede to the Treaties of Westphalia in October 1648.

## The Westphalian settlement

By 1648 the religious conflicts that fueled the Thirty Years' War had been tearing at the foundations of Europe's heteronomous order for over 130 years, and in this respect the 'Wars of Religion' significantly predate the violence precipitated by the Bohemian revolt of 1618. As we have seen, it was the Protestant Reformation that sparked and fueled these conflicts, animated as it was by a set of ideas about the individual's relationship with God, and about the relation between civil and religious authorities, that fundamentally challenged the transnational authority of both the Catholic Church and the Holy Roman Empire. With hindsight it is clear that these conflicts could be resolved only through a political settlement with two characteristics. First, a settlement would have to recognize the political authority and autonomy of princes and republics of diverse confessional orientations. Second, it would have to recognize the rights of individuals within those polities to some measure of liberty of conscience. The Peace of Augsburg was flawed from the start in recognizing only the first of these. Its cardinal principle of *cuius regio, eius religio* recognized the legitimacy of both Catholic and Protestant princes, and established their political rights in the critical area of defining the religion within their respective regions. But in doing the latter, while giving non-conforming subjects only the right of exit, the principle contradicted the rights of individuals to any liberty of conscience. The significance of the Westphalian settlement, and the key to its success in resolving almost a century and a half of religious conflicts, is that it contained within it both forms of recognition.

With regard to recognizing the political authority of both Catholic and Protestant princes, the Westphalian settlement confirmed explicitly the continued legal authority of the Treaty of Augsburg, as well as its antecedent, the 1552 Treaty of Passau. Article V.1 of the Treaty of Osnabrück states:

That the Transaction settled at Passau in the Year 1552 and follow'd in the Year 1555 with the Peace of Religion, according as it was confirm'd in the Year 1556 at Augsburg, and afterwards in divers other Diets of the sacred *Roman* Empire, in all its Points and Articles agreed and concluded by the unanimous Consent of the Emperor and Electors, Princes and States of both Religions, shall be maintain'd in its Force and Vigour, and sacredly and inviolably observ'd.[61]

The Treaties of Westphalia went well beyond these provisions, however, in recognizing the authority and autonomy of the German princes. To begin with, the 'Electors, Princes and States of the *Roman* Empire' were guaranteed 'free Exercise of their Territorial Right, as well in Spirituals and Temporals'.[62] More than this, they were also granted significant powers within the governing structures of the empire. The Treaty of Münster established an 'exact and reciprocal Equality amongst the Electors, Princes and States of both religions' in the empire, and their constituents were ensured 'without contradiction the Right of Suffrage in all Deliberations touching the affairs

---

[61] 'Treaty of Osnabrück of 24 October 1648' (Instrumentum Pacis Osnabrugentis, IPO), reprinted in Clive Parry (ed.), *Consolidated Treaty Index*, vol. I (New York: Dobbs Ferry, 1969), Article V.1.
[62] Ibid., Article VIII.

of the Empire',[63] especially the making or interpreting of Laws, the declaring of Wars, the imposing of Taxes, levying or quartering of Soldiers, and erecting new fortifications in the Territories of States. On top of all of this, the German states were also given the right to form alliances within and beyond the empire, providing these were not directed against the empire itself.[64]

These features of the Westphalian settlement are the ones most commonly highlighted, invoked as evidence of the treaties' importance in the constitution of an international order based on sovereign states. Highlighted less often is the settlement's recognition of the rights of individuals within emergent states to liberty of conscience, rights that significantly 'compromised' these states' sovereignty, as Krasner correctly observes.[65]

This recognition is most clearly expressed in Articles V.28 to V.30 of the Treaty of Osnabrück, articles explicitly devoted to 'Liberty of Conscience', something largely ignored by most commentators. The settlement ruled that 'Ecclesiastical Affairs' and the 'Politics with regard to them' were to be returned to the condition they were in in the year 1624. Using this date as the baseline, Article V.28 granted Protestants living in Catholic states, and Catholics living in Protestant states, liberty of belief and worship. It reads:

It has moreover been found good, that those of the Confession of *Augsburg*, who are subjects of Catholicks, and Catholick Subjects of the States of the Confession of *Augsburg*, who had not the publick or private Exercise of their Religion in any time of the year 1624, and who after the publication of the Peace shall profess and embrace a Religion different from that of the Lord of the Territory, shall in consequence of the said Peace be patiently suffered and tolerated, without any Hindrance of Impediment to attend their Devotions in their Houses and in private, with all Liberty of Conscience, and without any Inquisition or Trouble, and even to assist in their Neighbourhood, as often as they have a mind, as the publick Exercise of their Religion, or send their Children to foreign Schools of their Religion, or have them instructed in their Families by private Masters . . . [66]

Exercise of these rights was not without limit; minority religious groups were free to 'Exercise their Religion' on the condition that 'the said

---

[63] 'Treaty of Münster of 24 October 1648' (Instrumentum Pacis Monasteriensis, IPM), reprinted in Parry (ed.), *Consolidated Treaty Series*, vol. I, Article LXV.
[64] 'Treaty of Osnabrück', Article VIII.1.
[65] Krasner, *Sovereignty*, p. 77.     [66] 'Treaty of Osnabrück', Article V.28.

Vassals and Subjects do their Duty in all other things, and hold themselves in due Obedience and Subjection, without giving occasion to
any Disturbance or Commotion'.[67]

In recognizing the above rights, the Westphalian settlement went
well beyond the Peace of Augsburg, and just how far it went is evident
in the Treaty of Osnabrück's provisions governing what is to happen
if a prince changes his religion. Under the principle of *cuius regio, eius
religio* princes were licensed to define the religions of their territories,
which meant that if a prince changed his religion, or his successor professed a different faith, his subjects would have to change their religion
as well. The consequences of this for subject peoples were severe. In the
context of the Counter-Reformation and the struggle between Lutherans and Calvinists for Protestant ascendancy, the religious identities
of the German princes were often fluid, creating a heightened state of
religious insecurity for their peoples. In the Palatinate, for example,
Frederick III converted to Calvinism and, despite the Treaty of Augsburg recognizing only Lutheranism, forcibly converted his subjects.
When he died, his son Louis VI reestablished Lutheranism, and those
who refused to convert were exiled. Under Frederick IV, his successor,
Calvinism was again restored and imposed on a population that had
now seen three changes of religion in just over half a century.[68]

The Westphalian settlement clearly proscribed such practices. A
prince who changed his religion, or who acquired a new territory
where a different religion was practiced, was entitled to practice his
faith and to have preachers of his religion in his court. But he could
not demand that his subjects change their religion. Article VII of the
Treaty of Osnabrück states:

That if a Prince, or other Lord of a Territory, or Patron of any Church,
should afterwards go over to the Religion of another party, or acquire or
recover by Right of Succession, or by virtue of the present Transaction, or by
any other Title, a Principality or Dominion where the Religion of another
Party is publickly exercis'd at present, it shall be lawful for him without
controversy to have near himself, and at his abode or place or Residence,
private Preachers of his own Religion for his Court; but so that this may be
no Charge or Prejudice to his Subjects. But it shall not be lawful to change
the Exercise of Religion, or the Ecclesiastical Laws and Customs which shall
have been receiv'd formerly, nor to take the Churches, Schools, Hospitals,

---

[67] Ibid.       [68] Lecler, *Toleration and the Reformation*, pp. 277–8.

or the Revenues, Pensions and Salaries thereto belonging, from the first Possessors, and confer them upon those of his own Religion; and far less to oblige his Subjects under pretext of Right of Territory, Episcopal Right, that of Patronage, or any other, to receive Ministers of another Religion, or give any trouble or molestation to the Religion of others directly or indirectly.[69]

When these provisions are combined with those governing liberty of conscience, it is clear that the Westphalian settlement both upheld the principle of *cuius regio, eius religio* and severely circumscribed it. Under the Treaty of Augsburg, the principle established the prince's external and internal authority: externally it gave princes freedom from the transnational authorities of the Catholic Church and the Holy Roman Empire; internally it gave them the right to impose their religion on their subjects. The Westphalian settlement, in contrast, granted them only the first of these while placing significant limits on the second. Augsburg licensed plurality externally and homogeneity internally; Westphalia authorized plurality externally and toleration internally.

The principles laid down in the Treaty of Osnabrück on liberty of religious conscience found expression in the two other Westphalian treaties, though not in the same detail. The Treaty of Münster guaranteed the 'Electors, Princes and States of the *Roman* Empire... free exercise of Territorial Right, as well as Ecclesiastick', and it formally confirmed and ratified the Treaty of Osnabrück's articles on liberty of conscience.[70] Similarly, the Spain–Netherlands Treaty of May 1648 declared that the 'States-General of the *United Provinces*, and the Provinces thereof, with their dominions and dependencies, to be a free state'.[71] It said comparatively little on the question of religious freedom. But what it did say appears to follow the general principle that minority religious practices were to be tolerated so long as they didn't threaten civil order. Netherlanders in Spain and Spanish in the Netherlands were 'obliged to behave themselves modestly in points of religion, without giving scandal or offence'.[72]

---

[69] 'Treaty of Osnabrück', Article VII.    [70] 'Treaty of Münster', Article LXIV.
[71] 'Peace of Münster of 30 January 1648 between Spain and the United Provinces', reprinted in Parry (ed.), *Consolidated Treaty Series*, vol. I, Article I. Note that this treaty was signed in January but not ratified until 15 May 1648.
[72] Ibid., Article XIX.

The Westphalian settlement not only concluded the Thirty Years' War, it put an end to the religious conflicts that had plagued Europe since the beginning of the sixteenth century. Holsti writes:

The religious issue, the overriding source of increasing chaos, brutality, and intolerance throughout Europe for the preceding century, was resolved according to principles with which the rulers and dynasts of the day, if not the Popes, could live. No war occurring after 1648 – wars against the Ottomans excepted – derived primarily from religious issues. The Westphalia religious formula, moreover, was so successful that it served as a model for numerous other treaties, such as the Peace of Olivia (1660) ending the Swedish-Polish War.[73]

As F. H. Hinsley observes, the Treaties of Westphalia came to be seen 'as the public law of Europe'.[74] Over time, the principles they enshrined evolved into international social norms against which the domestic conduct of states could be judged. Evidence of this was the European response to Louis XIV's revocation of the Edict of Nantes, the edict recognizing the rights of the French Huguenots. The revocation was energetically condemned by the Protestant powers of Europe, and was seen as a clear violation of the norms enshrined in the Treaties of Westphalia. Not only did his demand that French Protestants convert to Catholicism violate the principles concerning freedom of belief and worship, his denial of their right to emigrate contradicted the *jus emigrandi* that dated back to the Peace of Augsburg.[75]

## Conclusion

As explained in the first part, the Westphalian settlement did not bring forth a fully formed sovereign order – it did not eradicate feudal bonds, destroy all transnational authority, or define the territorial reach of sovereign power. But it was a critical moment in the transformation toward such an order. In particular, it recognized the political agency and authority of a range of new polities, and it granted these states

[73] Holsti, *Peace and War*, p. 38.
[74] F. H. Hinsley, *Power and the Pursuit of Peace: Theory and Practice in the History of Relations between States* (Cambridge University Press, 1867), p. 168.
[75] Heather Rae, *State Identities and the Homogenization of Peoples* (Cambridge University Press, 2002), pp. 218–19.

legitimate powers that would come to be seen as the sole preserve of modern sovereign states. It was, in short, a crucial moment in the constitution of the membership of a new social order, a social order that would become the modern system of sovereign states.

Critical to this transformation was the politics of rights. The 'grund' idea animating the Reformation as a political movement was the individual's unmediated relationship with God, an idea that simultaneously challenged the authority of the Roman Catholic Church (and in turn the Holy Roman Empire) and provoked the central, unresolved controversies over issues such as justification. It was also the idea that made the Peace of Augsburg an unsatisfactory and unstable resolution of the conflicts attending the Reformation, an idea that the Westphalian settlement's provisions concerning liberty of conscience finally acknowledged. Ideas about individuals as integral moral agents, and the way in which these ideas fed violent conflict, undermined established authority structures, justified the secular power of the emerging German, Dutch, and Swiss states (while delimiting this power in critical ways), and ultimately defined the parameters of a stable resolution to the conflicts. They were thus central to this, the first wave of international systemic expansion.

This is not to deny, of course, the importance of other factors in shaping the Westphalian settlement, but it highlights the importance of rights politics as primary to both the conflicts that necessitated the Peace of Westphalia and the nature of their resolution. The default explanation of Westphalia emphasizes the protracted consequences of war-fighting – after thirty years of devastating conflict, the contending parties hammered out a peace that reflected their contrasting interests and relative political, economic, and military power. But this says nothing about the origins of conflicts that dated back to the first half of the sixteenth century, it leaves unexplained the key provisions of the Treaties of Westphalia governing religious freedom (other than to imply that these were in the 'interests' of contenders with sufficient 'power' to pursue them), and it contributes little to an explanation of why the Westphalian settlement so successfully removed religion as a source of war within Europe. To answer these questions, some appreciation of the importance of rights politics is required. A second, related account of Westphalia emphasizes the importance of Habsburg hegemony. Some argue that the rise of German and Spanish

Habsburg power threatened France, Sweden, the United Provinces, and the non-Habsburg principalities of the empire, and that these actors were waging a counter-hegemonic war. Others argue that it was Habsburg weakness that provoked the war, and that opportunism motivated the other protagonists. The problem with both of these explanations (beyond their mutually contradictory nature) is that it is difficult to construct a plausible account of Habsburg power as either a threat or an opportunity independent of questions of religion. It was not non-Habsburg princes who challenged the authority of the Holy Roman Empire, it was Protestant princes, and they challenged it because of the emperors' status as defender of the Roman Catholic Church. Only by forswearing any interest in the underlying sources of conflict within the Holy Roman Empire, or any interest in why the treaties resolved these sources, can the politics of rights be excluded from an account of the Westphalian settlement.

Having said this, the settlement was the product of nascent rights and it produced nascent sovereignty. As argued earlier, Europe's heteronomous order was rights based; it was a power structure bound together by ancient rights and attendant obligations, some based on custom, some on law, some on religious doctrine and tradition, and some on an amalgam of all these. It was, however, a hierarchical order, one in which a person's rights designated their position within a stratified social and political structure. It was not an order based on general individual rights, rights attached to persons as integral moral agents. What we see in the period from 1520 to 1648 is the gradual emergence of these kinds of rights, and they emerge in the area of religious freedom. For a political culture of individual rights to emerge, there has to be a concept of the individual as having primary moral value, and there has to be an associated belief that protecting certain spheres of individual freedom (and hence a person's status as an integral moral agent) justifies placing constraints on the nature and exercise of political power. The Reformation saw the emergence of both of these beliefs. It was the Treaties of Westphalia, however, that began the process of translating the Reformation's ideas of individual liberty of conscience into what we call today 'minority rights'. As this process was underway, the treaties also constituted the sovereignty of the state. Jean Bodin and others may have articulated a philosophical defense of sovereignty as early as the fifteenth and early sixteenth centuries, but sovereignty in law and practice was only partially achieved at Westphalia, with the ongoing notion of dynastic succession challenging territoriality well into the eighteenth century. Rights politics and the politics of state sovereignty thus emerged in tandem, and far from being parallel and independent, they were deeply entwined.

# 4 | *The independence of Spanish America*

By the middle of the eighteenth century the European political order had two dimensions. The first was the increasingly mature system of sovereign states within Europe itself. The Peace of Utrecht (1713–15) had clarified the territorial dimension of sovereignty, the absolutist conception of legitimate statehood prevailed, and the idea that European powers should work together to achieve order through the balancing of power had begun to take root. The second was the system of colonial empires maintained by Europe's maritime powers, the most extensive and well consolidated of which were the British, Spanish, and Portuguese empires in the Americas. Sovereignty at home and empire abroad was considered utterly natural by most Europeans, and in the first decades of the eighteenth century, by most Americans as well. Empire was considered a God-given extension of a monarch's domain, evidence of an imperial culture's superiority, and a vital resource in mercantilist struggles for state power. As the Holy Roman Empire continued its steady decline within Europe, the great overseas empires appeared as robust as their absolutist metropoles.

By 1825, however, the European empires in the Americas had all but collapsed. The collapse began with the Declaration of Independence by the United States in 1776, but its most dramatic phase occurred between 1808 and 1825 when the Spanish and Portuguese empires imploded, producing seventeen newly independent states. In less than two decades an international system comprising absolutist monarchies and their empires was replaced by a more variegated system, one populated by monarchies *and* republics, one of multiple regions of independent states, and one in which the locus of empire had shifted from the Americas to Asia and Australasia (and later Africa). The globalization of the system of sovereign states had begun.

This chapter argues that the politics of rights played a critical role in this transformation, a role most palpable in the collapse of the Spanish

Empire (the collapse that gave the international system the majority of its new members at this time). Rights politics did not, however, precipitate the collapse. It was the French invasion of Spain in 1807–8, the subsequent installation of Napoleon's brother as king, and the nature of the ensuing Spanish insurgency that catalyzed change. It was through the lens of rights, however, that Spanish Americans interpreted these developments, understood their interests, and fashioned their political responses. Yet the rights that they saw as violated and the rights they struggled to secure were a complex amalgam of old and new. The story is not a simple one of colonial peoples embracing the revolutionary ideals of their French 'liberators', the ideals of liberty, equality, and fraternity. Instead, Spanish Americans first interpreted the events of 1807–8 in terms of their medieval constitutional rights and traditional Spanish theories of sovereignty, rights and theories which held that sovereignty returned to the people if there was no legitimate monarch on the throne. Liberal ideas about individual rights came to the fore, however, at the insurgent General Cortes of Cádiz, where Peninsulares and 'Americanos' gathered to negotiate a constitution for a reformed, post-Napoleonic empire. The majority of delegates were committed to establishing a constitutional monarchy, with significant powers invested in representative forums. Yet a fundamental divide quickly emerged over the nature and terms of political representation. The Cortes was dominated by liberals, all of whom agreed that it was the individual who merited political representation, not traditional corporate bodies. The peninsular Spaniards and the Americans could not agree, however, on who constituted an 'individual' with a right to equal political representation: for the former, only those of Spanish blood qualified; for the latter, in addition to Creoles, Indians and freed slaves counted as well. After lengthy, acrimonious debate, the Americans were defeated in each key vote, producing the racially exclusive 1812 Spanish Constitution, and radicalizing the American insurgencies, turning them from reform to revolutionary secession.

The chapter is divided into four parts. After considering in greater detail the transformation of the international system that attended the independence of the Americas, I critically review the existing literature, within both International Relations and Latin American studies. I then turn to the central issue of the role of rights politics in the

Spanish Empire's collapse. The third part examines the eighteenth-century Bourbon reforms to imperial governance and economic extraction, which despite their systematic harshness, failed to provoke widespread calls for colonial independence. I then turn, in the fourth part, to the catalytic events of the Napoleonic usurpation of the Spanish crown, the spread of insurgencies across the empire, and the crucial divisions over the individual's right to equal political representation that turned the Americans from reform to revolution.

## Absolutism and Latin American independence

In 1648 the foundations of an absolutist system of sovereign states were visible to all. The Westphalian treaties had weakened the transnational authority of the Holy Roman Empire and the papacy, ordained the German states, the Swiss Confederacy, and the United Provinces with many of the rights we now associate with sovereignty, and reaffirmed the divine right of kings as the source of legitimate political authority. It was not until the middle of the eighteenth century, however, that absolutist international society stood fully formed. The preceding century had witnessed a significant growth in, and centralization of, the administrative structures of the major European states, and their frontiers had begun to resemble modern territorial borders. This was encouraged and sanctioned by developments in ideas of sovereignty. As explained in Chapter 3, the Westphalian settlement had defined the scope of sovereign rights – the areas of social life over which a sovereign could rightly exercise authority – but had left the geographical reach of those rights ambiguous. As the War of Spanish Succession (1701–13) so tragically demonstrated, the Westphalian settlement did little to diminish the general view that sovereign rights extended as far as the dynastic family tree. It was the Peace of Utrecht (1713) that eventually conjoined sovereignty and territoriality, establishing the principle that dynastic rights could be legitimately curtailed in the name of preserving a balance of power between sovereign states. These consolidations of state administration and sovereignty were licensed by the same conception of legitimate statehood that prevailed at Westphalia, the idea that a king's authority derived not from the consent of the people but from the command of God. In the words of Jean Domat, a leading French jurist in the reign of Louis XIV, 'It is from Him [God] that all who govern hold their power and authority, and it is God himself they represent in their functions.'[1]

This increasingly mature sovereign order had evolved in tandem with a by then well-established imperial order. As Edward Keene's excellent study demonstrates, by the eighteenth century Europeans were 'adopting one kind of relationship, equality and mutual interdependence, as the norm in their dealings with each other, and another, imperial paramountcy, as normal in their relations with non-Europeans'.[2] This sense of paramountcy applied to Europe's settler colonies in the Americas as well as subjects of non-European descent, particularly indigenous peoples.[3] In the former case, it was based on a denial of their independent national identities; in the latter, on their civilizational inferiority – the first a denial of difference, the second an insistence. The degree to which sovereignty at home and empire abroad had become the norm for Europeans of the eighteenth century is evident in the Treaty of Paris (1763) which ended the Seven Years' War, a war fought between all of the major European powers over continental and colonial territories. The treaty, signed by George III of Britain, Louis XV of France, Charles III of Spain, and acceded to by Joseph I of Portugal, licensed a complex series of colonial transfers between the signatories, most notably the transfer of French and Spanish territories in North America to Britain. In doing so the treaty simultaneously reaffirmed these monarchs' sovereignty and the taken for granted character of European colonialism – the European powers had fought over who should have which territories, but they never questioned their general sovereign rights to have such possessions. That such a treaty was signed merely thirteen years before the American Declaration of Independence indicates just how deeply – and unreflectively – these assumptions were held at Europe's courts.

The heyday of Europe's American empires was soon to pass, however. The independence of the 'thirteen United States of America' was swift, and George III's reaction hostile. Even after acknowledging

---

[1] This passage is taken from translated extracts of Jean Domat's *Le Droit Public*, reprinted in William F. Church (ed.), *Impact of Absolutism in France: National Experience under Richelieu, Mazarin, and Louis XIV* (New York: John Wiley & Sons, 1969), pp. 79–80.

[2] Keene, *Beyond the Anarchical Society*, p. 6.

[3] On the latter, see Paul Keal, *European Conquest and the Rights of Indigenous Peoples* (Cambridge University Press, 2003).

that Britain had little hope of recovering the colonies, he reportedly pledged 'never to acknowledge the independence of the Americans, and to punish their contumacy by the indefinite prolongation of a war which promised to be eternal'.[4] It was the collapse of the Spanish and Portuguese empires four to five decades later, however, that severed Europe's hold on the Americas, with Britain's 'Canadian' colonies left as the only substantial imperial holdings in the region. Between 1810 and 1825 these empires imploded, producing what would eventually become seventeen new sovereign states, all but two of them carved out of the Spanish Empire. The initial fracturing was by no means categorical. A number of early declarations of independence were temporarily reversed by Spanish military force, most famously in Venezuela. And the 'pan-Americanist' aspirations of a number of prominent revolutionaries led to the initial creation of a number of temporary confederate states, Simón Bolivar's project for Gran Colombia being the classic case. Within a relatively short period, however, the secessionist revolutions had given birth to what we now know as the sovereign states of Colombia, Paraguay, Venezuela, Argentina, Chile, Guatemala, Panama, Peru, Nicaragua, Mexico, Honduras, El Salvador, Costa Rica, Ecuador, Uruguay, Bolivia, and Brazil (from Portugal). Not only had the international system become bi-regional in the less than two decades, it was suddenly populated by a sizable number of republics as well as absolutist monarchies.

The impact on the social structure of the international system was significant. The immediate effect was to create a new axis of conflict and tension, one rooted in conflicting state identities. The European society of states was dominated by absolutist monarchies, with few yet to follow Britain's constitutionalist path. In the wake of Napoleon's defeat, the Congress of Vienna (1814–15) had reaffirmed the absolutist conception of legitimate statehood, and the Concert of Europe had resolved to combat liberal and nationalist revolutions, a project embraced with particular enthusiasm by the membership of the Holy Alliance (originally Russia, Austria, and Prussia). These latter states vehemently opposed the independence of the American colonies, which they saw as a direct challenge to the divine right of kings on which

---

[4] Quoted in George O. Trevelyan, *George the Third and Charles Fox: The Concluding Part of the American Revolution* (New York: Longmans Green, 1912), p. 4.

the absolutist order rested. Second, the independence of the Americas altered European balance of power politics. Until then, the colonies had been seen as integral elements of metropolitan material and social power, as much the objects of competition as European territories and peoples. Spain's and Portugal's losses in the Americas shifted not only the balance of material power but also the geographical dynamics of competition. Finally, the collapse of the Spanish and Portuguese empires furthered changes already underway in the institutional practices of international society, most notably those of diplomacy. The revolutionary governments of the United States and France had embraced the Enlightenment critique of 'old diplomacy', characterized as it was by secrecy, the sacrificing of national to monarchical interests, and an obsession with balance of power politics. Instead, they pledged that the national interest would guide foreign policy, and to disentangle themselves from political alliances and the European balance of power. The newly independent states of Spanish and Portuguese America embraced many of these ideals, even if their early vulnerability limited their capacities to realize them in practice. The most notable consequence, however, was for these diplomatic ideals to reinforce the separation of the Americas from European balance of power politics.

## Existing literature

Explaining why this expansion of the international system occurred has been of little interest to International Relations scholars. Holsti's ambitious study of armed conflicts and international order from 1648 has nothing to say on the subject, and Charles Kupchan's equally ambitious examination of imperial vulnerability leaves aside the collapse of the Spanish Empire.[5] Rodney Bruce Hall's study of the development of national collective identities examines the American and, particularly, French revolutions, but not the Spanish American.[6] And Jackson's analysis of European decolonization focuses exclusively on the twentieth century, a tendency broadly characteristic of most works

[5] Holsti, *Peace and War*; Charles Kupchan, *The Vulnerability of Empire* (Ithaca, NY: Cornell University Press, 1996).
[6] Rodney Bruce Hall, *National Collective Identity: Social Constructs and International Systems* (New York: Columbia University Press, 1999).

on decolonization and self-determination.[7] Even members of the English School, with their trademark interest in the expansion of international society, have added little more than bare description. Adam Watson's short essay on the subject sets out the broad contours of the expansion but offers no explanation.[8] While there has been a newfound interest in the Westphalian transformation, and the field continues its traditional interest in the twentieth century, the nineteenth century has remained largely the preserve of those interested in the Concert of Europe, British hegemony, and the new imperialism of the 'scramble for Africa'. Understanding the second of the international system's great expansions has thus been left almost exclusively to students of Latin American history and politics.

Victor Uribe has correctly referred to 'the enigma of Latin American independence', noting that despite the now voluminous literature on the topic 'independence remains an elusive subject'.[9] That this should be the case is hardly surprising, as the factors implicated in the demise of the Spanish Empire were multiple and deeply entwined, lending themselves to diverse interpretations and persistent debate. The literature is, however, in agreement about two things. The first is the rapid and dramatic nature of the collapse. In John Lynch's words,

> The revolutions for independence in Spanish America were sudden, violent and universal. When, in 1808, Spain collapsed under the onslaught of Napoleon, she ruled an empire stretching from California to Cape Horn, from the mouth of the Orinoco to the shores of the Pacific, the site of four viceroyalties, the home of seventeen million people. Fifteen years later she retained only Cuba and Puerto Rico, and new nations were already proliferating.[10]

The second point of agreement is that the collapse was catalyzed by exogenous events, namely the Napoleonic invasion of Spain. 'This change did not come about as a result of internal development either

---

[7] Jackson, *Quasi-States*. Karen Knop's *Diversity and Self-Determination in International Law* (Cambridge University Press, 2002) is a good recent example of the twentieth-century focus of most self-determination literature.

[8] Adam Watson, 'New states in the Americas', in Bull and Watson (eds.), *The Expansion of International Society*, pp. 127–42.

[9] Victor M. Uribe, 'The enigma of Latin American independence', *Latin American Research Review*, 32.1 (1997), 236, 255.

[10] John Lynch, *The Spanish American Revolutions: 1808–1826*, 2nd edn. (New York: Norton, 1986), p. 1.

in Spain or in Spanish America,' writes François-Xavier Guerra. 'It
followed Napoleon's invasion of Spain and the forced abdication of
King Ferdinand VII, rejected by the majority of Spaniards and Spanish
Americans in the name of a set of values which were still, in essence,
those of a traditional society.'[11]

Beyond these two points of consensus, numerous factors or variables have been identified to explain Spanish-American independence.
The most frequently invoked are the reforms to colonial governance
instituted by Spain's Bourbon monarchs in the eighteenth century, the
growth of nationalist sentiments among Creole elites in the Americas,
and the opportunity for revolution provided by the constitutional crisis
in Spain that followed the abdication of Ferdinand VII.[12] Additional
factors have included the failure of peninsular elites to find common
ground and adopt consistent policies toward insurgent politics,[13] the
varied responses to dissent by royal governments in the Americas,[14]
the erosion of traditional means of social control and integration,[15]
the empire's failure to accommodate demands by American economic
elites for extra-imperial free trade,[16] the examples provided by the
American and French revolutions, and the influence of the scientific,
economic, and political ideas of the Enlightenment.[17]

All of these factors were no doubt implicated in the process of
decolonization – this is not a story amenable to monocausal explanation. Alone, however, they leave three questions unanswered. Clearly
the suddenness of the revolutionary turn was directly related to the
Napoleonic invasion, the abdication of Ferdinand VII, Napoleon's
installation of Joseph I, and the nature of the ensuing empire-wide
insurgencies. But, first, why did key Spanish-American political elites

[11] Guerra, 'Spanish-American tradition of representation', p. 2.
[12] See Lynch, *The Spanish American Revolutions*.
[13] See Timothy Anna, *Spain and the Loss of America* (Lincoln: University of
Nebraska Press, 1983).
[14] See Jorge I. Dominguez, *Insurrection or Loyalty: The Breakdown of the
Spanish American Empire* (Cambridge, MA: Harvard University Press, 1980).
[15] See George Reid Andrews, 'Spanish American independence: a structural
analysis', *Latin American Perspectives*, 12.1 (1985), 105–32.
[16] See Peggy Liss, *Atlantic Empires: The Network of Trade and Revolution,
1713–1826* (Baltimore: Johns Hopkins University Press, 1982); John Fisher,
*Trade, War, and Revolution: Exports from Spain to Spanish America,
1791–1820* (Liverpool: Institute of Latin American Studies, 1992).
[17] See Carlos Fuentes, *The Buried Mirror: Reflections on Spain and the New
World* (Boston: Houghton Mifflin, 1992), pp. 233–48.

eventually choose independence as their response to these events? As David Bushnell points out, other options were available.

Spanish Americans could accept the rule of Joseph Bonaparte. Alternatively, they could swear obedience either to the provisional authorities thrown up by the Spanish movement of national resistance against the French or else to Ferdinand VII's sister Carlota.... Or, again, they could establish native American juntas to rule in the name of the captive Ferdinand exactly as his Spanish provinces had done [a move initially embraced but later abandoned in favor of independence].[18]

Second, why did the revolution come to engulf almost all of Spanish America? Comparative political scientists have devoted considerable attention to explaining why different colonies responded differently, why some were hotbeds of revolutionary struggle from the outset while others remained loyal until quite late in the process, in a number of cases 'embracing' independence only after having been 'liberated' by armies from other colonies.[19] But in emphasizing the particular these studies neglect one of the most striking features of the independence phenomenon – its universality. Third, why did the independence revolutions produce remarkably similar constitutionalist states, at least in the immediate aftermath of imperial collapse? Given Latin America's history of coup d'état, dictatorship, and constitutional crisis, it is understandable that scholars have focused on the region's failure to develop robust liberal democratic institutions. But the constitutionalist states created upon independence were liberal in intent and design, and certainly so by the standards of the time. Understanding why they proved so fragile is clearly important, but so too is understanding why they took the form they did in the first place.

To answer these questions we need to introduce the constitutive role played by ideas, in particular ideas about rights. To date, arguments about ideas and Spanish-American independence have taken three forms. The first, seldom advanced today, sees a direct causal connection between the political ideas of the Enlightenment (especially 'the rights of man') and the Spanish-American revolutions. The second, an often polemical response to the first, attributes the revolutions not to

---

[18] David Bushnell, 'The independence of Spanish South America', in Leslie Bethell (ed.), *The Cambridge History of Latin America*, vol. III: *From Independence to 1870* (Cambridge University Press, 1985), p. 95.
[19] See, for example, Dominguez, *Insurrection or Loyalty*.

the influence of Enlightenment philosophy but to traditional Spanish ideas and practices of political liberty.[20] The third, frequently paired with the second, acknowledges the influence of Enlightenment scientific and economic ideas but not political ones. It was ideas of rationality and experiential knowledge that Spanish Americans (and Spaniards in general) embraced, not the rights of man. And these ideas were embraced at the highest political levels, often 'for the very purpose of fortifying the political and social status quo'.[21] All of these approaches grant causal significance to ideas of some kind, but each is unsatisfying. The first because of its sheer simplicity – the ideational factors implicated in decolonization were far more complex than the inspirational effect of liberty, equality, and fraternity. The second because of its categorical refusal to acknowledge the very real role of liberal ideals in animating and justifying revolutionary action – both Bolivar and José de San Martin, the great revolutionary leaders, championed these ideals and repeatedly invoked them as the principal justifications for independence. And the third is unsatisfying in part for the same reasons as the second but also because it confuses level of social assimilation with political significance – it may well be true that on balance Spanish-American culture took more from Newton, Locke, and Descartes than Montesquieu, Voltaire, and Rousseau, but this does not mean that the latter were without political significance.

The argument advanced here differs from each of these positions, though it integrates several of their elements. I begin by rejecting the dichotomy often drawn between the influence of traditional Spanish ideas of political liberty and that of Enlightenment political ideas. Traditional ideas about sovereignty and the rights of peoples framed how Spaniards across the empire initially understood the Napoleonic usurpation, leading them to believe that without a legitimate monarch, sovereignty had returned to the people. But who were the 'people' and how were they to be represented in the deliberative institutions of a reformed, post-Napoleonic empire? It was in answering these questions that new liberal ideas about individual rights became important,

[20] An especially vigorous statement of this position is O. Carlos Stoetzer, *The Scholastic Roots of the Spanish American Revolution* (New York: Fordham University Press, 1979).
[21] Arthur Whitaker, 'The dual role of Latin America in the Enlightenment', in Arthur Whitaker (ed.), *Latin America and the Enlightenment*, 2nd edn. (Ithaca, NY: Cornell University Press, 1961), p. 6.

framing how peninsular Spaniards and Americans understood the issue of representation, but dividing them over the question of who constituted a rights-bearing individual. Traditional and new ideas were thus both implicated in the insurgent struggles that followed the usurpation, providing both common ground and the roots of fundamental division.

This argument is compatible with many of the theses on Spanish-American independence canvassed above, as it presents ideas about rights as a necessary, but not sufficient, condition of the transformation. It does, however, run against the grain of explanations that deny any significant role for ideas, arguments strongly rationalist in form, that see only material sources of interests, and that are blind to the politically constitutive role played by rhetoric and legitimation. Dominguez's thesis about patterns of insurgency and loyalty in the American colonies is a case in point. His project is to explain variations in the independence process, not its universality: 'The key question of the Spanish American experience in the first quarter of the nineteenth century', he writes, 'is why some colonies chose insurrection while others remained loyal – under the same prevailing international circumstances [including ideational conditions].'[22] As noted earlier, after exhaustively discounting other factors, he argues that 'political relations between elites participating in politics and the imperial and local governments responding to them were the decisive factors that led to insurrection or loyalty'.[23] No doubt such bargaining was important in shaping each colony's unique path to independence, but Dominguez has been criticized by historians for overzealously seeking a single explanatory variable and for reifying his cases in his emphasis on variation.[24] He has also been criticized for a lack of interest in actors' motives, and in the meanings they attributed to their actions.[25]

What concerns me here is Dominguez's treatment of the politics of legitimacy, one of the principal avenues through which ideas – particularly those of rights – condition political change. He begins by arguing

---

[22] Dominguez, *Insurrection or Loyalty*, p. 2.    [23] Ibid.

[24] For an overview of these criticisms, see Cheryl English Martin, 'Reform, trade, and insurrection in the Spanish Empire', *Latin American Research Review*, 19.3 (1984), 199–200.

[25] Richard Graham, 'Review: Jorge I. Dominguez, *Insurrection or Loyalty: The Breakdown of the Spanish American Empire*', *American Political Science Review*, 76.1 (1982), 164.

that legitimacy was central to the stability of the Spanish Empire, describing in some detail the 'Christian, Thomist political theory' that undergirded monarchical rule in Spain and the Americas.[26] The collapse of the Spanish Empire involved, at least in part, the collapse of this system of legitimation, and what Dominguez describes is a classic imperial crisis of legitimacy. At this point, however, the politics of legitimacy largely drops out of his story, referred to sporadically but not playing any central role in his analytical framework. We find, therefore, ideas and the politics of legitimacy sustaining the political edifice of empire, but absent from the politics that delegitimated that edifice and licensed the sovereign states that replaced it. That this should be so is curious indeed, as he notes explicitly that Enlightenment ideas were used to justify rebellion.[27] But here his position is not dissimilar to that of other scholars who downplay the constitutive role of ideas. It is commonplace for such scholars to admit that Enlightenment ideas were invoked as principal justifications for independence, but to follow this lead no further, as if ideas enlisted as justifications are politically inconsequential. But as we saw in previous chapters, ideas that succeed in justifying political action are politically powerful, making possible some forms of action and circumscribing others. David Bushnell denies that political ideology constituted a 'general cause' of the revolutions, but he goes so far as to describe Enlightenment ideas as 'weapons if nothing else'.[28] He fails to explore, however, what kind of weaponry these ideas were, why they were the preferred ideational armory of the revolutionary leaders, whether they were politically successful, and why. It is these questions that interest me here.

## The Spanish Empire and the Bourbon reforms

From the outset the organization of power in the Spanish Empire was informed by a distinctive conception of imperial title, a conception that would structure how Spanish Americans responded to the peninsular crisis of the early nineteenth century. In 1493 Pope Alexander VI granted the 'kings of Castile and Leon' title to all current and future dominions west and south of an imaginary line drawn from the Arctic to the Antarctic, 'one hundred leagues towards the west and south from

---

[26] Dominguez, *Insurrection or Loyalty*, pp. 11–15.    [27] Ibid., p. 122.
[28] Bushnell, 'The independence of Spanish South America', p. 107.

any of the islands commonly known as the Azores and Cape Verde'.[29] Three things were distinctive about this grant. First, in handing title to the Spanish monarchy, Alexander exercised his God-given authority to assign sovereign rights over the world's peoples and territories. Second, he granted title not to the emergent Spanish state but to the person of the monarch. The Indies thus became the personal patrimony of the Spanish crown, a point stressed repeatedly by monarchs over the next three centuries. When in 1680 the laws pertaining to the Indies were finally compiled in the *Recopilación de leyes de las Indies*, Charles II declared: 'By donation of the Holy Apostolic See and other just and legitimate titles, we are Lord of the West Indies, islands and mainland of the ocean sea, those discovered and those to be discovered, and [they] are incorporated into our Royal Crown of Castile.'[30] Third, the Spanish monarchy was an amalgam of the crowns of Castile and Aragon, an amalgam forged through the marriage of Ferdinand II and Isabella I in 1469. But Alexander's grant of title over the Indies was to the kings of Castile and Leon alone, not Aragon. 'Loyalty to the king meant loyalty to the Crowns of Castile and Leon, rather than to the Crown of Aragon, since the new lands were incorporated specifically into the two former Crowns.'[31]

The patrimonial nature of this imperial title had a significant effect on the structure of Spain's governance of the Americas. Because the new dominions were attached directly to the Spanish crown, their status was that of provinces not colonies, provinces notionally equal to those of peninsular Spain.[32] And because they were considered possessions of the Crown, the institutions created for their governance were elaborations and extensions of personal rule. This was most clearly apparent in the principal political institution of the Americas, the viceroyalty, the first two of which were established in New Spain and Peru in the first half of the sixteenth century, followed by New Granada and Rio de la Plata in the eighteenth century. 'The New Laws of 1542 institutionalized the new viceregal system of government: "the kingdoms of Peru and New Spain are to be ruled and governed by viceroys who represent our royal person". The viceroy, therefore, was the king's *alter ego*, holding court in his viceregal palace, and

---

[29] Pope Alexander VI, 'Inter caetera', 4 May 1493. Papal bull reprinted in Blair and Robertson (eds.), *The Philippine Islands 1493–1803*, vol. I. At www.gutenberg.org/files/13255/13255.txt (accessed 10 Oct. 2012).
[30] Quoted in Stoetzer, *Scholastic Roots*, p. 2.     [31] Ibid., p. 1.     [32] Ibid.

carrying with him something of the ceremonial aura of kingship.'[33] A second consequence of the imperial title's character was the relative underdevelopment of formal parliamentary or representative institutions in the Americas. In the centuries preceding the amalgamation of the Spanish crowns, the Kingdom of Aragon had evolved a set of well-articulated representative institutions, the most important of which were the Catalonian, Aragonese, and Valencian Cortes. Comprising the estates of the nobility, clergy, and towns, the Cortes were required to meet regularly, unanimity was mandated in each estate, and they had legislative (not merely advisory) power. 'The Cortes were therefore by the end of the Middle Ages powerful and highly developed institutions which played an indispensable part in the governing of the land.'[34] The story was very different, however, in the Kingdom of Castile, where although Cortes existed and functioned, they lacked the formal institutional power of their Aragonese counterparts. The Crown was under no obligation to summon the Cortes and they had no legislative power. Because the Indies were the patrimony of the Castilean monarchs, Cortes of any kind were never established there, let alone Cortes with the representative character of those in Aragon.

All of this suggests a highly centralized, authoritarian form of imperial rule. But this is only half the story, as other ideational and practical factors encouraged more qualified sovereignty and institutional latitude, if not decentralization. Alexander's papal grant provided Spanish monarchs with an ideological justification for the extension of their sovereignty to encompass the Americas. It did not, however, constitute a theory of sovereignty, only an argument about how just title had been acquired. For a Spanish theory of sovereignty one must look elsewhere, to the writings of Thomist political and legal theorists of the sixteenth and seventeenth centuries, theorists such as Francisco de Vitoria and Francisco Suárez.

The theory of sovereignty advanced by these authors was absolutist, but it had a twist with significant political implications. Absolutist conceptions of sovereignty generally hold that monarchs gain their political authority from God, establishing them 'as His lieutenants to

---

[33] Quoted in J. H. Elliott, 'Spain and America before 1700', in Leslie Bethell (ed.), *Colonial Spanish America* (Cambridge University Press, 1987), p. 66.
[34] J. H. Elliott, *Imperial Spain 1469–1716* (London: Edward Arnold, 1963), p. 17.

command the rest of mankind'.[35] They are granted such authority for a particular moral purpose – the preservation of a divinely ordained social order. In this schema, God invests monarchs with sovereignty directly so that they can protect society, understood as an organic whole.[36] Spanish theorists of sovereignty agreed with most of this, especially the idea that worldly political authority derived from God and that its purpose was the welfare of society. However, they did not believe that sovereignty passed directly from God to monarchs, unmediated. Instead, they held that God invested sovereignty in society (or more specifically 'political community'), and it was political community that granted monarchs sovereignty. Furthermore, because sovereignty was ordained by political communities, monarchs were under an obligation to govern in the common good.

Suárez provides a particularly clear articulation of this theory of sovereignty. Consistent with absolutist theory in general, Suárez insists that 'since the persons who wield this power within a human community are the ministers of God [or God's lieutenants], they accordingly administer a power received from God; and therefore, God is not only the chief Author of this power but its exclusive author'.[37] Sovereign power is first invested, however, in political communities, of which the world is divided into multiple forms, and which Suárez considers 'mystical' bodies.[38] Not only is the congregation of individuals into such communities entirely natural, so too is their possession of sovereign power, a power that does not exist in individuals, only in the political communities they form:

this power does not manifest itself in human nature until men gather together into one perfect community and are politically united. My assertion is proved as follows: the said power resides not in individual men separately considered, nor in the mass or multitude of them collected, as it were, confusedly, in a disorderly manner, and without union of the members into one body; therefore, such a political body must be constituted, before power of this sort is to be found in men, since – in the order of nature, at least – the

[35] Jean Bodin, *Six Books of the Commonwealth* (Oxford: Basil Blackwell, 1967), p. 40.
[36] Reus-Smit, *Moral Purpose*, pp. 95–7.
[37] Francisco Suárez, 'A treatise on laws and God the Lawgiver', in Francisco Suárez, *Selections from Three Works of Francisco Suárez, S.J.* (Oxford: Clarendon Press, 1944), Book III, ch. III.4, p. 379.
[38] Ibid., Book III, ch. III.6, p. 380.

agent of the power must exist prior to the existence of the power itself. Once this body has been constituted, however, the power in question exists in it, without delay and by the force of natural reason; and consequently, it is correctly supposed that it exists as a characteristic property resulting from such a mystical body, already constituted with just the mode of being [that it has] and not otherwise.[39]

While sovereign power is originally granted to a political community, Suárez holds that it must, of necessity, then be transferred to an individual, or group of individuals, within that community. His argument here is practical, not philosophical – while sovereignty is invested in a political community as a whole, 'infinite confusion and trouble would result if laws were established by the vote of every person'.[40] For this reason, sovereignty is always transferred by the community to a monarch, an aristocracy, or a democratic government, the first of which Suárez considered greatly superior. The upshot of all of this is that sovereign power 'resides immediately in the community; and, therefore, in order that it may justly come to reside in a given individual, as in a sovereign prince, it must necessarily be bestowed upon him by the consent of the community'.[41] While God is the source of sovereign authority, Suárez contends, 'its specific application as a certain form of power and government is dependent upon human choice'.[42]

The idea that legitimate sovereignty was ordained by the political community had implications for how it could be legitimately exercised. The essence of sovereign power is the capacity to make laws, and Suárez insists that laws should always be made for the common good. His reasoning is threefold. He argues, first, that it would 'be contrary to every consideration of rectitude that the common good should be subordinated to the private good' and, second, that since the happiness of the state is the end of the state, the common good should be the first principle of law.[43] His most important argument, however, is that because the political community invests the monarch with sovereign authority, the monarch should rule for the good of that community. When 'the power has been granted by men themselves', he writes, 'it is most evident that it has been granted not for the advantage of the

---

[39] Ibid., Book III, ch. III.6, pp. 379–80.   [40] Ibid., Book III, ch. IV.1, p. 383.
[41] Ibid., Book III, ch. IV.1, p. 384.   [42] Ibid., Book III, ch. IV.2, p. 382.
[43] Ibid., Book I, ch. IV, p. 92.

prince but for the common good of those who have conferred it; and for this reason, kings are called the ministers of the state.'[44]

As we shall see, this theory of sovereignty helped frame how Spanish Americans interpreted, and responded to, the Bourbon reforms of the second half of the eighteenth century and the peninsular crisis that attended the Napoleonic invasion of 1807. In response of the reforms, they affirmed the legitimacy of the monarchy but argued that Charles III's new imperialism was against the common good, a position clearly apparent in the catchcry of the Comunero Revolution of 1781: 'Long live the king and death to bad government.' In response to the peninsular crisis, Spanish Americans initially denied the usurper Joseph I's sovereign rights and pledged allegiance to Ferdinand VII. The reality, however, of the legitimate monarchy's abdication and its perceived replacement by usurpation eventually led them, together with the Peninsulares, to assert their own sovereign rights as a political community, thus licensing insurgency.

If the absolutist nature of Spain's imperial title was qualified by the Thomist theory of sovereignty, the monarchy's practical capacity to establish centralized, personal rule over the Americas was compromised by the attenuated and fragmented nature of actual imperial governance. Beneath the viceregal system existed a complex framework of lesser institutions, often with contradictory and overlapping functions and jurisdictions. In the first half of the sixteenth century, ten *audencias* were established, serving as the principal judicial bodies in the Indies. Below these were the officials who provided local government, variously termed *alcaldes*, *mayores*, or *corregidores*. Appointed for limited terms by the Crown or the viceroy, these officials governed town-centered rural districts. The towns themselves were ruled by *cabildos*, or local councils, and were generally presided over by the district *corregidor*. Any suggestion that these institutions were nested in a systematic hierarchy of political or judicial authority would be misleading. In reality,

often the lines of demarcation were not clearly drawn: different branches of government would overlap, a single official might combine different types of function, and there were endless possibilities for friction and conflict which was likely to be resolved, if at all, only by the lengthy process of reference

---

[44] Ibid., Book I, ch. V, p. 93.

to the council of the Indies in Madrid [the paramount peninsular institution for American governance].[45]

The *audencias*, for example, were designed as judicial institutions but over time developed many functions of government, and because their officers were appointed by the Crown for unlimited periods they evolved as centers of power separate from the viceroys.[46] The *cabildos* occupied a similarly complex political position. The institution had developed deep political roots in peninsular Spain, with town councils having gained considerable political powers and liberties during the Reconquista that expelled the Moors and the struggle by the Crown against the nobility, especially in Castile. In the Americas the *cabildos* became focal points for local, oligarchic politics. 'It was only by operating within this structure and resorting to lobbying and petitioning that the urban patriciates could hope to exercise any influence over governmental action and decree, for no other constitutional outlets were available to them.'[47]

The modalities of imperial rule in the Americas were, in sum, a curious blend of patrimonial assertion and absolutist ambition, on the one hand, and qualified sovereignty, institutional attenuation and contradiction, and local political autonomy, on the other. Alongside the idea of the papal grant of imperial title sat the idea that it was political communities that ordained monarchs with sovereignty; and within the formal structure of imperial governance were political spaces, interstices, that gave local political elites considerable room to maneuver: in Elliott's words, 'The presence of the state, therefore, while all-pervasive, was not all-commanding.'[48] This room to maneuver was more than a simple capacity facilitated by institutional gaps and contradictions, though. It came to be seen over time as an entitlement, a customary right. This perception was reinforced by the late medieval origins of institutions such as the *cabildo*, which had accrued significant political liberties against the Crown.

Over time the imperial system of rule established by the Habsburgs evolved a certain governance equilibrium. For all its limitations, its often overlapping and contradictory array of institutions and political relationships served the self-perceived interests of the principal actors – the Crown, the imperial bureaucracy, and Spanish-American

---

[45] Elliott, 'Spain and America before 1700', p. 64.   [46] Ibid., p. 69.
[47] Ibid., p. 71.   [48] Ibid., p. 75.

elites – and became embedded in a system of governance norms, which Lynch describes as a 'colonial consensus'.[49] The Bourbon ascent of the Spanish throne in 1700, and its confirmation after the Peace of Utrecht, marked the beginning of the end of this equilibrium. By the beginning of the eighteenth century, the Spanish state and empire were in a parlous condition, with a seriously weakened monarchy, a record of humiliating military defeats, and a dire economy. The Bourbons had little choice but to reform the imperial state and brought to their task absolutist principles and techniques honed in Louis XIV's France. It was not, however, until the reign of Charles III (1759–88) that these energies were focused, in any systemic way, on the Americas. The shift in imperial governance that Charles and his ministers forced was nothing short of a revolution, ushering in what has been termed the 'new imperialism' or 'second empire'. The colonial consensus, as well as the governance equilibrium, that had characterized the Habsburg era were destroyed, replaced by absolutist control.

By 1680, when the French and English states were consolidating their power internally and flexing their muscle internationally, the Spanish state was in a condition of advanced decline, with a crisis of government matched only by its decrepit economy. Heeren, the great nineteenth-century historian of the evolving society of states, wrote that in Spain 'all the germs of imperial corruption were so fully developed, that it is difficult to explain even the continuance of its political existence. But a great state can go a long way in the career of error, before it is overtaken by political death.'[50] Most commentators agree that Spain had reached the depths of its woes by 1680 – the low point of its economic recession – and that partially effective reforms were instituted by Charles II's ministers in the last two decades of the century, despite the monarch's mental and physical infirmity. Yet Lynch's characterization of late seventeenth-century Spain typifies how it has been seen: 'In the last decades of Habsburg rule Spain resembled a corpse, picked at by noble parasites and foreign marauders.'[51]

In the first half of the eighteenth century, the new Bourbon dynasty set about reforming the Spanish state, their goal being the creation of

[49] John Lynch, *Bourbon Spain: 1700–1808* (Oxford: Basil Blackwell, 1989), p. 333.
[50] Heeren, *A Manual*, p. 149.
[51] John Lynch, *Spain under the Habsburgs*, vol. II: *Spain and America 1598–1700* (Oxford: Basic Blackwell, 1969), p. 254.

a centralized absolutist state with the fiscal resources to sustain their territorial ambitions in Europe and beyond. Until the 1860s, however, they focused almost exclusively on the institutions of peninsular Spain, instituting a new system of government based on secretaries of state (Exchequer, Justice, War, Navy, and the Indies), abolishing traditional institutions in Aragon and Catalonia, concentrating the responsibilities of the old provincial councils in the Council of Castile, excluding the aristocracy from formal decision-making bodies, establishing a more uniform taxation system across the provinces, and reforming the military.[52] It was not until the reign of Charles III, and the humiliation of the Seven Years' War (1756–63), that the Bourbons focused, in any systematic and sustained way, on the empire, particularly the Americas. This is not to suggest that imperial reform had been off the table altogether, as significant reforms had been made, including the move to enhance royal control through the addition of the new viceroyalty in New Granada. It was the reforms instituted by Charles III, however, that revolutionized imperial governance.

Charles came to the Spanish throne after two and half decades as King of Naples and Sicily (1735–59), during which time he had successfully reformed the princely state along absolutist lines, grounding centralized royal authority in rational bureaucratic governance. He brought with him not only this experience but also a cadre of political elites whom he installed in senior ministerial positions in Spain. The imperial reforms he and his ministers instituted were animated by two objectives: to establish a more effective and direct system of absolutist political control over the 'colonies', as they were increasingly termed; and to boost the metropolitan economy by drawing more wealth out of the American periphery.

In pursuit of the first of these goals they introduced two key reforms. They began by replacing the old structure of governance with new framework. A fourth viceroyalty was established in River Plate in 1776, the institution of *visita general* was revived to police corrupt colonial rule, the practice of purchasing positions on the *audencias* was abolished, and a system of *intendants* was created, displacing the old system of *alcaldes*, *mayores*, and *corregidores*, which had also been corrupted by the purchasing of positions. From the point of view of

---

[52] D. A. Brading, 'Bourbon Spain and its American empire', in Bethell (ed.), *Colonial Spanish America*, p. 114.

Spanish Americas, however, the most insidious reform was the 'decre-olization' of imperial government, installing peninsular Spaniards in the place of native-born Spanish Americans. This was done by outlaw-ing the sale of offices, the principal way in which Creoles had attained government positions.

The object of the new policy was to de-Americanize the government of America, and in this it was successful. Sale of *audencia* offices was ended, the creole share of places reduced, and the appointment of creoles in their own districts virtually stopped. In the period 1751–1808, of the 266 appoint-ments in American *audencias* only sixty-two (23 per cent) went to creoles, compared with 200 (75 per cent) to *peninsulares*.[53]

These political reforms were paralleled by an equally ambitious set of economic reforms, strongly mercantilist in nature. The document that informed many of these reforms was José del Campillo y Cossío's *Nuevo sistema de gobierno económico para la América*, published officially in 1743. Campillo recommended the abolition of the impe-rial trading monopoly enjoyed by Cádiz, the opening up of shipping between Spanish and American ports, the destruction of manufacturing in the Americas (to reduce competition with metropolitan manufactur-ing and increase exports of manufactured goods to the colonies), and a new imperial taxation regime. Under Charles these ideas were manifest in far-reaching reforms, the most famous of which was the 1778 decree of *comercio libre*, a decree that allowed ports other than Cádiz to han-dle trade with the Americas, and permitted ordinary merchant vessels, not the traditional periodic fleets, to carry trade within the empire. In addition to this, a number of royal monopolies were established over key manufacturing and agricultural industries; direct control over the administration of colonial taxes replaced the old system of tax farm-ing, and key sales taxes were increased; and land was distributed to the Indians with the express purpose of increasing the colonial capacity to absorb metropolitan manufactured goods.[54] The overriding pur-pose of these reforms was to make the empire pay, to give the Bour-bon monarchy the same financial advantages that they believed the English, French, and Dutch were drawing from their empires. Charles

[53] Lynch, *Bourbon Spain 1700–1808*, p. 339.
[54] For overviews of these reforms, see Brading, 'Bourbon Spain and its American empire', pp. 132–49; John Leddy Phelan, *The People and the King* (Madison: University of Wisconsin Press, 1978), ch. 2; Lynch, *Bourbon Spain*, ch. 9.

III expressed this purpose succinctly in his 1776 *Cédula* creating the new viceroyalty of River Plate: 'To bring my royal revenues to their proper level'.[55]

In addition to these political and economic reforms, Charles and his ministers moved decisively to assert the power of the Crown over the Church. As elsewhere in Europe, the Catholic Church wielded significant social power, constituting an independent source of moral authority, a major landholder, a monopolistic provider of university education, and an entity with not insubstantial business interests. For a monarch determined to uphold the absolute powers of the state, it was thus a prime target. It was the Jesuits, however, who bore the brunt of Charles's discipline. As we saw in Chapter 3, the Society of Jesus was founded with the express purpose of defending the Pope, and had been a key force in the Counter-Reformation and in the prop-agation of the Catholic faith in North Africa, Asia, and the Americas. In the early 1760s Charles had a series of struggles with the Pope, and after one such incident – when the king blocked the publication of the Pope's condemnation of a work denying papal infallibility – he ruled that the Crown must approve all papal bulls or breves before their circulation, a ruling that was short-lived but reintroduced in 1768.[56] The struggle that brought the conflict to a head, however, occurred in 1766. Spain's losses in the Seven Years' War, repeated bad harvests between 1763 and 1765, and severe economic hardship in the winter of 1765–6 fueled high levels of public grievance, much of it targeted at Charles's Italian Secretaries of State for War and Finance and For-eign Affairs, the Marqués de Esquilache and Marqués de Grimaldi. Grievances turned to rioting when the former reasserted an old ban on the wearing of broad-brimmed hats and long capes, causing the worst internal violence since the War of Spanish Succession. It is unclear whether Charles genuinely believed that the Jesuits were behind this and earlier challenges, or whether scapegoating them gave him the justification he needed to destroy their influence. In 1767, following similar moves in France and Portugal, he expelled the Society from all Spanish territories. Like the decreolization of imperial government, this was seen as a direct attack on Spanish America, as the Jesuits,

---

[55] Quoted in Lynch, *Bourbon Spain*, p. 344.
[56] Richard Herr, *The Eighteenth Century Revolution in Spain* (Princeton University Press, 1958), p. 19.

among other things, had been responsible for educating most of the Creole elite and were themselves an influential part of that elite.[57]

## Rights politics and imperial crisis

In the case of the Westphalian settlement, emergent ideas about individuals' rights were catalysts, sparking the crisis that beset the Holy Roman Empire and the heteronomous order in which it was embedded. Ideas about liberty of conscience informed the Reformation, conflict over these ideas and their attendant political implications splintered Latin Christendom, and it was these ideas that had to be accommodated if peace in Europe was to be reestablished. The role played by ideas about rights in the independence of Spanish America differed markedly from this, however. As noted earlier, the collapse of the Spanish Empire was catalyzed by other factors, with ideas about rights conditioning how Spanish Americans responded to these factors. They appear, on first reflection, therefore to work as Weber's 'switchmen', as intervening variables that shape how actors respond strategically to the environmental challenges they encounter. But this misconstrues the nature of their impact. Ideas about rights did not spark the process of change in the Spanish Empire, but they determined the direction of that change, transforming a constitutional crisis in peninsular Spain into a crisis of empire. In this process ideas about rights framed how Spanish Americans understood the peninsular crisis, how they defined their interests, how they responded politically, and how they justified their responses.

### Catalytic factors

The Bourbon reforms were a direct attack on the governance equilibrium that had evolved under the Habsburgs, and were seen by Spanish Americans as seriously undermining their scope for independent political and economic action. Their effect was to accentuate Creole perceptions that they were a nation apart, a people with cultural, political, and economic needs distinct from those of peninsular Spaniards. They also

[57] On the expulsion of the Jesuits, see Magnus Morner, 'The expulsion of the Jesuits from Spain and Spanish America in 1767 in the light of eighteenth century regalism', *The Americas*, 23.2 (1966), 156–64; and *The Expulsion of the Jesuits from Latin America* (New York: Alfred A. Knopf, 1965).

fueled a heightened sense of grievance, a sense that Spanish Americans were victims of metropolitan exploitation. None of this translated, however, into a demand for independence. As the slogan 'Long live the king and death to bad government' indicated, Spanish Americans still conceived – both practically and normatively – of their political opportunities within a framework of imperial governance. Nor did they imagine at this time that the empire would soon be replaced by independent sovereign states. In Carlos Fuentes' words, 'Independence was far from self-evident as the nineteenth century dawned. A Spanish American on the first day of the year 1801 would have been gambling wildly if he had forecast that by 1821 Spain would have lost all of its possessions in the New World except two Caribbean islands, Cuba and Puerto Rico.'[58] Mark Burkholder and Lyman Johnson make a similar point: 'Yet despite the numerous difficulties of these years, almost no one in Spain or the colonies expected that in less than two decades the entire mainland empire in America would be independent of Spanish rule.'[59] It was not until 1807–8 that the Napoleonic invasion, the usurpation of the Spanish crown, and the resulting peninsular crisis catalyzed the empire's collapse.

In 1806 Napoleon declared a continental blockade of British imports, a move strongly resisted by the Swedes and Portuguese. Determined to gain control of the latter's ports, in October 1807 France and Spain signed the Treaty of Fontainebleau, dividing Portugal into three kingdoms. When the Prince Regent of Portugal maintained his refusal to join the continental blockade, in November 1807 Napoleon's army invaded Portugal through Spain. The Spanish, keen to acquire control of Portugal's territory and fleet, sent troops to aid the French. Napoleon's ambitions were partially thwarted by the escape of the Portuguese monarchy to Brazil, which denied Napoleon control of Portugal's American empire. But the full extent of his ambitions were soon revealed when in February 1808 French troops in Spain turned on France's ally, capturing key Spanish fortifications and occupying Barcelona. Intrigue then replaced war, with Napoleon manipulating the festering ambition of Charles IV's son and heir, Ferdinand, aristocratic hatred of Manuel Godoy, the king's First Secretary of State and

---

[58] Fuentes, *The Buried Mirror*, p. 234.
[59] Mark A. Burkholder and Lyman L. Johnson, *Colonial Latin America* (Oxford University Press, 1990), p. 290.

the Queen's assumed lover, and a string of popular uprisings against Godoy, eventually forcing Charles's abdication in Ferdinand's favor. Ferdinand's initial hope that Napoleon would support him was soon betrayed, however. Both he and Charles were removed to Bayonne where, on 5 May 1808, Napoleon forced both to abdicate, subsequently enthroning his brother Joseph as King of Spain and the Indies. After almost twenty years of waging an increasingly paranoid campaign to prevent the infiltration of French revolutionary ideas and to protect the monarchy against republican elements, Bourbon Spain fell to a French emperor clad in only the thinnest veil of liberty, equality, and fraternity.

The Napoleonic usurpation provoked insurgencies across the Spanish world that would, over the next decade and a half, change the face of Spanish politics, both on the peninsula and in the Americas. As early as May 2008 the insurgents had formed juntas in many cities to coordinate resistance and provide local governance, initially in the name of the deposed Ferdinand VII. Similar bodies sprang up across the Americas, based in most cases around the traditional locus of local government, the *cabildo*. For several months the peninsular juntas wrestled for leadership, with the juntas of Seville and Cádiz vying for recognition by Spanish Americans and Britain. In September 2008 a central junta was formed – the Suprema Junta Gubernativa del Reino – to provide paramount authority and coordinate the activities of local juntas, an institution promptly recognized by the American juntas. In 1809 the Suprema Junta proclaimed that the Americas were inherent components of the Spanish monarchy, not colonies, thus reversing a century of Bourbon practice. In 1810 a general 'Cortes' was called in Cádiz, which, although it would run parallel to the Suprema Junta, became the locus of insurgent government in the empire. The Cortes soon proclaimed that sovereignty resided in the nation, that the monarchy of Ferdinand VII was legitimate, and that the authority of the Cortes' deputies was inviolable. In 1812 the Cortes passed what has come to be known as the 'Cádiz Constitution', considered Spain's first post-absolutist constitution and one of the most liberal promulgated at the time.

These developments of 1808–12 catalyzed independence in Spanish America. But there was nothing about them that demanded secession, nothing intrinsic to their very nature that made independence the only possible response. As noted earlier, Spanish Americans could have accepted Joseph I's rule – they had, after all, accepted the conflict-ridden dynastic change from the Habsburgs to the Bourbons a century earlier. Alternatively, they could have accepted the authority of the insurgent juntas on the peninsula. And, lastly, they could have maintained their initial support for the American juntas that sprang up in the immediate aftermath of the usurpation, sustaining their loyalty until after Ferdinand's return to the throne in 1814. Spanish Americans did eventually turn from empire to sovereign independence, however. Why did this occur? Why did Spanish Americans take the path of independence? To answer this question we need to understand how they interpreted the events of 1808 to 1812. For it is the meanings they attached to these developments that conditioned their political responses. It is at this point in the story that ideas about rights began to shape political outcomes.

## The sovereign rights of peoples

In making sense of the Bourbon abdications and the Napoleonic usurpation, Spaniards across the empire drew on the traditional Spanish theory of sovereignty discussed earlier. Among the vast majority of Spaniards who rebelled against the French intruders, the prevailing opinion was that in the absence of a legitimate monarch sovereignty reverted to the people, as it was they who had invested such authority in the first place. 'Upon the abdication of the legitimate king, the *pactum translationis* was applied; civil authority reverted automatically to the people who had designated the king their ruler. The people were now legitimately empowered to take civil authority into their own hands, since there was no legitimate Spanish monarchy as long as the king did not return.'[60] This understanding of the reversion of sovereignty was articulated as readily and as stridently by Spanish Americans as Peninsulares. Mariano Moreno, the great Argentinian revolutionary, argued: 'In this reversion of powers (caused by the absence of the king) not only does each people assume the authority that all of them, acting together, had given to the king, but every citizen should be considered to be in the same state as that existing before the social contract was entered into.'[61]

[60] Stoetzer, *Scholastic Roots*, p. 157.
[61] Quoted in Víctor Andrés Belaunde, *Bolivar and the Political Thought of the Spanish American Revolution* (Baltimore: Johns Hopkins Press, 1938), pp. 98–9.

While these appeals to traditional understandings of sovereignty successfully undercut Joseph I's authority, as well as that of the rump imperial bureaucracy who might claim to govern in Ferdinand's name, they begged two questions that would divide peninsular Spain from the Americas: What is the nature of the 'people' to which sovereignty reverts? And how is this 'people' to be represented?[62] The idea of a sovereign people is one of protean flexibility, and historically it has been defined as narrowly as landed male aristocrats and as broadly as all citizens. But the question was particularly vexed in the case of the Spanish Empire. Did the inhabitants of the empire constitute one or more 'peoples'? And who counted as a member of a people? Were Creoles members, or Indians for that matter? Once this was settled, there was the question of how the views and interests of the people were to be represented. Again, there was a whole spectrum of possibilities, from direct democracy through republicanism or governance by the traditional estates to benevolent absolutism. This issue cut to the heart of the imperial structure of power and authority, resting as it did on a particular set of ideas about political representation.

Peninsular Spaniards were united in their answer to the first of these questions – the Spanish Empire was one: a single kingdom, a single people. This unitarian perspective was shared by those across the political spectrum, from liberals to absolutists. Nowhere was this more clearly stated than in the decree issued by the liberal-dominated Cortes on 15 October 1810. The Cortes upheld 'the unquestioned concept that the Spanish dominions in both hemispheres form one and the same monarchy, one and the same nation, and one and the same family, and that therefore those born in said European or overseas dominions are equal in rights to those of the Peninsula'.[63] It was this unitary conception of the Spanish people that was enshrined in the Constitution adopted by the Cortes on 19 March 1812, Article 1 of which states: 'The Spanish nation is the re-union of all the Spaniards of both hemispheres.'[64] It is worth noting that in the shift from the

---

[62] Guerra also sees these questions as critical to the politics of Spanish American independence, though poses them in a slightly different way. See Guerra, 'Spanish-American tradition of representation', p. 5.
[63] Quoted in Fernando Diaz-Plaja (ed.), *La historia de Espana en sus documentos, el siglo XIX* (Madrid: Instituto de Estudios Politicos, 1954), p. 96.
[64] 'Political Constitution of the Spanish Monarchy: promulgated in Cádiz, the nineteenth day of March 1812'. At www.cervantesvirtual.com/FichaObra.html?Ref=10794&portal=56 (accessed 1 Feb. 2008).

1810 decree to the 1812 Constitution the language of 'nation' has supplanted that of 'monarchy'. We should be careful here not read into such language contemporary understandings of nation. As José Carlos Chiaramonte points out, 'Political usage of the term at the time clearly knew nothing of the notion of nationality we today tag on to it...'[65] However, the Cádiz Constitution established Spain as a constitutional monarchy, and the liberals who dominated its drafting successfully sought to locate sovereignty in the hands of the nation (qua people). In fact, after Article 2 denies that the nation is 'the property of any family or person', Article 3 states explicitly: 'Sovereignty belongs to the nation, consequently it exclusively possesses the right of establishing its fundamental laws.'[66]

The consensus that this unitarian idea enjoyed on the peninsula did not extend to the Americas, where it was rejected by all but the absolutists. For their part, American absolutists – usually elites of Spanish birth, members of the imperial bureaucracy, or economic elites who benefited from the status quo – followed their peninsular counterparts in imagining that the dominions of the empire comprised a single kingdom. The vast majority of Americans, however, believed that the empire consisted of not one but several kingdoms or nations, each with an independent relationship to the Spanish monarchy. In defense of this interpretation they appealed, first, to Pope Alexander VI's original grant of the Indies to the Spanish monarchy in 1493. As far as most Spanish Americans were concerned, this meant that their relationship with the monarchy was independent of the peninsular kingdoms. They also appealed to the 1492 *capitulacion* between the Spanish monarchs, Ferdinand and Isabella, and Christopher Columbus. Signed in the new Christian settlement of Santa Fe, on territory recently liberated from the Moors, the compact permitted Columbus to 'discover' and 'gain' islands and 'firm lands' in the 'Ocean Seas', and appointed him 'their *Virrey* (Viceroy) and general governor on such islands and firm lands'.[67] Spanish Americans argued that this *capitulacion* constituted

[65] Chiaramonte is critical of much historiography of Latin American independence, which he contends has a nationalist agenda, and part of this agenda is to cast independence as the product of newly self-conscious nationalism. See José Carlos Chiaramonte, 'Principle of consent', 565.

[66] 'Political Constitution of the Spanish Monarchy'.

[67] 'Las Capitulaciones de Santa Fe', 17 April 1492. At http://webs.advance.com. ar/pfernando/DocsIglLA/CapsSantaFe.htm (accessed 10 Oct. 2012). Translated here from the Spanish by Gilberto Estrada Harris. On the nature of *capitulacions* as compacts or agreements establishing rights and obligations,

a contract between the Spanish monarchy and their ancestors, and like the original papal grant, it meant that their relationship with the monarchy was independent of the king's or queen's relationship with the peninsular kingdoms or provinces.

While this view prevailed among Spanish Americans, they were divided over its political implications. All agreed that under traditional Spanish theory, in the absence of a legitimate monarch they, as the people, had the right to the return of sovereignty. They also agreed that legally, as a consequence of the original papal grant and Ferdinand and Isabella's *capitulacion*, they were a rights-bearing people distinct from the people or peoples of the peninsula. Finally, they agreed that their status as an independent rights-bearing people undercut any claims by peninsular juntas, Cortes or other bodies to any natural authority over the Americas. Beyond these points, however, prevailing opinion divided between reformers, on the one hand, and revolutionaries, on the other, both of whom were liberal in political orientation. For the former, the separate status of the Americas did not foreclose membership of the empire under a common institutional framework; the issue for them was equality within such a framework. In the debates of the General Cortes they accepted the idea that the empire constituted a single monarchy, but not kingdom, and a single nation, but not people. The nature of the original papal grant and royal *capitulacion* meant that Americans were not subordinate to Spaniards and were thus entitled to nothing less than equal representation in any future, permanent Cortes. For the radicals, equality within the empire was a chimera, and the only logical consequence of the return of sovereignty was political independence. They refused the compromise language of the empire constituting a single monarchy and nation, and were rightly skeptical that Spaniards – liberal or otherwise – would ever grant them genuine equal representation. In the immediate aftermath of the Napoleonic usurpation, this division was manifest in the differences between the regional juntas that sprang up across the Americas, some of which asserted their autonomy but cooperated with the General Cortes, and others which denied its legitimacy, in a number of cases making early declarations of sovereign independence, most of which were short-lived.[68]

see Charles Gibson, 'Conquest, capitulation, and Indian treaties', *American Historical Review*, 83.1 (1978), 1–15.

[68] Stoetzer, *Scholastic Roots*, p. 166.

In addition to the divisive question of whether the empire comprised one or more 'peoples', there was the issue of how the 'people' should be represented. It is one thing to say that sovereignty reverts to the people, but how, in a reformed, post-Napoleonic empire, were the people to be represented: directly; through popularly elected representatives; through traditional estates or other corporate bodies; or through a monarch (constitutional or otherwise) who 'sees things more perfectly than they [the people] do . . . '?[69] The period between 1808 and 1812 saw a dramatic transition in the Spanish world from traditional to modern ideas of representation, with the liberal idea that it was individuals who required political representation ultimately prevailing.[70] Again, a division quickly emerged between Peninsulares and Spanish Americans. As noted above, liberals came to dominate the elite politics of both hemispheres, and they shared a belief in modern ideas of representation. But the idea that individuals were entitled to political representation was predicated on the notion that individuals were rational adults, and it is here that the disagreement emerged.[71] While liberal Peninsulares believed in the right of individuals to representation, they saw the issue through the lens of traditional Spanish conceits that denied the rational agency of Spanish Americans. And if Americans were not rational adults, they were not entitled to the same degree of representation as Peninsulares. Spanish Americans rejected this outright, with liberal reformers fighting unsuccessfully for equal representation in the General Cortes, and radicals seeing Spanish intransigence as just cause for revolution.

## Debate at Cádiz and the alienation of Spanish America

If being a political liberal means upholding the individual as the primary moral subject, society as an aggregation of said individuals, and the moral purpose of the state to be the protection of individuals' civil and political liberties, then Spanish reformers and radicals of the early nineteenth century were liberal in essence. But their liberalism was distinctive in a number of ways. Much has been made of the unbalanced

---

[69] Louis XIV on the 'rank superiority' of kings, quoted in R. W. Harris, *Absolutism and Enlightenment: 1660–1789* (London: Blandford Press, 1967), p. 76.

[70] Guerra, 'Spanish-American tradition of representation', 2–6.

[71] Forment, *Democracy in Latin America, 1760–1900*, pp. 15–65.

penetration of Enlightenment ideas into Spain and its dominions, with scientific and economic ideas taking root, encouraged by Enlightenment reformers within the Bourbon bureaucracy, but with political ideas gaining little purchase, actively censored by the very reformers who promoted the scientific transformation of social and economic life.[72] The fact is, however, that the political elites who dominated the reform process within Spain, and the reformers and radicals in the Americas, were deeply influenced by Enlightenment political ideas, particularly those of French origin. Where the earlier generation of Spanish Enlightenment reformers, of whom Gaspar de Jovellanos was representative, followed Montesquieu in admiring the English constitution and the gradualism of English constitutional change, the post-usurpation generation looked to early French revolutionary experience. Not only were they influenced by Rousseau's ideas of civil and political liberty, popular sovereignty, the general will, and law – that 'celestial voice' – as an engine of social change, but they saw in the constitutional phase of the French Revolution a model for an abrupt change from absolutism. 'The weight of Absolutism was such that, in their view, rupture with the past became necessary and in this area the sole existing experience was the French Revolution.'[73]

Peninsular and American liberals dominated the General Cortes that sat in Cádiz from 24 September 1810 to 4 May 1814. In large measure, this was because the Cortes sat as a single house, pressure by Jovellanos and the English having failed to get an additional upper house reserved for the nobility and clergy.[74] In the disorganized elections for delegates to the Cortes, these more conservative sectors of Spanish society secured little more than a third of the representatives, with the remaining two-thirds coming from the middle classes, broadly defined.[75] Of this two-thirds, a substantial minority were Spanish Americans, most of whom were liberal reformers. Between 1810 and 1814 sixty-four of the roughly three hundred deputies who served on the General Cortes

---

[72] On the influence of Enlightenment scientific and economic ideas over political ideas see Whitaker (ed.), *Latin American and the Enlightenment*. On the role of Enlightenment reformers in the Bourbon bureaucracy censoring radical political ideas, see Herr, *The Eighteenth Century Revolution in Spain*, chs. 8–12.

[73] Guerra, 'Spanish-American tradition of representation', 16.

[74] C. W. Crawley, 'French and English influences in the Cortes of Cadiz, 1810–1814', *Cambridge Historical Journal*, 6.2 (1939), 183.

[75] Dominguez, *Insurrection or Loyalty*, p. 10.

were Americans, and some of the most influential liberal voices came from their number.[76]

The peninsular and American liberals who served on the Cortes of Cádiz all embraced modern ideas of political representation, ideas which saw individuals, not corporate bodies, as the constituent units of political society, units that required representation in decision-making forums if the people were to be truly sovereign. The official position of the Cortes, expressed in a declaration of 11 February 1811, was that Spaniards and Americans were to enjoy equal political representation. But behind this apparent unanimity lay fundamental differences between Spanish and American liberals. While the Americans insisted on equal representation, the Spaniards resisted it. This was partly because equal representation would lead to American predominance in any future Cortes of the empire. It was also partly because Spaniards on the extraordinary Cortes wanted to deny the revolutionary juntas in the Americas the right to elect deputies to a central Cortes, and the revolutionary juntas, for their part, refused to accept the legitimacy of the Spanish Cortes anyway. But the principal reason for division between Spanish and American liberals was that they disagreed about who constituted a rational adult capable of exercising civic responsibilities. For the Americans on the Cortes, Spanish Americans were rational adults who could discipline their passions with reason, and this capacity for rationality, as well as their status as separate peoples (which was denied by the Spanish liberals), entitled them to equal representation. The Spaniards, in contrast, were still influenced by traditional Spanish prejudices that saw the majority of Spanish Americans as irrational children ruled by their passions. They were willing to concede that some Spanish Americans had reached adulthood, but since they constituted a minority of the population of the Americas, Americans should have less representation than Spaniards.[77]

This division fueled one of the most heated debates of the Cortes' negotiations toward the 1812 Constitution of Cádiz. In these debates, the American representatives argued passionately that all free American men should be granted citizenship and representation. The Spanish liberals sought to deny these by distinguishing between Americans of

---

[76] On one influential Spanish American, see Philip L. Asuto, 'A Latin American spokesman in Napoleonic Spain: José Mejia Lequerica', *The Americas*, 24.4 (1968), 354–77.

[77] Forment, *Democracy in Latin America*, pp. 57–60.

Spanish descent – the Creoles – and Indians and 'colored castes', by which they meant freed slaves and their descendants. While the Spanish fear that full citizenship and representation would lead to American domination of any future Cortes was a clear, often expressed motive, traditional prejudices led them to draw the line above Indians and freed slaves and to justify this discrimination in terms of the immaturity and irrationality of these peoples.

The Constitution of Cádiz is generally considered the most liberal of its time, and in the ferment of the early nineteenth century it was embraced by liberals across Europe as a model and held up by absolutists as a revolutionary threat to the *ancien régime*. It established Europe's most liberal constitutional monarchy. Sovereignty was placed firmly in the hands of the nation (Article 3), and the nation was 'obliged, by wise and just laws, to protect the liberty, property and all other legitimate rights, of every individual which composes it' (Article 4). While giving the king the power to execute laws (Article 16), it severely circumscribed his legislative and judicial powers. Legislation passed by the Cortes could be rejected by the king only three times, and if the Cortes approved it for a third year in succession, 'it shall be understood to have obtained his Majesty's assent, which, on being presented, it shall receive accordingly' (Article 149). The Constitution gave judicial tribunals the sole 'authority to administer justice in civil and criminal causes' (Article 242), and declared that 'Neither the King nor the Cortes can, under any circumstances, exercise the judicial authority, advocate a pending trial, or command a cause to be rejudged' (Article 243). It also outlawed the use of torture to extract confessions (Article 303), and mandated the humane treatment of prisoners and design of prisons (Article 297).[78]

The limits of the Constitution's liberalism were to be found, however, in how it dealt with the issue of equal representation of Spaniards and Americans. The General Cortes' debate on this issue was protracted and complex, moving through a series of phases. From the outset, the American deputies were determined to secure full and adequate representation for the overseas peoples of the empire. Their Spanish counterparts were equally determined, however, to limit overseas representation.

---

[78] 'Political Constitution of the Spanish Monarchy'.

The debate began before the Cortes had been officially installed, which required an initial vote of installation. The American deputies, most of whom had been elected from Creoles based in Spain, were deeply dissatisfied with their allocation of only thirty seats. On 25 September 1810 they submitted a draft decree calling for the election of additional American deputies, one for every 50,000 free subjects. The Spaniards on the Cortes used their sizable majority to defer consideration of the decree, arguing that discussing the matter was 'inopportune' and that the installation of the Cortes could not be held up.[79] The Americans were not deterred, though, and on 1 October 1810 they proposed another decree 'proclaiming the equality of "their natives and free individuals" with the Peninsular population'.[80] Again, the Spanish majority deferred consideration. Soon after, however, the deputies agreed that debate could proceed but only in secret sessions. Behind closed doors, the Spanish deputies moved to restrict American representation by excluding Indians, questioning the natives' status as humans and appealing to Aristotelian conceptions of Indians as natural slaves:

the Peninsular deputy Juan Pablo Valiente insultingly declared it was 'not known to what variety of animals Americans belonged ... ', observing that papal declarations had been necessary to establish the humanity of Indians, while Agustín de Argüelles [one of the leading Spanish liberals] recalled old opinions that the Indians were natural slaves according to Aristotelian doctrine, and Diego Muñoz Torrero protested against Indian equality on the grounds that it would require suppression of the native tribute.[81]

This effort to deny Indians the right to representation failed, however, because it conflicted with rights that Indians had long ago secured under the Laws of the Indies. With this path blocked, the Spaniards turned their attention to the free colored castes, former slaves of African origin. Despite rancorous debate, a compromise decree was eventually passed on 15 October 1810. Cited earlier, the decree upheld 'the unquestioned concept that the Spanish dominions in both hemispheres form one and the same monarchy, one and the same nation, and one and the same family, and that therefore those born in said European or overseas dominions are equal in rights to those of the

[79] James F. King, 'The colored castes and American representation in the Cortes of Cadiz', *Hispanic American Historical Review*, 33.1 (1953), 40.
[80] Ibid., 41.      [81] Ibid., 43.

Peninsula'.[82] The details of American political representation were
left utterly unresolved, deferred again to be dealt with 'opportunely'.[83]
Determined that an 'opportune' time should come sooner rather than
later, on 16 December 1810 the American deputies tabled eleven
demands, the first of which was a much watered-down call for equal
representation for 'natives derived from both hemispheres, Spaniards
as well as Indians, and the children of both'.[84] Despite the fact that
this demand excluded free men of color by implication, the Spanish
deputies again sought to defer debate. Only after the Americans successfully argued that failure to deal with the question of representation
was fueling revolution in the overseas provinces did Peninsulares back
down and allow debate. Despite its highly watered-down nature, the
Americans' first proposition was defeated in a preliminary vote on 18
January 1811. After two weeks of further debate, however, the Cortes
agreed to the principle of whites, Indians, and mestizos (those of mixed
descent) having equal representation, remaining silent on the question
of free colored castes. A proposal to have this principle applied to the
present General Cortes failed narrowly.[85]

Debate now turned to the wording of the future constitution, a drafting committee having been established on 23 December 1810. By the
time the draft was tabled, however, American opinion on the Cortes
had hardened, a consequence in part of the arrival of newly elected
deputies from Mexico and Central America to replace the 'substitutes'
who had been serving temporarily. The Americans were no longer willing to concede, even by implication, the denial of representation to free
colored castes. The draft constitution had been carefully crafted, however, to achieve the Spanish majority's objective of curtailing American
representation along racial lines.

Three articles of the draft were particularly important: Articles 5, 18,
and 22. The first of these defined who constituted Spaniards, members
of the Spanish nation. Here the drafters had been inclusive, the 1812
Constitution defining Spaniards as 'All free-men, born and bred up in
the Spanish dominions, and their sons' (Article 5.1), 'Foreigners who
may have obtained letters of naturalization from the Cortes' (Article
5.2), 'Those who, without it, have resided ten years in any village
in Spain, and acquired thereby a right of vicinity' (Article 5.3), and,

[82] Quoted in Diaz-Plaja, *La historia de Espana*, p. 96.
[83] King, 'The colored castes', 45.      [84] Ibid., 47.      [85] Ibid., 50.

crucially, 'The slaves who receive their freedom in the Spanish dominions' (Article 5.4). Not surprisingly, the Cortes accepted these articles
unanimously. The draft constitution took a discriminatory turn, however, when it came to Article 18, the article that defines which of these
many Spaniards were entitled to citizenship and, as a consequence,
political representation. Citizenship was granted to all those 'who,
by both lines, are of Spanish parents, of either hemisphere, and have
resided ten years in some village in the Spanish dominions' (Article
18). The implications of this were decidedly unclear. If freed slaves
were Spaniards, as per Article 5.4, then surely they were citizens as
well. But the lack of any specific declaration of their status raised
American concerns, concerns that were justified by the wording of
Article 22. According to this article, freed slaves had no automatic
right to citizenship, but as individuals their children could appeal to a
future Cortes for a Letter of Citizenship on the grounds that they had
demonstrated the necessary level of virtue. The original draft article
read as follows:

For those Spaniards who on either side derive their origin from Africa, the
door of virtue and merit is open. In consequence the Cortes may grant
letters of citizenship to those who have rendered eminent services to the
fatherland, or to those who distinguish themselves by their talent, application
and conduct, providing, so far as these latter are concerned, that they be the
offspring of legitimate marriages, the children of free parents, themselves
married to free women, and resident in Spanish dominions, and that they
exercise some useful profession, office, or industry and have a capital of their
own sufficient to maintain their homes and educate their children.[86]

The response from the American deputies was hostile, the earlier mod-
eration that produced their watered-down eleven propositions long
gone. They first attacked the notion that people worthy of being members of the Spanish nation should be denied citizenship. They condemned the idea that the Cortes would ever be in a position to assess
reasonably the many likely petitions. They criticized the notion that
peoples of disadvantaged castes should be expected to demonstrate
'eminent services'. And they argued that revolutionary juntas in the
Americas had already given Indians and colored castes equality, and a
failure by the Cortes of the empire to match this would further fuel the

[86] Quoted ibid., 53.

revolutions.[87] The Spanish liberals responded by accusing the Americans of having supported the exclusion of colored castes in their eleven propositions, and that the Committee on the Constitution had simply implemented the 15 October decree which, as we have already noted, lacked any details on American representation. They also challenged the integrity of the Americans, claiming that they were only interested in citizenship for Indians and colored castes so that they could secure a majority in any future Cortes.[88] In the end, however, they fell back on their majority in the General Cortes, conceding some minor changes to Article 22 (such as exchanging 'meritorious' for 'eminent') but curtailing debate and forcing a vote, which the Americans lost 108 to 36, many of them abstaining in protest.[89]

Articles 18 and 22 did not exhaust the discriminatory aspects of the draft constitution, however. Having the right to vote is the most direct form of political representation, but representation also comes, in a more attenuated form, through being counted in the process that determines the allocation of representatives. For instance, if it is decided that every 100,000 people are entitled to a representative, then being counted as part of that 100,000 people is a form of representation and, conversely, being excluded is an absolute denial of equal representation. Not satisfied with denying free colored men citizenship, the drafting committee sought to exclude them from the electoral count. Article 29 included in the count 'the people composed of those inhabitants who, by both lines, are natives of the Spanish dominions'. Since the ancestry of former slaves was traced to Africa not the Spanish dominions, this excluded them by definition. Those who had attained Letters of Citizenship from the Cortes were to be included, but the bar to colored castes doing this had already been raised by Article 22. The American reaction to this further constraint on American representation was again hostile. They pointed out that this would create a situation in which criminals who had been deprived of their citizenship would be counted while millions of Americans were excluded for no other reason than race. They also questioned why members of the Spanish nation were to be denied political representation. The Spanish deputies responded that Article 29 was consistent with Article 22, and that the test of 'virtue and merit' was necessary for all political representation, not just citizenship. The Peninsulares' ultimate response,

[87] Ibid., 53–7.      [88] Ibid., 57–8.      [89] Ibid., 59.

however, was to brook no compromise and simply outvote the American minority.[90]

It is tempting to see this struggle between peninsular and American deputies as one of narrow self-interest. The population of Spanish America was greater than that of peninsular Spain, and truly equal representation would have given the Americans a permanent majority in any future Cortes of the empire, something they desired as much as it was feared by the Spanish. Surely, therefore, their respective moral arguments about which Spaniards were rational adults deserving full representation were nothing more than rhetorical conveniences concealing far baser interests. Yet this misconstrues their positions. The Peninsulares' fear of Spanish-American domination and their denial that freed slaves constituted rational adults worthy of equal representation were deeply entwined – they feared Spanish-American domination in part because they considered most Spanish Americans culturally and racially inferior. Recall that a few short decades earlier Bourbon administrators had barred Creoles from the imperial bureaucracy on the grounds that they 'lack that mode of thinking, at once pure, sincere and impartial' required for government.[91] From this perspective, Indians and former slaves were completely beyond the pale. To be dominated by Americans, therefore, was to be dominated by one's inferiors, infusing the issue with heightened moral urgency. As for the American delegates, if their cultural attitudes had in reality been as discriminatory as those of their peninsular counterparts, and their goal nothing more than electoral domination, they could have adopted a different negotiating position. They could have supported, instead of opposed, Articles 18 and 22 of the Constitution, which together denied freed slaves citizenship, while continuing to oppose Article 29, which excluded free colored castes from the electoral count, arguing as they did that all Spaniards (as defined in Article 5) should be included.[92] This would have ensured Spanish-American domination of any future Cortes, but restricted political representation to Creoles and Indians.

Even if their respective positions had been motivated solely by strategic considerations – solely by the desire for numerical control of a

[90] Ibid., 60–3.   [91] Lynch, *Bourbon Spain*, p. 337.
[92] A similar strategy had been advanced unsuccessfully by southern slave-owning states in the negotiation of Article 1, Section 2, of the United States Constitution. 'United States Constitution', at www.usconstitution.net/const.html (accessed 10 Oct. 2012).

future Cortes – we are left with the question of why arguing to draw a line above or below Indians or freed colored men was rhetorically convenient. Ideas work to constitute political action at two levels: at the level of informing actors' interests, and at the level of providing justifications. When actors use rhetoric, ideas are working at the second of these levels; ideas or values are invoked to justify certain forms of action. Successful rhetoric is politically consequential because it is politically enabling – by licensing certain forms of action, it makes possible political outcomes that would otherwise have been foreclosed. For rhetoric to be successful, however, it must invoke ideas that have normative purchase within the prevailing social and cultural context. Invoking ideas or values that have no normative purchase makes poor rhetoric. The early nineteenth century was a period of ideological turmoil, however. Traditional ideas that had licensed three centuries of absolutism were now challenged by revolutionary liberalism. What we see in the debates over American representation is the protagonists searching for compelling rhetorical resources within this ideological turmoil. Because liberals dominated the General Cortes, they shared certain starting points, particularly the idea that it was individuals who should be represented not corporate bodies. But disagreements over who constitutes a rational adult deserving political representation are a feature of liberalism to this day, and those who argue for the line to be drawn more narrowly usually invoke traditional social values. (Recall late nineteenth- and early twentieth-century debates among liberals over whether women should have the vote.) In the Cortes' debates over political representation peninsular liberals reached back to invoke traditional Spanish ideas about civilizational hierarchy, and their American counterparts reached forward to invoke more modern ideas about the natural equality of all men and inalienable rights of man, often accusing the Peninsulares of violating their own liberalism.

## Revolution and collapse

If peninsular liberals hoped to secure the future of the empire and their own predominance within it by proclaiming the equality of all Spaniards while racially biasing the Constitution they were very much mistaken. The 1812 Constitution of Cádiz, and the negotiations that produced it, served only to polarize conservative and radical forces within the empire, ultimately fragmenting it. Not surprisingly, the

American liberals at the Cortes were deeply disillusioned. Their failure to secure equal political representation within a reformed empire
hardened radical opinion and fueled revolutionary struggles for independence. Conservatives at the Cortes were no happier. Outnumbered
by the combined Spanish and American liberals, they despised the
Constitution's liberal precepts – the envy of progressive forces across
Europe – and were committed to its revocation at the earliest possible
opportunity.

For the radicals in Spanish America, the initial underrepresentation
of Americans at the General Cortes was already evidence that reform
could not deliver political equality. This was clearly apparent in the
Venezuelan Declaration of Independence of 5 July 1811, which proclaimed the most famous of the early, if ill-fated, revolutions. The
Peninsulares had, it declared, 'promised us liberty, equality, and fraternity, conveyed in pompous discourses and studied phrases, for the
purpose of covering the snare laid by a cunning, useless, and degrad-
ing Representation'.[93] After the provisions of the Constitution were
set, and news filtered back to the Americas, radical sentiments such as
these became the norm, with the lack of equal political representation
seen as just cause for secession. As Jeremy Adelman explains,

The American printing presses responded with outrage at both the Regency
and Cortes for betraying their own principles. An anonymous writer in
Buenos Aires exclaimed in 1811 that 'we possess the basic rights to build
our own house, and we will work on our own fate as we can, for good or
for ill, so that our achievement will fit our ideal rather than that of a distant
power'.[94]

Overall, King observes, 'the denial of an equal basis of representation, more than any other act of the Cortes, encouraged and justified
incipient revolt in America, and the deliberate adoption of racial discrimination provided revolutionary leaders with a powerful appeal to
numerous colored elements of the population'.[95]

American anger at the Peninsulares' refusal to grant them equal
political representation articulated with broader grievances about

---

[93] 'Venezuelan Declaration of Independence', reprinted in Armitage, *The
Declaration of Independence*, p. 201.
[94] Jeremy Adelman, *Sovereignty and Revolution in the Iberian Atlantic*
(Princeton University Press, 2006), p. 197.
[95] King, 'The colored castes', 33.

imperial exploitation. As we saw earlier, although Spanish Americans had endured almost a century of harsh Bourbon rule, this had not provoked widespread calls for independence. But this was before the Napoleonic usurpation and the perceived return of sovereignty to the people(s), and before the formal Cádiz process to negotiate the terms of political representation in a reformed empire. In this new context, the issue of equal political representation framed how Spanish Americans understood other grievances, not least the economic ones. By the time of the usurpation, the Spanish Empire was experiencing a profound fiscal crisis, severely exacerbated by continued international conflict and the descent into insurgent warfare. Falling back on old extractive techniques, the General Cortes begged loans from Cádiz merchants in return for reasserting their monopoly over trade with the Americas. As 'the Spanish government backed into Cádiz it fell almost literally into the arms of merchants who had been arguing that commercial concessions to their colonies and the loss of their privileges were depriving Spain of its economic rents'.[96] The Cortes' reassertion of Cádiz's trading monopolies exacerbated Spanish Americans' longstanding economic grievances. Before the usurpation, better governance within existing imperial structures had been the preferred remedy for such concerns. After the usurpation, equal political representation of all free persons within reformed institutions was the only solution. And when the Cortes denied Spanish Americans such representation, the preference for 'voice' through equal representation was displaced in time by that of 'exit'.

The anger and alienation felt by Spanish Americans did not, however, produce an early wave of successful secessions. Venezuela declared independence in 1811, but the revolution was defeated a year later. Mexico seceded in 1813, but the new state lasted only two years. Of the early revolutions, only Paraguay remained independent from 1811. One reason for this was the centrifugal dynamics that arose during the Napoleonic period, in which weakened peninsular authority was matched by the increasing autonomy of local American juntas. Revolutionaries thus faced the double challenge of fighting royalist forces for the sovereign independence of the old administrative units of the empire while preventing local juntas from going their own way, either by carving out their own pockets of independence

---

[96] Adelman, *Sovereignty and Revolution*, p. 198.

or negotiating new associations within the empire.[97] Another reason was the not insignificant number of American loyalists. The upper echelons of the decaying imperial bureaucracy frequently remained loyal, as did much of the officer class of the imperial military. Recent immigrants of Spanish birth were often royalists, and in the grassland regions nomadic herdsmen often looked to the Crown to defend their rights against wealthy landowners.[98] What proportion of the Spanish-American population loyalists constituted in 1812 is difficult to determine, but there were distinct loyalist strongholds, such as in Peru (which had to be 'liberated' by San Martin's invading army), and elsewhere loyalists often commanded the resources needed to wage protracted counterrevolutionary war.

The turning point came when Ferdinand VII returned to the Spanish throne in 1814. Lobbied by conservatives to overthrow the 1812 Constitution, and supported by the traditional military elite who had been humiliated and sidelined by the insurgent armies' defeat of Napoleon, on 4 May he abolished the Cortes and annulled all of its decrees. Absolutism returned to the empire, and Ferdinand moved quickly to reinstate the traditional institutions of rule in the Americas and to eradicate the pockets of autonomy that had emerged during the insurgencies. This attempted reassertion of imperial rule has come to be known as the Reconquista, a counterrevolutionary project that favored the often savage exercise of military force over institutional compromise. In 1815 Ferdinand dispatched to the Americas the largest expeditionary force in the empire's history, the immediate aim of which was the destruction of notions of popular sovereignty and constitutionalism. In Adelman's words,

The concept that the people were in any sense sovereign was the root of all evil. To make matters worse, mulattos, blacks, and Indians added to the 'damage' by treating themselves as citizens with equal rights. All this had to be extirpated by the Crown with the same zeal as the Inquisition before it, by force of arms if necessary where it most deeply burrowed.[99]

Under the command of Field Marshal Pablo Morillo, the force set sail in February 1815, charged first with pacifying Venezuela and then

[97] Ibid., pp. 258–67.
[98] John H. Elliot, *Empires of the Atlantic World: Britain and Spain in America 1492–1830* (New Haven: Yale University Press, 2007), pp. 381–4.
[99] Adelman, *Sovereignty and Revolution*, p. 272.

moving south to subdue New Granada. Marred by low morale, mis-adventure, and an unclear mandate, and meeting unexpectedly high levels of resentment and resistance, Morillo's tactics became increasingly brutal, evident most clearly in his savage suppression of Cartagena between August and October 1815. While this brutality achieved early military victories, its overall effect was to hasten the process of revolutionary change. 'In effect, the ends and means of the restoration pushed colonists – even those who had once hung onto their Spanish loyalties, especially after the reforms of 1812 – to rally behind a cause that promised to break the Atlantic chains altogether.'[100]

Struggles for independence in the Americas continued until 1825, but this belies the rapidity of the empire's collapse. It was between 1816 and 1821 that most of the implosion occurred. Some of the units that gained independence in this period were larger aggregations that eventually fragmented into smaller, more enduring sovereign states – the experiment with Gran Colombia being the prime example. But of present-day sovereign states, Argentina, Chile, Colombia, Costa Rica, El Salvador, Guatemala, Honduras, Mexico, Nicaragua, Panama, Peru, and Venezuela all trace their independence to this period, with Paraguay occurring earlier and Ecuador and Bolivia soon after.

Of our three great waves of systemic expansion, only in this wave did *de facto* sovereignty so clearly precede *de jure*. In ending 120 years of religious conflict, the Treaties of Westphalia gave legal recognition to a given set of nascent sovereign states, and in doing so stabilized a particular practical configuration of political authority. *De jure* and *de facto* sovereignty emerged entwined. With post-1945 decolonization, international recognition of colonial peoples' right to self-determination facilitated the creation of new states. *De jure* sovereignty preceded *de facto*. In the Spanish-American case, by contrast, subject peoples had to wrest independence from imperial Spain, only later gaining international recognition. At the time, US recognition policy was based explicitly on the 'de facto' principle. In the words of the Committee on Foreign Affairs of the House of Representatives, 'For a nation to be entitled, in respect to foreign states, to the enjoyment of these attributes, and to figure directly in the great political society, it is sufficient that it is really sovereign and independent, that is, that it governs

---

[100] Ibid., p. 277.

itself by its own authority and law.'[101] By 1822 the US was satisfied that the new Latin American states had achieved such independence, and formal recognition came as part of the 1823 Monroe Doctrine. Throughout the independence struggles, Britain had remained neutral, frustrating both Madrid and the revolutionaries. The latter's repeated calls for assistance were ignored or rebuffed, while the former's pleas for Parliament to outlaw private British assistance for the independence movements produced only a partial and belated response. It was not until 1825, when the independence of the Latin American states was an irreversible fact, that Britain formally recognized their sovereignty.[102]

## Conclusion

Individual rights are not something that one immediately identifies with the history of Latin American states. Military coups, violent dictatorships, and systematic human rights violations come more readily to mind. The evolution of the Latin American human rights regime, the success of human rights struggles in transforming dictatorships into democracies, and the development of tribunals for prosecuting the crimes of former heads of state, all point to the importance of individual rights in the more recent history of Latin America.[103] But these positive developments are cast against a dark background: a century or more of constitutional upheaval, short-lived experiments in democracy, the imposition of military rule, and the sacrifice of human rights to personal ambition and reason of state.

Yet individual rights, and the struggles they animated, did play an important role in the development of Latin American states. This played out, however, in the immediate prehistory of these states; in

---

[101] Quoted in Gregory Weeks, 'Almost Jeffersonian: US recognition policy toward Latin America', *Presidential Studies Quarterly*, 31.3 (2001), 493.

[102] The classic work on British policy is C. K. Webster, *Britain and the Independence of Latin America 1812–1830* (London: Octagon Books, 1970). See also D. A. G. Waddell, 'British neutrality and Spanish-American independence: the problem of foreign enlistment 1', *Journal of Latin American Studies*, 19.1 (1987), 1–18.

[103] On these developments, see Kathryn Sikkink, *The Justice Cascade: How Human Rights Prosecutions Are Changing World Politics* (New York: Norton, 2011); Margaret Keck and Kathryn Sikkink, *Activists beyond Borders* (Ithaca, NY: Cornell University Press, 1998); and Kathryn Sikkink, *Mixed Signals: US Human Rights Policy in Latin America* (Ithaca, NY: Cornell University Press, 2004).

their emergence from the wreck of the Spanish Empire. As we have seen, Napoleon's usurpation of the Spanish crown sparked a crisis in the empire. But there was nothing about this event itself that determined the nature of the crisis, or that led inexorably to the independence of Spanish America. What mattered was how the inhabitants of the empire understood the usurpation, how this informed their interests, and how it shaped their responses.

Old ideas mattered. The usurpation was understood through the lens of traditional Spanish theories of sovereignty, which held that in the absence of a legitimate monarch sovereignty returned to the people. But did the empire comprise one or more peoples? The Peninsulares and the Americans disagreed, the latter defending their integrity as separate peoples by appealing to the original papal grant. This itself did not condemn the empire, however; Spanish-American reformers remained loyal providing they could secure equal political representation in a post-Napoleonic empire. But it was precisely this that they were unable to secure.

In the heated debates of the General Cortes, nothing was more central than the question of political representation, and it was here that new ideas about individual rights became critically important. Dominated by liberals, the Cortes rejected the notion that it was traditional estates and corporate bodies that were entitled to representation (a core element of the regime of unequal entitlements that sustained imperial hierarchy). They agreed instead that it was the individual who had a right to representation. The Peninsulares and Americans divided acrimoniously, however, over the fundamental question of who constituted an individual; a rational adult worthy of such a right. Reconfiguring the regime of unequal entitlements that undergirded the empire, the Peninsulares forced through a constitution that defined large sectors of the Spanish-American population as irrational children unworthy of fundamental political rights. This constitutional inscription of disrespect and discrimination radicalized the American struggles for equal rights, convincing a growing number of Spanish Americans that exit was the only option, perceptions further accentuated by the Reconquista's savage suppression of the pockets of autonomy Americans had carved out during the French occupation.

# 5 | *Post-1945 decolonization*

Of the five great waves of systemic expansion, post-1945 decolonization was the greatest. In the space of twenty-six years all of Europe's territorial empires collapsed, fragmenting into seventy-six new sovereign states by 1970, forty-five emerging after the 1960 United Nations Declaration on Granting Independence to Colonial Countries and Peoples. What makes this wave distinctive, however, is not only the sheer numbers involved (of both empires and successor states), it is that more than individual empires disintegrated: the institution of empire itself collapsed. The deeply rooted and utterly pervasive understanding that territorial empire was not only a legitimate system of rule but a morally desirable one was swept away. From this point on, empire and imperialism were words of opprobrium, synonyms for domination, exploitation, and injustice. The universalization of the sovereign state was all but complete.

As this transformation was unfolding, a second revolution was underway: the international recognition and codification of human rights. Indeed, it is with post-1945 developments that most accounts of international human rights begin. As Beth Simmons puts it, 'The second half of the twentieth century was the first time in history that human rights were addressed in a systematic manner by the international community.'[1] Each of the principal components of the 'international bill of rights' were negotiated during this period. The Universal Declaration of Human Rights was promulgated by the United Nations in 1948, and after two decades of intense negotiations, the legally binding International Covenant on Civil and Political Rights and International Covenant on Economic, Social and Cultural Rights were signed in 1966, coming into effect ten years later. As the sovereign state

---

[1] Beth A. Simmons, *Mobilizing for Human Rights: International Law in Domestic Politics* (Cambridge University Press, 2009), p. 23.

became the sole legitimate form of rule, sovereignty itself was qualified by a new set of international norms.

For most observers, these momentous developments had little if anything to do with one another. Accounts of decolonization stress a myriad of factors, but the politics of human rights is seldom mentioned. Similarly, histories of the international human rights regime ignore, to all intents and purposes, the politics of decolonization. This neglect is in part the product of deeply engrained yet underscrutinized assumptions: that if decolonization was about rights, it was about collective rights not individual rights; and that the international codification of human rights was a Western project, compromised or rounded out (depending on your point of view) by the Soviet bloc's emphasis on social and economic rights – colonial and postcolonial peoples had no role in this process. The analytical quarantining of human rights and decolonization is not all the result of underscrutinized assumptions, though. Recent work by scholars such as Samuel Moyn vigorously denies, first, that the post-1945 politics of human rights was particularly significant, and second, that it had anything to do with decolonization. In Moyn's words, 'Given the uncertainty of the meaning and the marginal power of the idea of human rights in the 1940s, it is better to regard the eventual force of anticolonialism at the UN as its own distinctive tradition – one that the rise of human rights in the more contemporary sense would have to displace.'[2]

This chapter advances an alternative perspective on decolonization and human rights, one in which the two post-1945 revolutions are deeply interconnected. What needs explaining in this case is the aforementioned universality: the fact that it wasn't a single empire that collapsed, but all of them. The answer lies, I suggest, in the delegitimation of the institution of empire. In the immediate aftermath of World War II, this condominium of ideas and practices remained largely intact: the imperial powers routinely and unashamedly reasserted the notion that empire was a civilizational responsibility; the Declaration Regarding

---

[2] Moyn, *The Last Utopia*, p. 86. Other vigorous denials that decolonization had anything to do with human rights include A. W. Brian Simpson, *Human Rights and the End of Empire: Britain and the Genesis of the European Convention* (Oxford University Press, 2001); and Reza Afshari, 'On the historiography of human rights: reflections on Paul Gordon Lauren's *The Evolution of International Human Rights: Visions Seen*', *Human Rights Quarterly*, 29.1 (2007), 1–67.

Non-Self-Governing Territories contained within the United Nations Charter largely reaffirmed this; the right to self-determination proclaimed after Versailles had never been granted to non-European peoples, and Churchill had insisted that they were also excluded from any such rights expressed in the Atlantic Charter of 1941. Between 1945 and 1960 this institutional complex was successfully dismantled, undercutting the normative foundations of individual empires. While local anticolonial struggles contributed to this process, it was largely an achievement of newly independent postcolonial states working within the emergent human rights forums of the United Nations. Contrary to common wisdom, these states played a key role in the negotiation of both the Universal Declaration and the two covenants on human rights, taking positions diametrically opposed to the Soviet Union and more liberal than Western powers. It was here that they reconstructed the collective right to self-determination, arguing that it was a necessary prerequisite for the satisfaction of individuals' civil and political rights. The net result was a tectonic shift in international legitimacy. By pushing for the strong international codification of human rights, and by grafting the right to self-determination to these emergent norms, postcolonial states not only reasserted this right in universal terms, they undermined the normative foundations of empire.

The following discussion proceeds in several steps. After examining the broad contours of post-1945 decolonization, I explore the limits of existing accounts, focusing in particular on their inability to explain the universality of imperial collapse. This is followed by a detailed engagement with Moyn's argument in *The Last Utopia*, constituting as it does a particularly vigorous denial that human rights and decolonization were in any way connected. I then turn to the empirical heart of the chapter. I begin with a brief analysis of the preceding wave of systemic expansion; that which followed the Versailles settlement. This is important not only because collective rights were particularly pronounced in this case, but because the fate of the self-determination regime established then was crucial for what transpired later. The bulk of my discussion focuses, however, on the relation between struggles for individual rights and post-1945 decolonization, concentrating in particular on the political contestation surrounding the negotiation of the two international covenants and the reconstruction of the right to self-determination.

## The collapse of empire

On 26 February 1885 the major European powers, along with Turkey and the United States, signed the General Act of the Berlin Conference, the purpose of which was to bring a modicum of order to the Europeans' 'scramble' for colonial territories in West Africa. That the European powers had a right to acquire such territories was taken as given; the problem was one of coordination. The parties sought 'to regulate the conditions most favourable to the development of trade and civilization in certain regions of Africa, and to ensure to all nations the advantages of free navigation on the two chief rivers of Africa flowing into the Atlantic Ocean'. They also wished 'to obviate the misunderstanding and disputes which might in future arise from new acts of occupation (prises de possession) on the coast of Africa'. Coordination such as this not only served the interests of the imperial powers, it was upheld as a civilizational responsibility: it was essential, the Act declared, to 'furthering the moral and material well-being of the native populations'.[3]

Ninety years later the problem faced by European powers was no longer one of coordinating their colonial acquisitions: it was adjusting to a rapidly evolving postcolonial international order. They emerged from World War II committed to retaining their colonial territories, seeing empire as essential to postwar economic recovery. But by 1975 the British, French, Dutch, Portuguese, Belgian, and Italian empires had all but disintegrated, replaced by a host of new states in Africa, Asia, and the Pacific. Some colonies gained independence shortly after the war, the most notable being British India. And there was a steady flow of newly independent states throughout the 1950s. It was after 1960, however, that the collapse accelerated. Of the seventy-six new sovereign states that emerged between 1946 and 1975, forty-five gained independence after the 1960 Declaration on Granting Independence to Colonial Countries and Peoples. Between 1946 and 1960 new states emerged at a rate of 1.26 per year, but in the period 1960 to 1975 the rate was 3.86 per year. What began as a trickle became a flood.

---

[3] 'General Act of the Berlin Conference on West Africa', 26 February 1885. At http://africanhistory.about.com/od/eracolonialism/l/bl-BerlinAct1885.htm (accessed 21 Sept. 2012).

Europe's territorial empires were constructed in tandem with the development of the European system of sovereign states, and this paired development was sustained by deeply held beliefs that sovereignty at home and empire abroad was both a natural and morally appropriate way to organize political authority on the globe. As Keene observes:

In the family of civilized nations, the main point of international and political order was understood as being to encourage respect for the equality and independent sovereignty of individual states or nations. . . . Outside the family of civilized nations, however, other forms of international political organization and different legal rules were deemed appropriate, in keeping with the belief that here the central purpose of international order was to promote the civilization of decadent, backward, savage, or barbaric peoples.[4]

Two interlinked institutional forms thus structured the distribution of political authority in Europe and its non-European territories: the institution of sovereignty and the institution of empire. As we have seen, the expansion of the system of states involved the gradual displacement of the latter by the former, with crises of legitimacy in individual empires leading to fragmentation and the proliferation of new states. But while postcolonial states made their presence felt in the system from the first half of the nineteenth century onward, the institution of empire endured, rationalized by leading liberals like John Stuart Mill and reaffirmed and reasserted by international accords such as the Berlin General Act.[5]

What do I mean, though, by the 'institution of empire'? An institution is a stable set of norms, rules, and principles that 'define the meaning and identity of the individual' and shape 'patterns of appropriate economic, political, and cultural activity engaged in by those individuals'.[6] It follows that the institution of empire is a set of norms,

---

[4] Keene, *Beyond the Anarchical Society*, p. 7.
[5] John Stuart Mill, 'A few words on non-intervention' (1859). At www.libertarian.co.uk/lapubs/forep/forep008.pdf (accessed 23 Sept. 2012). On liberal rationalizations for empire, see Uday Singh Mehta, *Liberalism and Empire: A Study in Nineteenth-Century British Liberal Thought* (University of Chicago Press, 1999); and Jennifer Pitts, *A Turn to Empire: The Rise of Imperial Liberalism in Britain and France* (Princeton University Press, 2005).
[6] John W. Meyer, John Boli, and George M. Thomas, 'Ontology and rationalization', in George M. Thomas, John W. Meyer, Francesco Ramirez, and John Boli (eds.), *Institutional Structure: Constraining State, Society, and the Individual* (London: Sage, 1987), p. 12.

rules, and principles that shapes and licenses a 'system of interaction between two political entities, one of which, the dominant metropole, exerts political control over the internal and external policy – external sovereignty – of the other, the subordinate polity'.[7] Individual empires are structured by 'internal' institutions of empire, the regimes of unequal entitlements emphasized in previous chapters. But since the sixteenth century Europe's individual empires had also been sustained by an 'external' institution of empire: a set of intersubjective beliefs and attendant social practices that established empire in general as a legitimate form of rule, a rightful way of distributing political authority. The original papal grant of the Indies to the crowns of Castile and Leon was an early component in the construction of this institution; the General Act of the Berlin Conference, the Mandates system of the League of Nations, and the United Nations Trusteeship system were all subsequent components.

After 1945 multiple empires experienced internal crises of legitimacy. But as anticipated in the Introduction, what was unique about this period was that the 'external' institution of empire collapsed. By 1970 the United Nations General Assembly had passed Resolution 2621, declaring that 'the continuation of colonialism in all its forms and manifestations is a crime' (Article 1) and upholding 'the inherent right of colonial peoples to struggle by all necessary means at their disposal against colonial powers which suppress their aspirations for freedom and independence' (Article 2).[8] This reflected in part the changed balance of power within the General Assembly, where postcolonial states could now outvote the imperial powers and their Western sympathizers. But a normative shift had nonetheless occurred, and the most revealing evidence of this is the changed voting behavior of Western powers. As we shall see below, in the early 1950s the imperial powers, supported by the United States, Australia, and others, vigorously opposed any United Nations resolutions that cast the right to self-determination as a necessary prerequisite for the recognition and protection of individual human rights. But a decade later the very same

---

[7] Doyle, *Empires*, p. 45.
[8] United Nations General Assembly, 'A/RES/2621: Program of action for the full implementation of the Declaration on the Granting of Independence to Colonial Countries and Peoples'. At http://daccess-dds-ny.un.org/doc/ RESOLUTION/GEN/NR0/348/86/IMG/NR034886.pdf?OpenElement (accessed 23 Sept. 2012).

states were unwilling to pay the reputational of costs of voting against the 1960 Declaration on the Granting of Independence to Colonial Countries and Peoples (Resolution 1514), either abstaining or voting in favor. The institution of empire had been successfully displaced by a newly reformulated and reasserted right of self-determination.

The collapse of the institution of empire simultaneously empowered colonial peoples in their struggles with particular imperial powers, placed a moral burden on imperial powers to hasten decolonization while discrediting 'Algerian' style strategies of forced retention, aided metropolitan opponents of empire, and licensed a role for the United Nations in negotiating transitions to independence. Violent struggle was needed to force the imperial powers out of a number of colonies: Algeria, Indonesia, and Indo-China the most protracted. But two things are worth noting. First, most of these violent struggles occurred in the early years of postwar decolonization, well before the institution of empire had been fully discredited. Even in Algeria, which did not gain independence until 1962, the French ability to sustain the war domestically had waned by the late 1950s and de Gaulle had opened the door to independence by 1959, the year before the United Nations passed Resolution 1514. Second, in the majority of cases new states did not win independence by force of arms. Indeed, most former colonies – Gabon, Burkina Faso, Samoa, Malawi, Guinea, Madagascar, Gambia, Lesotho, Barbados, etc. – lacked the material or organizational capacity to wage sustained insurgencies. Moreover, in many of these cases, especially after 1960, the imperial powers withdrew in haste, often leaving national institutional structures poorly suited to the challenges of self-government. Overall, as Jackson argues, the collapse of the institution of empire, driven in large measure by the reassertion of the right to self-determination, led to a proliferation of 'weak' states, ordained with 'juridical' (or *de jure*) sovereignty but frequently lacking the empirical characteristics of viable states.[9]

## Existing accounts

There is an enormous literature on post-1945 decolonization, some focusing on particular empires, some on the general phenomenon, and all of it throwing up a myriad of contending arguments and

---

[9] Jackson, *Quasi-States*, p. 83.

explanations. How well, though, does this variegated literature deal with the distinctive feature of imperial fragmentation in this period – its aforementioned universality? Although an imperfect division, the literature falls into three broad categories: the first emphasizing the salience of local nationalist movements, the second, metropolitan capacities and priorities, and the third, the nature of the international context. None of these, I suggest, adequately addresses the issue of universality.

From the late nineteenth century onward, movements for imperial reform emerged across Europe's empires, transforming over time into explicit campaigns for political independence. The Indian National Congress was founded in 1885, the South African Native National Congress in 1912, the National Congress of British West Africa in 1920, and the Indonesian National Party in the same year. Not surprisingly, one strand of the literature on decolonization stresses the role of such movements.[10] Unpersuaded by arguments that emphasize metropolitan policies or the international context, Anthony Low argues, for example, that decolonization

all but invariably required first the growth of nationalist sentiments and nationalist forces within a colonial territory itself. Whilst in reality international aspects were rarely of great significance, what was then of prime importance were the particularities of the imperial responses which to a major degree determined the nature of the confrontation which then ensued – though hardly the eventual outcome.[11]

Nationalist impulses provoking context-specific imperial responses thus drove decolonization, understood as a complex tapestry of locally instigated, largely autogenous social processes. At one level, the salience of such factors is difficult to deny: without anticolonial

---

[10] The United States Central Intelligence Agency emphasized the strength of local nationalist movements as early as 1948. It reported: 'The primary cause of the breakup of the European colonial empires is the growth of native nationalism in these areas, simultaneously with the decline in power and prestige of the colonial powers.' Central Intelligence Agency, *The Breakup of the Colonial Empires and Its Implications for US Security*, 3 September 1948. At www.foia.cia.gov/sites/default/files/document_conversions/89801/DOC_ 0001166383.pdf (accessed 10 Mar. 2013).

[11] D. A. Low, *Eclipse of Empire* (Cambridge University Press, 1993), p. xii. Other works emphasizing local nationalist movements include Hedley Bull, 'The revolt against the West', in Bull and Watson (eds.), *The Expansion of International Society*, pp. 217–29; and Geoffrey Barraclough, *An Introduction to Contemporary History* (Harmondsworth: Penguin, 1967), ch. 6.

pressure from below the twentieth-century politics of empire would have run an entirely different course. And in a number of headline cases, such as British India, the strength of local agitation did make continued imperial rule politically, if not militarily, unsustainable. Yet the very diversity of local impulses, the fact that they varied in organizational capacity, degree of unity, available material resources, political objectives and imperial setting, means that such accounts are better suited to explaining the particularities of individual colonial crises than the universality of post-1945 decolonization.

A second set of explanations shifts the focus on to the metropole, emphasizing either material incapacity, deliberate policy choices, or both. One of the most frequently cited reasons for postwar decolonization is the weakness of the war-ravaged European powers. 'They were exhausted,' as Gann and Duignan put it.[12] There are, however, two problems with this argument. First, the material incapacity of the imperial powers was not felt equally across all colonies. As R. F. Holland writes, 'Western Europe's status and capacity . . . was clearly on the wane for most of the twentieth century, and violently so after 1945, but whether that status fell in relation to Upper Volta or the Gold Coast/Ghana is very doubtful.'[13] Second, material incapacity did not, it seems, encourage imperial retrenchment. Indeed, often the reverse was the case, with empire seen as essential to postwar recovery. For instance, 'it seems likely', John Darwin argues, 'that the economic repercussions of the Second World War encouraged a revival of British interest in parts of their colonial empire and in imperial integration generally.'[14] The notion that decolonization resulted from material incapacity is sometimes accompanied by a second proposition: that the imperial powers engineered decolonization to allow a more cost-effective form of 'informal empire'. In W. R. Louis and R. Robinson's words, 'The formal Empire contracted in the post-war years as it had once expanded, as a variable function of integrating countries into the international capitalist economy.'[15] Decolonization was

---

[12] Gann and Duignan, *Burden of Empire*, p. 72.
[13] R. F. Holland, *European Decolonization, 1918–1981* (London: Macmillan, 1985), p. 300. A similar observation is made by John Gallagher in *The Decline, Revival and Fall of the British Empire* (Cambridge University Press, 1982), pp. 73–4.
[14] Darwin, *Britain and Decolonization*, p. 20.
[15] W. R. Louis and R. Robinson, 'The imperialism of decolonization', *Journal of Imperial and Commonwealth History*, 22.3 (1994), 495.

thus a case, according to Nicholas Tarling, of 'adaptation rather than abandonment'.[16] This sits uncomfortably, however, with the tenacity with which the imperial powers clung to their colonial territories. Not only did they fight a number of bloody colonial wars, but as we shall see, they used every argument they could muster, in every available institutional forum, to maintain the moral standing of empire as a legitimate system of rule. Any argument that decolonization was a metropolitan strategy to reconstitute European power and influence needs to deal with these seemingly contradictory facts.

If accounts stressing local anticolonial forces and imperial capacities and policies help us little in understanding the universality of post-1945 decolonization, what of those emphasizing international context? Several of these arguments were addressed in Chapter 1 and need no revisiting here: imperial rivalry, the changing structure of the world economy, incorporation into an international society, and the socializing effects of world culture. There remain, however, two prominent lines of reasoning, one emphasizing the geopolitical transformation that accompanied the end of World War II, the second stressing revolutions in international norms.

The first of these is nicely summarized by Darwin:

The whole face of international politics seemed to have been transformed after 1945, when the complex pattern of pre-war rivalries gave way to the stark simplicity of a bi-polar world in which Cold War (at varying temperatures) had become the dominant influence on international politics. In this new nuclear landscape of competing ideologies and vast land powers, sustained by colossal expenditure on scientific weaponry, colonial empires appeared as quaint survivors of a bygone age, to be quickly dismantled lest they be knocked to pieces in the turbulent wake of the superpowers.[17]

Arguments such as this are usually accompanied by claims about the anticolonialism of the system's new titans. One of the few things the United States and the Soviet Union had in common, it is argued, was their disdain for old-style European imperialism and commitment to the principle of self-determination, articulated decades earlier by both Wilson and Lenin. Two things thus conspired to push the European

[16] Nicholas Tarling, *The Fall of Imperial Britain in South-East Asia* (Oxford University Press, 1993), p. 2.
[17] John Darwin, *The End of the British Empire: The Historical Debate* (Oxford: Basil Blackwell, 1991), p. 56.

powers toward decolonization: the material structure of the international system, in which they were relegated to second rank status, and the superpowers' common ideological cause. But while one would be unwise to discount such factors entirely, they bear less weight than they seem to. Both the Ottoman and Austro-Hungarian empires endured for considerable periods despite being cast as 'the sick men of Europe', propped up time and again by contending first rank powers. More importantly, though, the Cold War standoff between the superpowers had a contradictory impact on decolonization. On the one hand, the Soviet Union's opposition to Europe's empires gave anticolonial nationalists new sources of material support and ideological sustenance. But equally importantly, the Cold War greatly diluted Washington's former anticolonialism, significantly reducing the pressure on Britain and the other imperial powers. It was 'far from obvious', Darwin argues, 'that the only power strong enough to demolish the British empire had any interest in doing so. Indeed, simply in terms of great power politics, there seemed little reason why the British should not play an "Austrian" hand indefinitely, provided they kept their heads.'[18]

The second line of reasoning, which emphasizes international normative change, is advanced by Jackson, Philpott, and Neta Crawford, though each in their own distinctive way. For Jackson, the rapidity and universality of decolonization was a consequence of a fundamental change in the norms governing which political entities are entitled to recognition as fully independent sovereign states. Prior to the late 1950s and early 1960s only those countries which demonstrated 'empirical sovereignty' – 'the wherewithal to provide political goods for [their] citizens'[19] – were accorded sovereign status. The so-called 'standard of civilization' was used to determine such achievement, and the European powers ensured that the membership of the international system was an exclusive, jealously guarded right. This old 'positive sovereignty' game, Jackson argues, has since been supplanted by a new 'negative sovereignty' game, under which weak states have been granted 'juridical sovereignty' without exhibiting any of the trappings of empirical statehood. Only through reference to this change in the meanings attached to the sovereignty game, Jackson contends, can we explain the nature and speed of European decolonization. Moreover, it was the triumph of the right to self-determination,

---

[18] Ibid., p. 58.    [19] Jackson, *Quasi-States*, p. 29.

which lay at the heart of the new negative sovereignty regime, that
spurred this dramatic expansion of the system. 'Anti-colonialism', he
concludes, 'looks more and more like a sea change in international
legitimacy.'[20]

Philpott also attributes decolonization to a normative transformation after 1945, the second of two great 'revolutions in sovereignty'.
Each of these revolutions revised the underlying 'constitution' of international society, establishing systemic norms about what constitutes
a legitimate political entity and what kinds of political communities
can become such entities.[21] As we saw in Chapter 3, the first revolution occurred with the Peace of Westphalia, which 'defined the legitimate polities mainly as states, possessing the quality of sovereignty'.[22]
For three centuries, however, the evolving system of sovereign states
formed the hub of a network of expansive empires, and the colonies
that comprised these empires were denied sovereign recognition. The
revolution that occurred after 1945 retained the sovereign state as
the legitimate political entity but radically revised the norms concerning which polities could become states. 'In this new constitution of
international society – global sovereign statehood – the second face
of authority prescribed that all colonies were entitled to sovereign
independence.'[23] For Philpott, what caused this revolution was the
spread of two key ideas: anticolonial nationalism, 'the idea that a
colony is a nation, a group of people that has a common identity
and history and is entitled to a state of its own', and 'racial equality, holding that colonialism by its very nature subordinated Asian,
African, and Central American peoples to European rulers, implying
their inferiority and perpetuating their domination'.[24] These ideas were
internalized and mobilized by diverse anticolonial critics – 'couriers of
ideas' – who used 'reputational social power' to alter the cost-benefit
calculations of imperial elites, ultimately leading them to relinquish
empire in the interests of the state. The key locus of change, for
Philpott, was within the British and French colonial establishments,
as these were by far the largest of Europe's empires. In each case,
however, the revolutionary ideas of colonial nationalism and racial
equality articulated differently with established ideas: a stated commitment to eventual self-government in the British case, and assimilation

[20] Ibid., p. 83.    [21] Philpott, *Revolutions in Sovereignty*, p. 15.
[22] Ibid.    [23] Ibid., p. 153.    [24] Ibid., p. 161.

in the French. These different articulations, Philpott argues, explain the marked differences between how the British and French managed decolonization.[25]

Like Jackson and Philpott, Crawford sees decolonization as the product of a fundamental normative change. Indeed, she goes so far as to argue that 'the end of formal colonialism as a legitimate practice is perhaps the biggest change in the structure and practice of international relations in the last 500 years'.[26] What drove this transformation, she contends, was over a century of normative argument. 'Whereas colonialism had been the dominant practice, or norm, for thousands of years, supported by strong ethical arguments, colonialism was denormalized and delegitimated in the twentieth century because anti-colonial reformers made persuasive ethical arguments.'[27] Such arguments must be understood as social processes that move through several key phases: they 'denormalize and delegitimize dominant beliefs and practices', they 'articulate an alternative that meets normative criteria', they animate political action, and in time they become institutionalized, 'altering structures of the world and the starting point for new ethical arguments'.[28] The processes of ethical argument that eventually undermined colonialism originated well before the post-1945 period, dating back to debates over the moral legitimacy of slavery and forced labor. These practices, Crawford argues, 'were among the defining characteristics of colonial practice and understanding their demise is vital for understanding decolonization'.[29] During the nineteenth century a combination of new religious arguments against slavery and more secular ideas about the 'rights of man' undermined slavery's legitimacy and gnawed away at the moral architecture of colonialism itself. A second important step came with the Mandates system of the League of Nations, which was not only a consequence of public pressure for a more moderate form of colonialism, but which also established a set of institutional practices that deconstructed colonial rule.[30] By 1945, therefore, the delegitimation of colonialism was already well underway: in fact, 'Post-World War II decolonization may be considered the implementation and extension of already articulated normative

---

[25] Ibid., pp. 161–7.
[26] Neta C. Crawford, *Argument and Change in World Politics: Ethics, Decolonization, and Humanitarian Intervention* (Cambridge University Press, 2002), p. 2.
[27] Ibid., p. 4.    [28] Ibid., p. 7.    [29] Ibid., p. 159.    [30] Ibid., p. 288.

beliefs and arguments.'[31] Four things were distinctive, though, about post-1945 developments: the growth of anticolonial movements in the core and periphery, the delegitimation of 'scientific racism' and social Darwinism, the dwindling of public support for the maintenance of empire, and the institutional mechanisms of the United Nations Trusteeships system, which embodied the earlier 'reform' colonialism of the League's Mandate regime.[32] It was in this context, Crawford contends, that colonialism was finally and fully delegitimated.

Nothing in what follows questions the central insight of Jackson's, Philpott's, and Crawford's work: that the practice of colonialism suffered a profound crisis of legitimacy after 1945, and that this goes a long way to explaining both the rapidity and universality of decolonization. I have concerns, however, about particular elements of each of their arguments. Jackson provides a detailed account of the apparent revolution in the rules of the sovereignty game, from 'positive' to 'negative' sovereignty, but he provides no explanation of this transformation. The rehabilitation of the right to self-determination plays a central role in his account, but why did this occur when it did and with such salience? Philpott goes some way to overcoming this limitation, showing how ideas about anticolonial nationalism and racial equality were mobilized by anticolonial 'couriers', ultimately changing British and French interests in empire. Once these states had given up the game, the old 'Westphalian' constitution of international society was finished, replaced by universal state sovereignty. But while struggles over the legitimacy of empire within Britain and France were clearly important, they do not, in and of themselves, explain changing international norms about empire. In fact, Britain and France fought the reconstitution of such norms at the international level until the very end. As far as the construction of new intersubjective meanings to structure the membership of the international system was concerned, they were on the losing side. Furthermore, the politics shaping these meanings was occurring not within their metropoles but in international forums. Crawford's account takes us several steps closer to grasping this politics. Not only does she trace the long history of the transimperial ethical arguments that eventually undercut the legitimacy of colonialism, her emphasis on the institutional politics of the Mandate and Trusteeship systems places international normative developments front and center.

[31] Ibid., p. 292.    [32] Ibid., p. 293.

The problem is, however, that she neglects the principal site in which ethical arguments were mobilized to delegitimize empire after 1945: the evolving human rights forums of the United Nations. It was in these forums that older ideas about the 'rights of man', which feature so prominently in the earlier parts of Crawford's account, were elaborated and codified, and it was there, for the large part, that the right to self-determination was redefined in universal terms.

## The irrelevance of human rights?

Before proceeding it is worth considering the claims of those who explicitly deny that decolonization had anything to do with human rights. As noted in the Introduction, this is a default assumption of many commentators. There are those, however, who are more categorical in their denials. Brian Simpson writes, for example, that 'the anti-colonial movement was not in essence a human rights movement. Its primary aim was not to reduce the power of the state over the individual, and this is the central idea which underlies the [human rights] movement, and which leads to the pressure for international mechanisms of protection...'[33] Equally categorically, Reza Afshari argues that 'anti-colonial struggles even among those who had already imagined their nationhood, heroic as they were, remained in essence a single issue struggle, lacking the necessary human rights consciousness'.[34] Jackson takes the argument one step further, claiming that the development of the international human rights regime was a response to decolonization and the proliferation of weak states in the developing world.[35] The new 'negative' sovereignty game gave colonies an unconditional right to self-determination, resulting in a marked increase in authoritarian, human rights violating states. This 'new sovereignty game is... complicated by the emergence of a cosmopolitan regime which seeks to establish the legal status of humans in international

[33] Simpson, *Human Rights and the End of Empire*, p. 300.
[34] Afshari, 'On the historiography of human rights', 44.
[35] I have critiqued this argument elsewhere, not least for its chronological inaccuracies. The construction of the international human rights regime did not occur in the wake of decolonization, its principal instruments were either proclaimed or under negotiation well before the flood of new states that followed 1960. See Christian Reus-Smit, 'Human rights and the social construction of sovereignty', *Review of International Studies*, 27.4 (2001), 519–38.

relations against the sovereign Leviathan. *This norm is not part of the sovereignty game but is a reaction to it: human rights are intended to curb sovereign rights'* (emphasis added).[36] Important as these arguments are, the following discussion concentrates on the most recent, and most fully elaborated, denial that human rights mattered: Moyn's argument in *The Last Utopia*.

Moyn presents a revisionist history of human rights, in which they become a force in world politics only after 1970. The pursuit of human rights, he contends: 'is a recognizably utopian program: for the political standards it champions and the emotional passion it inspires, this program draws on the image of a place that has not yet been called into being. It promises to penetrate the impregnability of state borders, slowly replacing them with the authority of international law.'[37] Yet human rights as a utopia did not capture the public imagination, or animate a global social or political movement, until after two other utopian projects – communism and nationalism – had lost their allure. '[F]ar from being the sole idealism that has inspired faith and activism in the course of human events,' Moyn writes, 'human rights emerged historically as the last utopia – one that became powerful and prominent because other visions imploded.'[38] This did not happen until well into the 1970s, however. The long history of the 'rights of man', so often seen as an antecedent of modern human rights, was in reality something quite different: it was a statist project, not about building authority beyond the state: 'Far from being sources of appeal that transcended state and nation, the rights asserted in early modern political revolutions and championed thereafter were central to the construction of state and nation, and led nowhere beyond until recently.'[39] Contrary to conventional narratives, efforts to codify international human rights after 1945 were weak, Moyn argues. 'The percolation of the phrase in wartime, the Universal Declaration, and associated developments like the European Convention on Human Rights (1950) were minor byproducts of this era, not main features. Human rights were already on the edge of the stage in the postwar moment, even before they were pushed off entirely by Cold War politics.'[40]

---

[36] Jackson, *Quasi-States*, p. 44. Jackson reiterates these claims in *The Global Covenant: Human Conduct in World Politics* (Oxford University Press, 2000), pp. 303–4.

[37] Moyn, *The Last Utopia*, p. 1.    [38] Ibid., p. 4.

[39] Ibid., p. 12.    [40] Ibid., p. 46.

An important step in Moyn's argument is the claim that human rights had nothing to do with post-1945 decolonization, which had largely run its course by the mid-1970s. 'There was a truncated principle that decolonization universalized. But it was that of collective liberation, not human rights.'[41] Indeed, according to Moyn, the collective right to self-determination and the human rights of individuals cannot share the stage: the more of one, the less of the other. From the outset, 'human rights entered the global rhetoric in a kind of hydraulic relationship with self-determination: to the extent the one appeared, and progressed, the other declined, or even disappeared'.[42] Moyn admits that references to human rights peppered the arguments of anticolonialists, but stresses their infrequency and relegates them to what he sees as the irrelevant realm of rhetoric.[43] Furthermore, he argues that wherever self-determination and human rights were invoked together, the former was always the primary value. 'Already by 1955, the appeal to UN principles meant an appeal to a concept of human rights that had gone through a conceptual revolution, with self-determination becoming the chief and threshold right – "a prerequisite," as the Bandung Final Communiqué put it, "of the full enjoyment of all fundamental Human Rights."'[44] Below I question Moyn's understanding of what 'prerequisite' meant in such statements, but what matters here is that he sees the use of human rights to justify self-determination as nothing more than a new iteration of the old practice of invoking the rights of man to license state power. 'Any attempt . . . to place anticolonialism in human rights history must face up to an era when the human rights idea had no movement and anticolonialism, a powerful movement, typically took the new "human rights" in the original, collectivist direction of earlier rights talk.'[45] Only when decolonization was complete, when the sovereign state had been universalized, did human rights come of age. This momentous development simultaneously took the wind out of nationalism's sails and freed the West of its imperial baggage, creating space for a new international human rights politics. 'The hard fact to contemplate', Moyn concludes, 'is that human rights experienced their triumph as a widespread moral vernacular after decolonization

---

[41] Ibid., p. 86.    [42] Ibid., p. 88.
[43] When discussing W. E. B. DuBois's use of the language of human rights, for example, Moyn writes that 'it represented merely a tool, not the essence of his thought and his activism, even when he appealed to it'. Ibid., p. 103.
[44] Ibid., p. 108.    [45] Ibid., p. 107.

not during it – and because of it perhaps only in the sense that the loss
of empire allowed for the reclamation of liberalism, including rights
talk, shorn of its depressing earlier entanglements with oppression and
violence abroad.'[46]

There is much in Moyn's work that I agree with. He is right to stress
the pro-empire orientation of the early United Nations. He is right that
in the politics of decolonization, rights talk took the sovereign state
as its institutional referent. And he is right that in the wake of decolonization, the politics of international human rights changed form,
evincing new modes of transnational activism and focusing increasingly on the augmentation of international institutional authority. His
central claims are not so robust, however. He is wrong to claim that
human rights mattered in world politics only after 1970, and he is
wrong to claim that they played little if any role in decolonization.

*The Last Utopia* is a good example of how underlying conceptual
assumptions shape historical arguments, conditioning what the historian (or the International Relations scholar, for that matter) sees and
emphasizes. Moyn's argument rests on the assumption that human
rights matter only when they animate a global political movement.
Until they inspired the hearts and minds of the world's peoples, until
they animated national and international activism, and until they
informed the construction of legal authority beyond the sovereign
state, human rights were 'peripheral on the world stage'.[47] If this
assumption is wrong, however, if the politics of human rights can
take diverse forms and have significant political consequences even in
the absence of a global political movement, then Moyn's argument
collapses and the history of human rights looks very different. In what
follows, I argue that the politics of human rights has indeed taken such
diverse forms, and that it was at work in significant and consequential ways after 1945. This is not only because the principal, legally
binding components of the international bill of rights were negotiated
during this period, including the International Covenant on Civil and
Political Rights and its First Optional Protocol (which Moyn barely
mentions). But because it was in the context of these negotiations that
the collective right of self-determination was reasserted and redefined
in universalist terms.

[46] Ibid., p. 117.    [47] Ibid., p. 8.

This brings me to the second problem with Moyn's account: his claim about the 'hydraulic' relationship between human rights and self-determination, in which the strengthening of one entails the weakening of the other. Nowhere do I deny the very real tensions between collective and individual rights, the subject of numerous scholarly explorations. Nor do I deny, more specifically, the tensions between national self-determination and the protection of individuals' human rights, with the former often serving as a bar to the latter, and the latter compromising the former. Yet Moyn's 'displacement' thesis, in which human rights come to the fore only in the wake of decolonization, obscures the crucial interconnection between self-determination and human rights in the two decades following World War II. Moyn speaks of the right to self-determination as though its meaning has been unchanged. But, as we shall see, in reality the principle emerged from World War II politically and ethically denuded. The post-Versailles notion that it was ethnically defined nations that enjoyed the right to self-determination had been undermined by the savagery of the Nazi campaign for an ethnically homogeneous greater Germany. And it was, in any case, a principle poorly suited to the emancipatory politics of anticolonialism: non-European peoples were formally excluded from its purview, and most of these peoples were ethnically and culturally heterogeneous. The right to self-determination thus has had to be reconstituted after 1945, given a new set of meanings better suited to the exigencies of anticolonialism. As we shall see, newly independent postcolonial states did this by grafting the right of self-determination on to emergent human rights norms, arguing that the former was a necessary 'prerequisite' for the latter.

Moyn misreads this, though. According to the Oxford English Dictionary, 'prerequisite' means 'required as a previous condition'. No normative hierarchy is implied. Yet Moyn takes it to mean 'normatively primary', as though the right of self-determination was a more important value than human rights. But this is not at all what early postcolonial states were saying in UN forums when they argued that self-determination was a 'prerequisite' for the satisfaction of basic human rights. Because Moyn misses altogether the fact that the right to self-determination had to be reconstituted after 1945, he fails to understand what these states were doing discursively. Communicative action theorists have long observed that when seeking to justify a new value, actors will appeal to existing, higher order values. As Agnes Heller explains, in justifying their chosen value they appeal 'to values higher than those which they want to justify, by proving that the latter are but an interpretation of the higher values, or that they can be related to these higher values without logical contradiction'.[48] What early postcolonial states were doing, therefore, was trying to reassert the normative validity of the right to self-determination by casting it as necessary to the satisfaction of human rights. As we shall see, this could only be done once human rights had been legally codified at the international level, a project in which the very same postcolonial states played a prominent role.

The final problem with Moyn's thesis concerns his claim that there is a fundamental difference between the political struggles for the 'rights of man' which characterized the early modern period through to decolonization, and the contemporary politics of human rights. The first was about constructing the authority of the state, the second about transcending and containing it. My concern here is not that Moyn is wrong, but that he fails to grasp how these two manifestations of rights politics are related in the long history of struggles for general individual rights. To begin with, 'the rights of man' and 'human rights' are both species of general rights – individuals hold them not because of some contract or custom but because they are said to constitute a particular kind of moral being. What changes over time is who, among all biological humans, are thought to constitute such beings. In the case of human rights, it is at least theoretically all members of the human species. The expansion of the 'zone of application', from its very circumscribed ambit in early modern Europe, occurred gradually and always through intense political struggle. Second, general individual rights are institutionally dependent; their recognition and protection require an enabling or executing institutional architecture. Historically, as the cases in this book demonstrate, empires have been principal sites of struggle for the recognition of these rights. And when empires have proven incapable of accommodating new rights claims, disaffected subject peoples have turned to the sovereign state as the institutional alternative. Yet the state itself has also proven a suboptimal guarantor of general individual rights, and this has spurred the development of institutional norms and practices at the international

---

[48] Agnes Heller, *Beyond Justice* (Oxford: Basil Blackwell, 1987), p. 239.

level, seeking to compromise and qualify sovereign authority. This is not, however, a development categorically different from the focus on the state which characterized the politics of the 'rights of man'. Instead, it is the latest manifestation of an institutional imperative inherent to the politics of general individual rights.

## The fourth great wave

Like Jackson, Philpott, and Crawford, I attribute the near simultaneous breakup of Europe's colonial empires to a normative revolution; in my case, to the demise of the institution of empire, and the advent of universal state sovereignty. This revolution was a consequence of the reassertion and reformulation of the collective right to self-determination, an achievement of newly independent postcolonial states which played a key role in the negotiation of the international bill of rights and then successfully grafted the right to independence to emergent human rights norms. The nature of this argument affects how the following discussion proceeds. I begin with a brief analysis of the wave of expansion that followed the Peace of Versailles. This is important because it is the one case in which collective, not individual, rights were central. Furthermore, as noted above, the nature and fate of the self-determination regime established with Versailles affected what transpired after 1945. I then turn to the role that new states played in the negotiation of key human rights instruments, particularly the two international covenants. This lays the foundations for the final discussion of how the right to self-determination was reconstituted in universalist terms.

### Post-Versailles

In the wake of World War I, a third great wave of systemic expansion occurred, a consequence this time of the defeat and collapse of the German, Austro-Hungarian, and Ottoman empires. As indicated above, it was here that the rights of ethnically defined 'nations', not individuals, were crucial. In the struggles preceding Westphalia, the fundamental conflict concerned the nature of individuals, their relationship to God, and the degree to which the Church could legitimately mediate that relation. The collective identities of 'Protestant' and 'Catholic' were constituted by this confessional struggle, and the resulting identities were transnational not national. In the collapse of the Spanish Empire, inhabitants of the Americas rebelled in the end because their rights, as individuals, to equal political representation were flagrantly disregarded. But although the Americans' sense of cultural distinctiveness had grown during the eighteenth century, it had not coalesced into a sense of 'national' identity. Indeed, as Chiaramonte observes, in Latin America ideas of nationality and nation were not the cause of independence, 'they were the result of a long-drawn-out process sparked off by it'.[49] With the third wave of systemic expansion, in contrast, recognition of the rights of ethnically defined nations was primary, serving as an organizing principle of the post-Versailles international order and animating local political struggles.

When carving up the territories of the defeated empires, the victorious powers upheld the principle that all 'nations' had a right to self-determination. In his 'Fourteen Points' speech, Woodrow Wilson proclaimed 'the principle of justice to all peoples and nationalities, and their right to live on equal terms of liberty and safety with one another, whether they be strong or weak'.[50] While not enshrined in the Treaty of Versailles itself, this principle was instituted in a series of postwar accords, the net result being the creation of more than twenty new sovereign states. In determining which 'peoples' constituted 'nations' entitled to the right to self-determination, an ethnic conception of nationality was applied. As Rupert Emerson observes, 'the peoples involved in the Wilsonian period were ethnic communities, nations, or nationalities primarily defined by language or culture'.[51] Although excluded from the final draft of the Covenant of the League of Nations, Wilson's third draft was explicit in seeking to make the ongoing sanctity of any new territorial boundaries conditional upon stable 'racial conditions'.[52] This emphasis on the racial and cultural integrity of nations reflected the prevailing view that successful sovereign states were ethnically homogeneous. For Wilson, democracy could function

[49] Chiaramonte, 'Principle of consent', p. 565.
[50] Woodrow Wilson, 'Address to a Joint Session of Congress on the Conditions of Peace', 8 January 1918. At wwi.lib.byu.edu/index.php/President_Wilson%27s_Fourteen_Points (accessed 3 Oct. 2012).
[51] Rupert Emerson, 'Self-determination', *American Journal of International Law*, 65.3 (1971), 463.
[52] See Ray Stannard Baker, *Woodrow Wilson and World Settlement*, vol. III (London: Heinemann, 1923), p. 119.

properly only when a population was bound together by linguistic and cultural affinities.[53] And for Vladimir Lenin, 'multinational' states were 'always those whose internal constitution has for some reason or other remained abnormal or underdeveloped'.[54] Not all ethnically distinct peoples were entitled to self-determination, however. Ethnic minorities 'trapped' inside the new European states had no right to secession, and their most basic rights depended on the notoriously weak Minority Rights Treaties. 'The result', Hannah Arendt explained, 'was that those peoples to whom states were not conceded, considered the Treaties an arbitrary game which handed out rule to some and servitude to others.'[55]

The situation was no better for peoples living in Europe's overseas empires, who, as noted earlier, were deemed civilizationally unfit for self-determination, regardless of whether they were ethnically homogeneous or not. Nowhere was this more apparent than in the creation of a separate international regime to govern the colonial territories of the defeated powers: the Mandate system of the League of Nations. Crawford is correct to argue that the very existence of this system indicates a shift in attitudes toward colonialism, in the sense that there was now widespread recognition that a degree of international oversight was required to protect the rights and ensure the well-being of colonial peoples. She is also correct that 'the Mandate system grew to be more than its framers – or the mandatory powers – intended, ultimately striking a wedge in the colonial system'.[56] This having been said, though, the Mandate system rested on the firm conviction that colonial peoples were civilizationally backward, unready for independence and needing the ongoing tutelage of the imperial powers, acting under the League's oversight. According to the Covenant of the League of Nations, the colonial peoples of the defeated powers 'were not yet able to stand by themselves under the strenuous conditions of the modern world' and 'the well-being and development of such peoples

---

[53] Alfred Cobban, *The Nation State and Self-Determination* (London: Collins, 1969), p. 71.
[54] Vladimir I. Lenin, 'The right of nations to self-determination', in V. I. Lenin, *Collected Works*, vol. XX (Moscow: Progress Publishers, 1964), p. 387.
[55] Hannah Arendt, *Imperialism* (New York: Harvest, 1968), p. 150.
[56] Crawford, *Argument and Change in World Politics*, p. 264.

form a sacred trust of civilization'.[57] Article 22 went on to specify
the responsibilities of the Mandatory powers, which included ensur-
ing freedom of conscience and religion, prohibiting slavery, and preventing the building of military fortifications. What is not mentioned,
however, is any responsibility on the part of these powers to prepare
colonial peoples for eventual independence. In the wake of World War
I, therefore, non-European peoples were not only formally ineligible
for the right to self-determination, there was not even a promise on the
horizon.

As noted above, this self-determination regime did not survive World
War II. The idea that ethnically defined nations had a right to sovereign
statehood, and that granting this right would enhance international
peace and security, was shattered by Hitler's genocidal war for an ethnically homogeneous greater Germany. As Eric Hobsbawm observes,
the 'logical implication of trying to create a continent neatly divided
into coherent territorial states each inhabited by a separate ethnically
and linguistically homogeneous population was the mass expulsion
and extermination of minorities'. In this respect, Hitler was 'a logical
Wilsonian nationalist'.[58] Furthermore, as suggested earlier, the post-
Versailles right to self-determination was ill-suited to the exigencies
of post-1945 anticolonialism. Not only were the colonial peoples of
Africa, Asia, and the Pacific outside the civilizational perimeter within
which such a right was thought to apply, few if any of them were
ethnically homogeneous (at least as they were defined by established
colonial boundaries). For both of these reasons, existing formulations
of the right to self-determination emerged from World War II morally
and politically bankrupt. In the Atlantic Charter of 1941, Britain and
the United States had declared their respect for 'the right of all peoples to choose the form of government under which they will live'.[59]
But beyond Churchill's adamant denial that this applied to colonial
peoples, it was no longer clear what such a right meant or who was
entitled to it.

---

[57] 'Covenant of the League of Nations', Article 22. At www.unhcr.org/
    refworld/pdfid/3dd8b9854.pdf (accessed 3 Oct. 2012).
[58] Eric J. Hobsbawm, *Nations and Nationalism since 1780* (Cambridge
    University Press, 1990), p. 133.
[59] 'Atlantic Charter', 14 August 1941. At http://avalon.law.yale.edu/wwii/
    atlantic.asp (accessed 3 Oct. 2012).

## *A brief word on rhetoric*

Before proceeding to post-1945 developments, a word is needed on the question of rhetoric. Those who deny that human rights played a role in decolonization frequently admit that anticolonialists employed the language of rights but claim that this was little more than rhetoric. In Jan Eckel's words, 'those activists and states that did base their claims on human rights did not so much express their commitment to universal norms as appropriate them for their specific anticolonial policies'.[60] In a similar vein, Andreas Eckert argues that 'commitment to human rights remained rhetorical, however, often sacrificed in the name of ideology, traditions or institutions'.[61] These claims are not completely wrong. As explained in Chapter 2, one of the features of the post-1945 wave of systemic expansion is the important role that ideas about rights played as justificatory resources. What is interesting about those who see rights talk as simply rhetoric, however, is that they show surprisingly little interest in the analytical significance of their own observations. When they say that anticolonialists' use of rights language 'remained rhetorical' they are saying that it was nothing more than cheap talk, neither connected to their underlying interests nor causally significant. And in casting rights discourse as nothing more than rhetoric, they explore it no more. 'Rhetoric' in these accounts is an analytical full stop.

Yet rhetoric is neither cheap talk nor politically insignificant; it is a purposive social practice, employed by actors deliberately and artfully because successful rhetoric is politically enabling. All actors, Quentin Skinner observes, 'possess strong motives for seeking to legitimise any conduct liable to appear questionable',[62] and this was especially true of anticolonialists seeking independence from empire. As we have seen, in the immediate wake of World War II, empire remained an internationally legitimate form of rule and independence for non-European colonies was far from accepted. Anticolonialists thus had a significant

---

[60] Jan Eckel, 'Human rights and decolonization: new perspectives and open questions', *Humanity: An International Journal of Human Rights, Humanitarianism, and Development*, 1.1 (2010), 113.

[61] Andreas Eckert, 'African nationalists and human rights, 1940s and 1970s', in Stefan-Ludwig Hoffmann (ed.), *Human Rights in the Twentieth Century* (Cambridge University Press, 2011), p. 284.

[62] Quentin Skinner, *Visions of Politics*, vol. I: *Regarding Method* (Cambridge University Press, 2002), p. 155.

interest in reversing this balance of legitimacy. Yet shifting the terms of social and political legitimacy is difficult and requires the rhetorical reinterpretation and rearticulation of established meaning systems. 'Innovating ideologists', Skinner argues, have 'to show that a number of favourable terms can somehow be applied to their seemingly questionable actions'.[63] The first thing to note about successful rhetoric, therefore, is that it has one eye to the past, to established values and modes of argumentation. In Skinner's words, 'All revolutionaries are to this extent obliged to move backwards into battle.'[64] There are several ways that innovating ideologists can tailor established meanings to license their projects: neutral terms can be turned into favorable ones and used to describe what the actor wants to achieve; unfavorable terms can be turned into neutral ones for the same purposes; and questionable actions can be portrayed in new ways, showing that they embody values previously seen as unrelated. As we shall see, anticolonialists working in United Nations forums used a rhetorical strategy of grafting, casting empire as a fundamental violation of human rights and self-determination as a necessary condition for their recognition and protection. International human rights norms were only emergent at this time, however, and newly independent states had to play an active role in their codification before they could graft on a reconstituted right of self-determination.

Because successful rhetoric helps legitimate political action, it is empowering. Yet the artful use of rhetoric is also constraining. Far from cheap talk, rhetoric has costs. When actors claim that their actions are consistent with, or that they embody, a given set of principles, their subsequent actions must bear some relation to the principles they invoked. As Skinner observes, even when actors are not motivated by the values they assert, 'they will find themselves committed to behaving in such a way that their actions *remain compatible* with the claim that their professed principles genuinely motivated them'.[65] History is replete, of course, with cases where rhetoric was followed by incompatible behavior. Skinner's point, however, is not that transgressions from purported principle do not occur; it is that they carry with them costs, reputational costs in particular. Acting in ways that contradicts one's rhetoric is to expose oneself to accusations of hypocrisy; to be hoist with one's own petard, as the saying goes. One might argue that

[63] Ibid., p. 149.    [64] Ibid., pp. 149–50.    [65] Ibid., p. 155.

this is precisely what has happened with the early efforts of postcolonial states to codify international human rights norms. Irrespective of whether their rhetoric reflected their underlying motivations, they assisted in the construction of an international human rights regime that would in time serve as a normative resource for critics of authoritarian rule in postcolonial states.

## Rights in local struggles

In the Westphalian and Spanish-American waves of systemic expansion, ideas about individual rights helped ferment crises of imperial legitimacy, provided justificatory resources in struggles over legitimate political authority, and constituted deal-breakers, principles that had to be recognized if attempts to resolve imperial crises were to succeed. But as argued in Chapter 2, the balance between these was markedly different in the post-1945 wave. Here too many empires collapsed, spanning too many diverse societies, to sustain strong claims that ideas about individual rights fermented local crises of legitimacy or served as deal-breakers in all empires. The emphasis in this wave is thus on the role that ideas about individual rights played as justificatory resources, particularly at the international level where they were deeply implicated in the delegitimation of the institution of empire. This having been said, though, claims that human rights played little if any role in animating local anticolonial struggles are frequently overstated. Ideas about rights were important in a number of key local struggles, most notably in British South Asia and British and French sub-Saharan Africa. They were also at work in Egypt, although this was far from the norm in the Middle East where Arab and Islamic cultural politics were especially prominent. Two examples illustrate this.

The anticolonial struggle in British India is often divided into several phases, the first centered on agitation by Western educated elites for equal access to employment within the imperial bureaucracy.[66] Thoroughly imbued with liberal ideas about individual rights, this group pressed their right to racial equality in what was at first a moderate campaign for imperial reform. The Indian National Congress

---

[66] Munmun Jha, 'Nehru and civil liberties in India', *International Journal of Human Rights*, 7.3 (2003), 104.

('Congress' hereafter) was founded in this context, and while the ideas animating its eventual campaign for sovereign independence broadened significantly to encompass indigenous cultural beliefs (evident in the Hindu reform movement), the emphasis on individual rights remained an abiding feature of Indian anticolonial politics. Concerns about rights became especially prominent, however, after the 1918 publication of the British government's Sedition Report, and the subsequent enactment of its principal recommendations in the 1919 Anarchical and Revolutionary Crimes Act. Responding to the proposed constraints on basic civil liberties, Congress drafted a Declaration of Rights and insisted it be included in a new Indian constitution. Adopted at a special session in Bombay in 1918, the declaration enshrined a host of fundamental rights, including freedom of speech, expression, and association, equality before the law, and trial by jury.[67] Ten years later, following increased repression of the anticolonial struggle, Congress established a working group to draft a constitution for an independent India. The resulting Nehru Report, published in 1928, again emphasized the fundamental freedoms requiring constitutional protection.[68] At its 1931 meeting, Congress adopted the oft-cited Karachi Resolutions, which not only sought to explain the meaning of *Swaraj* (or self-rule) for the Indian people, but returned to the theme of fundamental freedoms, setting out a list of basic rights of all citizens.[69]

These early declarations, draft constitutions, and resolutions were all antecedents of the 1947 Constitution of India, Part 3 of which details a comprehensive set of fundamental individual rights, including the right to equality before the law, to freedom of speech, to protection of life and liberty, and to freedom of religion.[70] Several things are worth noting here. First, the constitutional codification of individuals' fundamental rights indicates that delegates to the Indian Constituent Assembly considered them sufficiently important to establish them as

[67] Ibid., 106.
[68] The report was named after Motilal Nehru, the working group's chair and father of India's first Prime Minister, Jawaharlal Nehru.
[69] Om Gautam, 'Human rights in India', in Peter Schwab and Admantia Pollis (eds.), *Toward a Human Rights Framework* (New York: Praeger, 1982), pp. 173–4.
[70] The fundamental rights set down in the Constitution are strikingly similar to those later codified in the International Covenant on Civil and Political Rights. See Vijayyashri Sripati, 'Human rights in India – fifty years after independence', *Denver Journal of International Law and Policy*, 26.1 (1997–8), 102–4.

formal legal constraints on the authority of the newly independent Indian state. Second, as we have seen, Moyn argues that if human rights had anything to do with decolonization their role was akin to earlier struggles for the rights of man, where the aim was the construction of state authority not its limitation. Yet although anticolonialists in India appealed to Indians' fundamental rights when campaigning for independent statehood, thus implicating rights in the institutional transition from empire to the sovereign state, they also understood these rights as human rights and saw them as necessary constraints on the authority of the state. This is clearly apparent in Jawaharlal Nehru's comments when he founded the Indian Civil Liberties Union in 1936. 'It is obvious', he said, 'that questions of civil liberties only arise when there is a conflict between the public or certain sections of it, and the executive government...A democracy can only function properly if public opinion constantly checks government and prevents it becoming too autocratic.'[71] Third, the fundamental rights set down in the Constitution are all civil and political, and are distinguished from 'directive principles of state policy', which are social and economic in nature and detailed in Part 4. The reason for this distinction is that delegates to the Constituent Assembly held that only civil and political rights were justiciable, defensible in a court of law.[72] Interestingly, this is precisely the position India subsequently adopted at the United Nations when calling for two separate international covenants, one on civil and political rights, the other on economic, social, and cultural rights.[73]

Appeals to individuals rights also featured in anticolonial struggles in sub-Saharan Africa, although the situation was more complex than in India. This is nicely illustrated by the independence struggle in colonial Nigeria, richly detailed in Bonny Ibhawoh's study *Imperialism and Human Rights*.[74] British rule in Nigeria rested on an ever more elaborate regime of colonial laws, portrayed as an enlightened extension to

[71] Quoted in Jha, 'Nehru and civil liberties in India', 109.
[72] Matthew George, 'Human rights in India', *Howard Law Journal*, 11 (1965), 292; Sripati, 'Human rights in India', 95.
[73] Roger Normand and Sarah Zaidi, *Human Rights at the UN: The Political History of Universal Justice* (Bloomington: Indiana University Press, 2008), pp. 206–12. It is worth noting that this is the only issue on which India and the United Kingdom agreed in the negotiation of the two international covenants.
[74] Ibhawoh, *Imperialism and Human Rights*.

colonial subjects of the rights and liberties enjoyed by British citizens. Ibhawoh writes:

The colonial legal system was an effective instrument for fostering colonial hegemony and guaranteeing the maintenance of social order on a scale conducive to colonial interests. The discourse of rights was particularly influential in this regard. Rights talk, within the context of the colonial legal system, was one of the many discourses employed by the colonial state to rationalize and legitimize empire.[75]

Yet this was contradicted by countervailing legal practices that revealed the regime of unequal entitlements that in fact characterized imperial hierarchy: the use, for example, of a Collective Punishment Ordinance (1912) to punish entire communities for the crimes of individuals,[76] an Unsettled District Ordinance (1912) to detain and punish individuals considered of 'undesirable character and reputation',[77] and a Seditious Offences Ordinance (1909) to limit freedom of the press.[78] In responding to these autocratic practices, Nigeria's Western-educated elite turned the discourse of individual rights back on their colonial masters.

[I]n their opposition to these coercive laws, African elites employed the same rhetoric of rights and liberties that the colonial authorities found so appealing in other contexts. However, the language of rights as employed by African elites who dominated public debates was not merely a form of oppositional discourse. As it was to colonial authorities in rationalizing empire, the language of rights along with 'self-determination' and 'development' became powerful tools for the nationalist cause.[79]

As in India, the early phase of agitation focused on imperial reform; on ending the discriminatory exclusion of the Western-educated elite from positions within the colonial bureaucracy, for example. During World War II, however, the agenda shifted from reform to sovereign independence. Churchill's denial that the Atlantic Charter applied to colonial peoples angered Africans, who believed that their contribution to the war effort had earned them greater respect. In 1943 the National Council for Nigeria and the Cameroons (NCNC) responded by publishing a 'Freedom Charter' that not only set down a range of fundamental individual rights held by all Nigerians, but also affirmed

---

[75] Ibid., p. 55.     [76] Ibid., pp. 64–6.     [77] Ibid., p. 66.
[78] Ibid., pp. 70–5.     [79] Ibid., p. 64.

the Atlantic Charter's expressed commitment to the right to national self-determination.[80]

The subsequent history of individual rights in Nigeria is entangled with centrifugal cultural politics. In 1951 the British instituted a process of constitutional reform, directly involving Nigerians. This encouraged the development of local political parties, which increasingly took on ethnic and regional characteristics, with the major parties controlled by the Hausa-Fulani, Yoruba, and Igbo cultural groups. While the campaign for national independence continued, minority groups started to fear persecution after Britain's departure, and there were calls for dividing the colony into several successor states. In 1957 the British established the Willink Commission to explore the validity of these fears. It concluded that there was indeed a high risk of persecution, but recommended against dividing the colony. Instead, it recommended the inclusion of a Bill of Rights in any future constitution of an independent Nigeria, trusting that the codification of a set of fundamental rights held equally by all Nigerians would protect minorities and aid national integration.[81] With the broad support of nationalist politicians, the 1960 Constitution of the Federation of Nigeria thus came to enshrine a comprehensive list of civil and political rights, including the rights to life and personal liberty, freedom of conscience, and freedom of expression. Like many of the early postcolonial constitutions in Africa, this early document did not survive the subsequent traumas of state- and nation-building. But as Ibhawoh observes, the rights provisions of the 1960 Constitution, and the Freedom Charter before them, were part of a politics of individual rights that were deeply rooted in the nature of the colonial legal order, its manifest contradictions, and in the mobilization of rights claims by the Western-educated elite.[82]

These examples alone cast doubt on overdrawn claims that the politics of individual rights played little role in local anticolonial struggles. Claiming that rights were implicated in all local anticolonial struggles would be unsustainable, but so too is the reverse. In notable cases, Western-educated 'indigenes' internalized liberal ideas about individual rights to liberty and challenged the hypocrisy of colonial administrations that spoke the language of enlightened rule but practiced discrimination. As in the Spanish case, they initially sought

---

[80] Ibid., pp. 155–6.    [81] Ibid., pp. 162–6.    [82] Ibid., p. 152.

imperial reform, or rights within empire, but were eventually radicalized as imperial governments failed to accommodate their rights claims, responded to agitation with heightened suppression, and treated them with disrespect after loyal wartime service.

## Postcolonial states and the international human rights regime

It is widely assumed that the construction of the international human rights regime was a Western project, and that newly independent postcolonial states played no meaningful role in negotiating its principal instruments. 'It should not be forgotten', Adamantia Pollis and Peter Schwab argue, 'that the San Francisco Conference which established the United Nations in 1945 was dominated by the West, and that the Universal Declaration of Human Rights was adopted at a time when most Third World countries were still under colonial rule. Thus to argue that Human Rights has a standing which is universal in character is to contradict historical reality.'[83] While not all scholars use the purported lack of postcolonial involvement to challenge the universality of international human rights norms, the conventional narrative highlights nonetheless the critical role of Western liberal powers, constrained and cajoled by the Soviet bloc with its emphasis on social and economic rights. Yet although this narrative has assumed the status of common wisdom, it is strikingly at odds with the historical record. Postcolonial states that gained their independence in the immediate aftermath of World War II, often in alliance with states that freed themselves from empire in previous waves of systemic expansion, not only played a decisive role in negotiating the Universal Declaration and the two international covenants, their positions were frequently opposed to the Soviet Union and more liberal than the Western powers.[84]

---

[83] Adamantia Pollis and Peter Schwab, 'Human rights: a Western construct with limited applicability', in Christine M. Koggel (ed.), *Moral and Political Theory*, vol. I of *Moral Issues in Global Perspective*, 2nd edn. (Peterborough: Broadview Press, 2006), p. 62.

[84] The following discussion is an elaboration of an argument I first published in Reus-Smit, 'Human rights and the social construction of sovereignty'. In the same year, Susan Waltz published an important article highlighting the role of 'small states' in negotiation of the Universal Declaration of Human Rights, and more recently Roland Burke has published a valuable book on the role of postcolonial states in the development of the international human rights regime. See Susan Waltz, 'Universalizing human rights: the role of small states

Notable here is the priority newly independent postcolonial states gave civil and political rights, over and above the social and economic rights they are usually seen as emphasizing. When, in debates on the Universal Declaration, the Soviet Union tried to subordinate the former rights to social and economic concerns, India replied that it 'would never agree to restricting political rights in order to realize social aims, however notable those might be'.[85] Three years later, when the Soviet Union called for a single international covenant that would prioritize social and economic rights, India and Lebanon supported proceeding with two treaties. We have already seen that in negotiating the Indian Constitution, the Constituent Assembly clearly distinguished between these civil and political 'rights' and social and economic 'directives of policy', arguing that only the former were justiciable. In calling for two international covenants, India and Lebanon went one step further, insisting that 'the two groups of rights were not of equal importance, the full enjoyment of economic, social and cultural rights being... dependent on the assurance of civil and political rights'.[86] Together with leading Western powers, these states successfully overturned a prior UN decision and forced the drafting of two separate covenants.[87]

Postcolonial states were also at the forefront of efforts to ensure the universal application of international human rights norms, bringing them into direct conflict with the major Western powers. This was apparent in two controversial areas. The first concerned the attempt by the United States, with principal support from Australia and Canada, to have a federal state clause inserted into the two international covenants. Their reasoning was that in many federal states the central government did not have the authority to uphold all of the

in the construction of the Universal Declaration of Human Rights', *Human Rights Quarterly*, 23.1 (2001), 44–72; and Roland Burke, *Decolonization and the Evolution of International Human Rights* (Philadelphia: University of Pennsylvania Press, 2010).

[85] United Nations, *Yearbook of the United Nations 1948–49* (New York: UN Office of Public Information, 1949), p. 533.

[86] United Nations, *Yearbook of the United Nations 1951* (New York: UN Office of Public Information, 1951), p. 483.

[87] The former decision, which provided for one covenant encompassing both civil and political and economic and social rights, was contained in General Assembly Resolution 421 (V), 4 December 1950: A/RES/421 (V). It was overturned by General Assembly Resolution 543 (VI) on 5 February 1952: A/RES/543 (VI).

rights set down in the draft covenants; they fell instead within the jurisdiction of provincial authorities. The legal obligation of federal states
to uphold international human rights thus had to be limited with a
formal exemption. The push for a federal state clause was roundly
criticized by other states, however. In 1950 the Indian representative,
who had obvious reasons to be sympathetic to the concerns of federal
states, told the Third Committee of the General Assembly that 'the
United States should take responsibility for its importance in international affairs and consider amending its Constitution to enable it to
meet the growing demands of international participation'.[88] Addressing the same meeting, Pakistan's delegate said that it 'would be unjust
for some powerful States to hide behind the federal clause, thus depriving their signatures and even the covenant of any meaning'.[89] Three
years later, as debate dragged on, the representatives of the Domini-
can Republic, Egypt, Iraq, and Mexico argued 'that such a clause
was out of place in covenants on human rights, the universality of
which should be assured'.[90] The United States, Canada, and Australia
responded by claiming that 'to omit the federal clause would constitute an insuperable barrier to ratification of the Covenant by federal
states'.[91] To this, some states replied that including such a clause would
deter non-federal states from signing the covenants, fearing that they
would be assuming greater obligations than their federal counterparts.
Other states countered the United States by arguing that it was better
to have a strong treaty with few ratifications than a weak one with
more. While the possibility of a federal clause remained on the table
for the next decade, its proponents failed to overcome the opposition.
In fact, the final texts of both covenants are clear: 'The provisions of
the present Covenant shall extend to all parts of federal States without
any limitations or exceptions.'[92]

[88] Quoted in Normand and Zaidi, *Human Rights at the UN*, p. 405.
[89] Quoted ibid., p. 227.
[90] United Nations, *Yearbook of the United Nations 1953* (New York: UN Office
of Public Information, 1953), p. 385.
[91] Ibid.
[92] This is codified in Article 50 of the International Covenant on Civil and
Political Rights, 16 December 1966, At http://untreaty.un.org/cod/avl/ha/
iccpr/iccpr.html (accessed 8 Nov. 2012). And Article 28 of the International
Covenant on Economic, Social and Cultural Rights, 16 December 1966, At
http://treaties.un.org/Pages/ViewDetails.aspx?chapter=4&lang=en&mtdsg_
no=IV-3&src=TREATY (accessed 8 Nov. 2012).

The second area of controversy concerned Britain's proposal to insert a 'colonial clause' in the covenants, effectively limiting the obligations of imperial powers to uphold new human rights norms in their dependent territories. They argued that some of these territories had reached a level of self-government such that they, not the imperial metropoles, were the authorities responsible for upholding human rights. The metropoles should not, therefore, be bound legally to protect such rights within these territories. Speaking in favor of the clause, Britain, Australia, Belgium, Brazil, Canada, France, Greece, New Zealand, and the United States claimed that

some Non-Self-Governing Territories had reached a stage in their development toward self-government which placed them in a position to enact, through their own autonomous organs, the laws covering those matters covered in the draft Covenant, and that the metropolitan powers could not automatically adhere to the Covenant on behalf of such territories under their administration without consulting these legislative organs.[93]

Since the violation of civil and political rights was a key grievance of many anticolonial movements, it is not surprising that Britain's move met with hostility from postcolonial states, this time joined by China and the Soviet bloc. Addressing the Sixth Session of the Commission on Human Rights in 1950, Chile, China, India, Mexico, and Peru argued that a colonial clause 'would allow the possibility of discrimination, without the colonial people having any vote in the matter'.[94] In subsequent debates in the Third Committee of the General Assembly, opponents questioned whether any dependent territories actually enjoyed the purported level of self-government, and claimed that Britain's arguments were a thinly veiled attempt to avoid having to uphold the human rights of its colonial subjects. The Philippines described the proponents' arguments as 'specious' and Syria insisted that their 'only purpose, of course, is to prevent the application of the covenant on human rights to colonial territories'.[95] Such was the opposition to the proposed clause, that on 4 December 1950 the General Assembly passed Resolution 422 (V) instructing the Commission on Human

---

[93] United Nations, *Yearbook of the United Nations 1950* (New York: UN Office of Public Information, 1950), p. 525.
[94] Ibid., p. 522.
[95] United Nations, 'General Assembly, Third Committee, summary records', General Assembly Document A/C.3/SR.296, 1950, p. 169; and General Assembly Document A/C.3/SR.294, 1950, p. 153.

Rights to include the following article in both covenants: 'The provisions of the present Covenant shall extend to or be applicable to a
signatory metropolitan State and to all the territories, be they Non-
Self-Governing, Trust or Colonial Territories, which are being administered or governed by such metropolitan State.' While this wording
never appears in the final texts, the Resolution put an end to proposals
for a colonial clause and its intent is covered by Article 2.1 of the
International Covenant on Civil and Political Rights.

In addition to helping ensure the universal applicability of the international covenants, postcolonial states also worked hard to bolster
their enforcement mechanisms. Throughout the negotiations of the
Universal Declaration and the covenants, leading postcolonial states
argued consistently that the protection of human rights was an international concern which limited the domestic jurisdiction of states.
In the Third Committee's debate on the draft Universal Declaration,
Pakistan stated that 'it was imperative that the peoples of the world
should recognize the existence of a code of civilized behavior which
would apply not only in international relations but also in domestic
affairs'.[96] In a sadly prophetic statement, the Chilean representative
told the General Assembly that 'no one could infringe upon the rights
proclaimed in it [the Universal Declaration] without becoming an out-
cast from the community of states'.[97] These attitudes were reflected
in the position that postcolonial states took on the right of individuals and non-state actors to petition the United Nations directly on
human rights violations by their states, an issue that lay at the heart of
debates about implementation and enforcement. While the Soviet bloc
countries opposed all enforcement measures on the grounds that they
violated the domestic jurisdiction of states, and the United States and
Britain argued that only states should have the right to petition, leading postcolonial states insisted that individuals and non-governmental
organizations must have direct access to United Nations forums. After
unsuccessfully trying to have the right of petition enshrined in the
Universal Declaration, a coalition of small Western states and postcolonial countries pushed to have the right recognized in the International Covenant on Civil and Political Rights. Addressing the Third
Committee in 1953, Denmark, India, Iraq, Israel, Mexico, and Syria

[96] United Nations, *Yearbook of the United Nations 1948–1949*, p. 527.
[97] Ibid., p. 52.

argued that 'without the inclusion of provisions extending the right of petition to individuals, groups and non-governmental organizations, the whole value of the Covenants would be in question'.[98] The issue remained unresolved for over a decade, resuscitated in the final debates before the covenants were adopted by the General Assembly in 1966. Again, the lead was taken by postcolonial states. Nigeria put a motion that the International Covenant on Civil and Political Rights include an optional article giving individuals the right to petition, and when this was defeated in favor of a separate Optional Protocol (proposed by Lebanon), Nigeria produced the draft text that with minor revisions was adopted by the General Assembly alongside the two covenants.[99]

## Grafting the right to self-determination

'In the 1950s, 60s, and 70s,' Daniele Archibugi argues, 'the principle of self-determination was interpreted mainly as the right of peoples to become states, a reiteration of the conceptual and legal categories used to reorganize European society after World War I.'[100] While the first part of this is true – that it was about peoples gaining sovereign statehood – the second part misses altogether the conceptual reconstitution that the right to self-determination had to undergo in this period. As explained earlier, the idea of the right to self-determination emerged from World War II morally and politically bankrupt. The notion that it was a right of ethnically defined nations had been discredited by the Nazi Holocaust and was ill-suited to the needs of anticolonial struggles in the non-Western world, which had been formally excluded from its purview, and where the colonial peoples seeking independence were ethnically heterogeneous. If it was to be any use in legitimating the dissolution of Europe's empires, therefore, the right to self-determination had to be rehabilitated, its content redefined and its normative foundations reconstructed. It was in the negotiations of the international covenants on human rights that this process of rehabilitation took place.

[98] United Nations, *Yearbook of the United Nations 1953*, p. 386.
[99] Erik Mose and Torkel Opsahl, 'The Optional Protocol to the International Covenant on Civil and Political Rights', *Santa Clara Law Review*, 21.1 (1981), 275–6.
[100] Daniele Archibugi, 'A critical analysis of the self-determination of peoples: a cosmopolitan perspective', *Constellations*, 10.4 (2003), 494.

Between 1950 and 1960, postcolonial states successfully grafted the right to self-determination on to emergent international human rights norms, casting it as a necessary precondition for the satisfaction of individuals' civil and political rights. The connection between the two was first articulated in 1950 by Afghanistan and Saudi Arabia. Laying the groundwork for the eventual inclusion of the right to self-determination in Article 1 of both international covenants, they successfully moved a motion in the Third Committee of the General Assembly calling on the Commission on Human Rights to study 'the right of peoples and nations to self-determination'.[101] Frustrated with the commission's failure to initiate such a study, in 1951 the representatives of Afghanistan, Burma, Egypt, India, Indonesia, Iran, Iraq, Lebanon, Pakistan, the Philippines, Saudi Arabia, Syria, and Yemen, among others, called on the General Assembly to compel the commission to insert an article on the right to self-determination into the draft covenants. They argued that this inclusion 'would give moral and legal support to peoples aspiring to political and social independence and would be a valuable contribution to international peace and security'. More importantly, they contended that 'no basic human rights could be ensured unless this right were ensured'.[102] In response, the commission not only inserted the requested articles in both covenants, it asked the General Assembly to pass a separate resolution encouraging states to uphold the right. Adopted in 1952, Resolution 637 (A) explicitly tied the right to self-determination to individual human rights – 'the right of peoples and nations to self-determination is a prerequisite for the enjoyment of all fundamental human rights'.[103]

Not surprisingly, these moves were opposed by the imperial powers, backed by other Western states, including the United States. A collective right to self-determination had no place in covenants on individual rights, they argued, and establishing such a right contradicted the 'sacred trust' that the United Nations Charter placed on states responsible for non-self-governing territories, a trust that required the administering powers to nurture colonial peoples, raising them up to

---

[101] United Nations, *Yearbook of the United Nations 1950*, p. 529.
[102] United Nations, *Yearbook of the United Nations 1951*, p. 485.
[103] United Nations General Assembly, 'The Rights of Peoples and Nations to Self-Determination', A/RES/637 (VII), 16 December 1952, Preamble.

the point where they were ready for independence.[104] All of these arguments were rejected by postcolonial states. In particular, they insisted that the Charter's provisions on non-self-governing territories had to be interpreted in the context of Articles 1.2 and 55, the first of which upholds 'the principle of equal rights and self-determination of peoples', while the second mandates 'universal respect for, and observance of, human rights and fundamental freedoms'.[105] Moreover, they insisted that although Article 11 of the Charter invested administering powers with a 'sacred trust' to govern non-self-governing territories until they were ready for independence, this did not mean 'that they would be owned by such states'.[106] When it came to the vote, Resolution 637 (A) was adopted with forty states in favor, fourteen against, and six abstentions. Australia, Belgium, Canada, France, the Netherlands, South Africa, the United Kingdom, and the United States, among others, all voted against it.

Debate persisted throughout the 1950s. Having successfully placed the right to self-determination in Article 1 of the draft international covenants, postcolonial states turned to a series of related issues, notably establishing two United Nations commissions: the first to examine the right of nations to 'permanent sovereignty over their natural wealth and resources', the second to consider 'alleged denials or inadequate realization of the right to self-determination'. While the General Assembly established the first of these in 1958, the second never saw the light of day, with debate repeatedly postponed. As postcolonial states pursued this agenda, leading Western powers tried unsuccessfully to dilute the endorsement by the United Nations of the right to self-determination in the draft covenants. In response to the commissions sought by postcolonial states, they sought unsuccessfully to establish a rival commission to 'conduct a thorough survey of the concept of self-determination'.[107] They also advanced a series of arguments, each designed to undercut the notion of a 'right' to self-determination. They repeatedly asserted, for example, 'that the Charter of the United Nations did not go beyond recognition of the principle of

---

[104] United Nations, *Yearbook of the United Nations 1952* (New York: UN Office of Public Information, 1952), p. 441.
[105] Ibid., pp. 441–2.   [106] Ibid., p. 442.
[107] United Nations, *Yearbook of the United Nations 1958* (New York: UN Office of Public Information, 1958), p. 212.

self-determination, and they could not agree that a right was involved'. Postcolonial states responded, however, that the draft international covenants had clearly established that self-determination was a fundamental right.[108] A second line of argument concerned the relationship between the right to self-determination and the preservation of international peace and security, a primary mandate of the United Nations. In response to the initial proposal for a commission to examine 'alleged denials or inadequate realization of the right to self-determination', the British representative argued that 'self-determination was a political principle which might have to be subordinated, in its application, to other principles, in particular the maintenance of international peace. It would be impossible, he said, to find a solution which would be applicable in all cases.'[109]

Despite these attempts at rollback, by the end of the decade it was clear that postcolonial states had successfully rehabilitated the right to self-determination, cast in this manifestation as a necessary prerequisite for the recognition and satisfaction of individual human rights. The culmination of this process was the 1960 Declaration on the Granting of Independence to Colonial Countries and Peoples, generally considered the crucial United Nations resolution on decolonization. It not only begins by reaffirming 'faith in fundamental human rights, in the dignity and worth of the human person, and in the equal rights of men and women and of nations large and small', but Article 1 declares that 'subjection of peoples to alien subjugation, domination and exploitation constitutes a denial of fundamental human rights'.[110] The declaration's adoption reflects the numerical advantage postcolonial states had come to enjoy in the General Assembly, especially when they had the support of the Soviet bloc. The nature of its adoption suggests, however, that over the previous decade postcolonial states had achieved a normative revolution. As noted above, when Resolution 637 (A) was passed in 1952, most Western states voted en masse against it. But in 1960 many of the same states voted in favor of the declaration, and

---

[108] United Nations, *Yearbook of the United Nations 1957* (New York: UN Office of Public Information, 1957), p. 204.

[109] United Nations, *Yearbook of the United Nations 1954* (New York: UN Office of Public Information, 1954), p. 209.

[110] United Nations General Assembly, 'The Declaration on the Granting of Independence to Colonial Countries and Peoples', A/RES/1514 (XV), 14 December 1960, Article 1.

the remainder (including Australia, Belgium, France, Portugal, Spain, Britain, and the United States) abstained, unwilling to pay the reputational costs of opposing a declaration supported by 90 percent of UN member states.

## Conclusion

Between 1945 and 1970 the Asian, African, and Pacific pieces of the global system of sovereign states were put in place, with the bulk of new states in these regions gaining independence after 1960. This rapid and near simultaneous fragmentation of Europe's great colonial empires was in part the result of crises of legitimacy that unfolded within individual empires, but it was also the product of a more general crisis of legitimacy that befell the institution of empire itself. In the space of fifteen years, empire went from being a morally acceptable system of rule to a synonym for domination, a 'crime' in the words of General Assembly Resolution 2621. Newly independent postcolonial states brought about this delegitimation of empire by rehabilitating the right to self-determination, effectively portraying it as a prerequisite for the recognition and protection of human rights. By grounding the right to self-determination on the fundamental rights of the individual, they gave it universal foundations, breaking past links with civilizational achievement and ethnic homogeneity – self-determination was now a right held by all colonial peoples because all colonial subjects were human beings with basic human rights, recognition of which was incompatible with the persistence of imperial rule.

Delegitimating empire was not the only thing postcolonial states achieved, however. As we saw in previous chapters, for most of the history of struggles for individual rights it has been entirely normal to claim that you have fundamental rights like freedom of religious conscience and equal political representation because of your nature as a moral being, while simultaneously denying that other human beings meet this standard. Only through repeated political struggles has the realm of inclusion been pushed ever further outward to the point where after 1945 all human persons were, both theoretically and legally, included. These struggles were waged on diverse fronts by women, workers, religious minorities (or majorities), and others. But, as we have seen above, postcolonial states also played a key role in this universalization of general individual rights, contributing first to the strong international codification of civil and political rights and, second, to fighting the idea that there could be imperial zones of the international system in which such rights did not apply.

In contrast to the Spanish case, where the Latin American colonies gained *de facto* sovereignty before *de jure*, with post-1945 decolonization the latter permitted the former – international recognition of colonies' right to self-determination, and subsequent recognition of their status as sovereign states, facilitated the construction of state institutions and capacities. Several scholars have interpreted this as establishing a categorical sovereignty regime, in which old notions that sovereign recognition depended on meeting substantive measures of 'civilized' statehood were stripped away. We see this in Jackson's aforementioned argument about the advent of the 'negative sovereignty' regime, and it is also evident in George Schwarzenberger's claim that the right to self-determination rests on 'pristine sovereignty in the form of lawlessness'.[111] In a similar vein, Donnelly argues that self-determination meant 'a right of colonial territories to recognition as sovereign states within colonial borders. Considerations of justice were thus banished from decisions on membership of international society.'[112] Yet the paired rehabilitation of the right to self-determination and codification of international human rights norms described here problematizes such claims. Postcolonial states did indeed reject the notions that civilizational achievement or readiness for self-government were legitimate barriers to self-determination, and after independence many of these states vigorously opposed international efforts to scrutinize their often appalling human rights practices. But in reconstituting the right to self-determination, many of these very same states played a crucial role in building an international human rights regime that compromised sovereignty.

[111] George Schwarzenberger, *International Law*, vol. II: *The Law of Armed Conflict* (London: Stevens & Sons, 1968), p. 207.
[112] Jack Donnelly, 'Human rights: a new standard of civilization?', *International Affairs*, 47.1 (1998), 13.

# Conclusion

Have struggles for the rights of individuals affected the nature and dynamics of world politics? Yes, but not only in the ways commonly suggested. Scholarship to date has focused on the regulatory and constitutive effects of international human rights norms; on their cascading proliferation over time, and on their impact on national human rights practices, with transnational advocacy networks mobilizing international legal norms to alter the terms of political legitimacy, delimiting the scope of rightful state action.[1] Nothing in this book questions the importance or veracity of this research. What it does, however, is point to a deeper, structural effect of rights politics; to the impact of struggles for individual rights on the globalization of the system of sovereign states.

Over the course of three and a half centuries, the system globalized through a series of great imperial implosions, in which one or more empires fragmented into a host of successor sovereign states. The most important of these implosions were driven, in significant measure, by struggles for the recognition of general individual rights. In the Westphalian case, it was the struggle for liberty of religious conscience. In the Spanish-American case, the cause was equal political representation. And in the post-1945 case, subject peoples sought recognition of their fundamental civil and political rights. In each case, the emergence of new ideas about individual rights generated crises of imperial legitimacy by challenging the regimes of unequal entitlements that sustained imperial hierarchy. Initially subject peoples sought imperial reform – or rights within empire – but when the empires in question proved incapable of accommodating their new rights claims, they turned from

---

[1] Both rationalist and constructivist work has clustered within this broad framework. See, for example, Simmons, *Mobilizing for Human Rights*; and Risse, Ropp, and Sikkink (eds.), *The Power of Human Rights*, and Thomas Risse, Stephen Ropp, and Kathryn Sikkink (eds.), *The Persistent Power of Human Rights* (Cambridge University Press, 2013).

voice to exit, each time embracing the sovereign state as the institutional alternative empire.

The impact of these struggles on the structure of the evolving international order was profound. In the fifteenth century, prior to the conflagration ignited by the Reformation, the Holy Roman Empire was embedded within a heteronomous configuration of power and authority. From the seventeenth until the twentieth centuries, sovereignty was the prevailing organizing principle in Europe (and later in the Americas), but it was formally conjoined to the imperial rule of large sectors of the non-Western world. And from 1970 onward, sovereignty became the global organizing principle, licensing the division of the world into centralized, territorially demarcated states. In helping drive this three-phase transition, struggles for individual rights brought about fundamental changes in the spatial configuration of political authority. In doing this they also altered the prevailing structure of political agency. The formal hierarchical ordering of metropolitan and peripheral polities was replaced, in the final phase, by a global system of constitutionally independent, legally equal, sovereign states. And while diverse forms of hierarchy still characterize relations between juridically equal sovereigns, they are either informal, revealed in practices rather than declared principle, or the product of socially sanctioned distributions of special responsibilities.[2]

This concluding chapter explores some of the conceptual, theoretical, and analytical implications of the book's central argument.[3] I am particularly concerned with four issues: the relationship between individual rights and contentious politics, the light the argument sheds on agency in the construction of the international system, the implications for how we think about the nature, dynamics, and future of the liberal international order, and what the argument means for understanding the cultural politics of international human rights.

---

[2] See Mlada Bukovansky, Ian Clark, Robyn Eckersley, Richard Price, Christian Reus-Smit, and Nicholas J. Wheeler, *Special Responsibilities: Global Problems and American Power* (Cambridge University Press, 2012).

[3] A number of the implications discussed here draw on ideas that I have rehearsed in a number of earlier publications. See, in particular, Christian Reus-Smit, 'Human rights in a global ecumene', *International Affairs*, 87.5 (2011), 1205–18; and Christian Reus-Smit, 'On rights and institutions', in Charles R. Beitz and Robert E. Goodin (eds.), *Global Basic Rights* (Oxford University Press, 2009), pp. 25–48.

## Individual rights and contentious politics

In debates about human rights and world politics, consensus about international human rights norms is often taken to be the measure of whether ideas about individual rights matter. Skeptics deny the political veracity and normative standing of human rights by emphasizing their contested nature; by stressing the tension between such ideas and more base material interests, by emphasizing how alien human rights are to non-Western cultures, and by showing how they exist in diverse ideational universes, where rival beliefs and values often predominate. Advocates of human rights respond by pointing to the very real levels of international agreement on basic international human rights norms. Donnelly argues, for example, that norms codified in the Universal Declaration of Human Rights, especially those relating to equal concern and respect, now constitute 'principles that are widely accepted as authoritative within the society of states'.[4]

The level of global support for the concept of human rights, and for the norms set down in the major international legal instruments, is clearly important – if support is high, establishing the illegitimacy of rights-violating practices will, in all likelihood, be easier than if support is low. Yet the focus on levels of consensus misses an essential feature of the politics of individual rights, human rights included. General individual rights are inherently contentious and they breed contentious politics. Let me explain this in two steps.

First, the very idea of a general individual right is politically dynamic, capable in itself of generating division and controversy. The proposition that an individual can have a right simply because he or she constitutes an integral, fully developed moral being – a 'rational adult' in the political discourse of the Cortes of Cádiz – begs the crucial question of who, among all biological humans, constitute such beings. As we have seen, the earliest impulses were to define the zone of application narrowly, to see only a small subset of all humans as morally qualified. In the first of our three cases, for example, only Christians of certain confessions met the standard: Muslims, Jews, and heretics were outside the zone. Yet the perimeter of the zone of application is inherently unstable. Any attempt to differentiate between human beings

---

[4] Jack Donnelly, *Universal Human Rights in Theory and Practice*, 2nd edn. (Ithaca, NY: Cornell University Press, 2002), p. 38.

on the basis of their purported qualities as moral beings is necessarily subjective, and thus always open to challenge. And because rights are empowering, and their denial disempowering, there are always excluded persons, often constituting large sectors of a given population, with strong incentives to contest the boundary between inclusion and exclusion. This is what Spanish Americans were doing when they argued that Indians and freed slaves were individuals worthy of equal political representation, and what twentieth-century colonial peoples were doing when they sought equal civil and political rights within empire and when they pushed for the universal application of international human rights norms. These struggles to expand the zone of application are of a piece, however, with cognate struggles by unpropertied males, women, peoples of color, indigenous peoples, gays and lesbians, and many others, all of whom have fought for recognition as moral beings worthy of general individual rights.

Second, as suggested in Chapter 2, general individual rights are usefully conceived as power mediators; normative principles that materially weak actors can invoke to alter the power relationship between themselves and materially advantaged actors or institutions. When one appeals to a prisoner's right not to be tortured, one is invoking a principle of humane conduct to prevent actions that the prisoner has no material capacity to prevent. Rights, as Vincent argued, are 'a weapon of the weak against the strong'.[5] Because individual rights are power mediators, they come to the fore within, and are generative of, highly contentious politics. When rights are invoked to alter power relations, they challenge existing social and political hierarchies – hierarchies in which privileged actors are usually deeply invested. We saw this in each of our three cases, where the spread and mobilization of new ideas about individual rights brought into question the regimes of unequal entitlements that sustained imperial hierarchy. Rights claims, and the struggles they animate, provoke contention by confronting the prevailing terms of political legitimacy; by casting as unjust social institutions, relationships, and practices once considered morally acceptable, even desirable. Yet predominant actors and institutions seldom respond to such challenges passively; indeed they often compensate for losses of legitimacy by relying more heavily on their material capacities, frequently through heightened levels of coercion. After the failure of the

[5] Vincent, *Human Rights and International Relations*, p. 3.

Diets of Regensburg, Charles V turned to war in his efforts to reassert control of the Holy Roman Empire, and after returning to the Spanish crown in 1814, Ferdinand VII launched a series of savage wars to crush the American insurgencies and embryonic republics. As we saw in Chapter 5, in both Nigeria and India the British responded to the anticolonial movements with increased suppression. And even within the human rights forums of the United Nations, where efforts by postcolonial states to delegitimize the institution of empire could not be met with coercion, intense contestation characterized negotiations.

Yet it is through such contentious politics that the contours of evolving international social orders become most visible, even palpable. As noted in Chapter 1, when scholars want to show the existence of society among states, or to assess the qualitative nature of such society, they have focused, by and large, on settled norms and institutional practices. This was encouraged from the outset by Bull's oft-quoted definition, in which an international society is said to exist when a group of states 'conceive themselves to be bound by a common set of rules in their relations with one another, and share in the workings of common institutions'.[6] When one can see such rules and institutions, one knows society among states exists. It has also been encouraged by the tendency, discussed in Chapter 2, to see international society existing when sovereignty comes to be based on mutual recognition. Again, when one can see sovereignty resting on norms and practices of reciprocal recognition, society among states is thought to exist. This emphasis on settled norms as the marker and measure of international society is evident not only in the ongoing debate between pluralists and solidarists, a debate revolving around the qualitative nature of the norms and practices that bind the international social order together, but also in the debate between those who think international society exists and those who reject the concept. The standard move among skeptics is either to deny the existence of settled international norms altogether, or more commonly, to deny that such norms exist outside the Western, liberal core.

While international social orders are structured by settled norms and routinized practices, social and political life within such orders is also characterized by ongoing contestation. Indeed, it is contestation that often reveals what is most at stake in a given order, including

---

[6] Bull, *The Anarchical Society*, p. 13.

how legitimate political authority is distributed, and what the bounds are of legitimate political action. Contestation is also a window on the dynamics of social and political change, which are often obscured by an emphasis on settled norms and practices.

For example, if the sovereignty of states does indeed rest on mutual recognition, as I would certainly agree, then the preceding chapters bring into sharp focus the dependence of such recognition on substantive conceptions of legitimate statehood: divine right, level of civilization, and, in a more complicated way, the recognition and protection of fundamental human rights. They have also highlighted how expansion of the community of recognized sovereign states has been the product of struggle, generally from below. The rational process of incorporation highlighted by the English School was not a feature of the great waves of expansion; nor was the simple diffusion of world cultural norms emphasized by sociological institutionalists. Change came through concrete struggles that generated crises of legitimacy in individual empires and then in the institution of empire itself. These struggles did more than increase the number of recognized states, though. Preceding chapters have also shown how the great waves of systemic expansion brought with them fundamental changes in the substantive conceptions of legitimate statehood undergirding mutual recognition. Prior to the Reformation a legitimate state was a Catholic state, but both the Peace of Augsburg and the Westphalian settlement expanded this to include states of a number of Protestant confessions. Before the fragmentation of the Spanish Empire a legitimate state was an absolutist state, but the collapse forced the recognition of republics. And prior to 1960 a legitimate state was one that met the standard of civilization, but the rehabilitation of the right to self-determination stripped away this criterion.

## Agency and change

In conventional accounts of international change, the principal agents are great powers. Their material capabilities are said to give them greater influence over political outcomes, their number and relative power determine a system's polarity, establishing the structural conditions for conflict and cooperation, and transitions between rising and falling great powers are considered a principal axis of change. 'For more than three hundred years,' Kenneth Waltz writes, 'the drama of modern history has turned on the rise and fall of great powers.'[7] Yet the preceding chapters have told a drama-laden story of a major transformation in world politics – the globalization of the system of sovereign states – in which the principal agents were not great powers, they were actors normally written out of the narrative of international change, subject peoples struggling in diverse imperial settings, and newly independent postcolonial states working within the institutional framework of the United Nations.

As noted in the Introduction, it is common to distinguish between 'systems' and 'systemic' change.[8] The first occurs when there is a shift in organizing principles, from heteronomy to sovereignty, for example, or sovereignty to hierarchy. When such a shift occurs, we are said to have moved from one kind of international system to another. The second form of change – systemic change – occurs within a system, and is generally thought to involve a shift in polarity, from multipolarity to bipolarity, or bipolarity to unipolarity. In this book, and in *Moral Purpose* before it, I have been primarily concerned with systems change. But in *Moral Purpose* I broke such change down into two different forms: 'configurative' change, and 'purposive' change.[9] The latter takes place when there is a change in prevailing conceptions of legitimate statehood, when one set of understandings about the moral purpose of the state is displaced by another. A prime example of such change was the nineteenth-century shift from an absolutist conception of legitimate statehood to a liberal constitutionalist one. Configurative change, in contrast, occurs when there is a shift in organizing principle, when there is a transformation in the deep norms governing how power and authority are distributed among a system's diverse polities. Like others, I have to date seen the sixteenth- and seventeenth-century transition in Europe from heteronomy to sovereignty as the quintessential example of such change.

While the distinction between configurative and purposive change remains heuristically useful, preceding chapters suggest new ways of thinking about how these forms of change have unfolded historically. The first insight concerns timing. The proposition that the nineteenth

---

[7] Kenneth Waltz, 'The emerging structure of international politics', *International Security*, 18.2 (1993), 44.
[8] Gilpin provided the classic statement of this distinction in *War and Change*.
[9] Reus-Smit, *Moral Purpose*, p. 164.

century witnessed a major purposive change in underlying conceptions of legitimate statehood is not in question here – divine right was
displaced in this period by emergent liberal constitutionalist norms.
Our discussion poses a more serious challenge, however, for established notions of configurative change. The sixteenth and seventeenth
centuries did not witness a simple transition from heteronomy to
sovereignty, and not because sovereignty has forever been compromised or qualified. As we have seen, heteronomy gave way not to
sovereignty as an organizing principle, but to sovereignty conjoined to
empire. The sixteenth to twentieth centuries saw the balance between
sovereignty and empire shift toward the former, as individual empires
fragmented into successor sovereign states. Yet the hybrid principle
itself persisted until the second half of the twentieth century, replaced
only then by universal state sovereignty. From this perspective, configurative change looks less like a moment, often associated with the Peace
of Westphalia, than a process extending over four to five centuries.

This brings me back to the issue of agency, the second insight. The
long process of configurative change was punctuated and propelled
by crises within particular empires, in which imperial hierarchy was
rejected in favor of sovereignty, and in the final phase, by the delegitimation of the institution of empire more broadly. The principal agents
in this succession of crises and fragmentations were subject peoples. Far
from sitting on the sidelines as great powers engaged in 'competitive
decolonization', or being passive recipients or enactors of world cultural or international social norms, these peoples – led by local social
and political elites – embraced new ideas about individual rights, mobilized these in concrete struggles against the prevailing maldistribution
of entitlements, and pursued sovereign statehood when empires failed
to recognize their new rights claims. To a significant extent, therefore,
configurative change was change from below.

Yet in undermining the legitimacy of individual empires, and encouraging their fragmentation in multiple new sovereign states, subject
peoples also contributed to the purposive transition of the nineteenth
century. In *Moral Purpose* I attributed this change in international
norms of legitimate statehood to political revolutions and constitutional developments within major states. Once these developments
had taken root domestically, they were then transposed into the international realm, informing new liberal constitutionalist discourse of

legitimate statehood and appropriate institutional practices. I still see this as a principal engine of nineteenth-century purposive change, but preceding chapters reveal a second influence: the changing membership of the community of recognized states. As explained in Chapter 4, the implosion of the Spanish Empire brought a host of new republics into the system, diluting the influence of the absolutist powers. Old conceptions of legitimate statehood were thus caught in a pincer movement, squeezed between domestic political transformations, on the one hand, and the changing nature of the community of states, on the other. And since the agency of subject peoples was crucial in bringing about this latter change, it contributed as well to a reconfiguration of underlying norms of legitimate statehood.

Because this is an argument about the political importance of ideas, it falls within the broad rubric of constructivism. Yet it is not the conventional constructivist story of social norms shaping actors' identities, interests, and behavior through socialized logics of appropriateness. As new ideas about individual rights spread in each imperial context, and subject peoples accepted them as meaningful constructions of their rightful social and political entitlements, they encouraged new understandings of the self, informed new political interests, and licensed new forms of struggle. But these ideas were not established social norms, they were revolutionary; they challenged prevailing regimes of unequal entitlements. Even in the post-1945 case, where norms concerning individual rights were well established in the metropoles, the notion that they extended equally to colonial peoples was highly subversive. And at the international level, until the negotiation of the Universal Declaration and the international covenants on human rights, little in the way of human rights norms existed. This is a story of revolutionary ideas being mobilized to challenge the most basic norms governing the global distribution of power and authority. In this respect, the argument is a form of what Kathryn Sikkink usefully calls 'agentic constructivism', as it 'is concerned with how agents – that is, real people and organizations – promote new ideas and practices'.[10] Like the Argentinian activists Sikkink studies, subject peoples 'were not following any logic of appropriateness. They were being consciously and explicitly "inappropriate".'[11]

[10] Sikkink, *The Justice Cascade*, p. 237.    [11] Ibid., p. 238.

## The liberal international order

The rights featured in this book – to liberty of religious conscience, equal political representation, and civil and political rights more generally – are all part of a broader panoply of liberal freedoms, even if sixteenth-century expressions of the first of these were at best instances of what Skinner terms 'liberty before liberalism'.[12] Given the impact of these rights on configurative and purposive international change, one would expect them to have influenced how we think about the nature and development of the present liberal international order. Yet this has not been the case. Prevailing accounts neglect altogether processes of configurative change, taking the universal system of sovereign states as given. And with this significant blind spot, it is hardly surprising that individual rights, and the struggles they animated, receive little attention. Recognizing this dimension of change, along with the social forces that produced it, leads to a very different understanding of the liberal international order, however.

John Ikenberry presents one of the most influential accounts of the liberal international order. Bull famously defined international orders as purposive arrangements of states,[13] and Ikenberry adopts broadly the same position – international orders, he writes, are the settled rules and arrangements that guide the relations of states.[14] A liberal international order, he argues, is one that 'is open and loosely rule based. Openness is manifest when states trade and exchange on the basis of mutual gain. Rules and institutions operate as mechanisms of governance – and they are at least partially autonomous from the exercise of state power.' In its ideal form, 'liberal international order creates a foundation in which states can engage in reciprocity and institutionalized cooperation'.[15] International orders, in general, come in three forms, Ikenberry contends. There are balance of power orders, in which order is a byproduct of competition between great powers; hierarchical orders, which are 'organized around the domination of a powerful state'; and constitutional orders, that rest on rules and institutions that reflect the common interests and enlightened self-interest of the major powers.[16] Our present international order is a combination

---

[12] Quentin Skinner, *Liberty before Liberalism* (Cambridge University Press, 1997).
[13] Bull, *The Anarchical Society*, ch. 1.   [14] Ikenberry, *Liberal Leviathan*, p. 47.
[15] Ibid., p. 18.   [16] Ibid., pp. 55–62.

of the second and third of these: it is institutionalized and rule based, but it also rests on the power and authority of the United States – it is a 'liberal hegemonic order', he argues.[17] As will be clear from these definitional moves, great powers are considered the principal agents in the production and reproduction of international orders, and in the present order, the hegemonic agency of the United States has been crucial.

Here is not the place for a comprehensive assessment of Ikenberry's account.[18] Two observations are sufficient. First, Ikenberry defines international orders as arrangements of sovereign states, and understands this arrangement in terms of the prevailing architecture of settled rules and practices. Yet the arrangement of political units in an international order is more than the rules and practices that entwine them. It concerns how they stand in relation to one another; how they are differentiated, as Ruggie explained in his oft-cited critique of Waltz.[19] The way in which units are differentiated in a heteronomous order differs markedly from how they are differentiated in an order based on sovereignty. This is not simply an issue of classification, enabling us to distinguish between heteronomous, sovereign, or other kinds of orders. It is crucial for understanding fundamental change. So long as the arrangement of an international order is understood narrowly, in terms of its manifest rules and practices, only systemic change is visible – configurative change is off the radar altogether. It leaves us without even the most basic conceptual apparatus necessary to understand how the patterns of differentiation that characterize international orders emerge over time. While this is a problem for the analysis of all kinds of international orders, it is especially problematic for understanding the present liberal international order. The story of this order is not one of liberal rules and practices evolving within an established system of sovereign states, in which the differentiation of the constituent political units was settled. Indeed, as we saw in preceding chapters, at the very same time that the architecture of liberal rules and practices was being constructed under the hegemonic

---

[17] Ibid., p. 16.
[18] For a more detailed engagement, see Christian Reus-Smit, 'The liberal international order reconsidered' in Rebekka Friedman, Kevork Oskanian, and Ramon Pacheco-Pardo (eds.), *After Liberalism* (London: Palgrave, 2013).
[19] Ruggie, 'Continuity and transformation', p. 274.

leadership of Britain and then the United States, a profound configurative transformation was taking place, with the conjoined organizing
principles of sovereignty and empire eventually displaced by universal
sovereignty. More than this, the golden era of liberal institution building, from 1945 until the early 1970s, was also the most dramatic phase
of configurative change – embodied in post-1945 decolonization and
the delegitimation of the institution of empire.

Second, if we expand our conception of international orders to
include how their constituent political units are differentiated, and
if we see the development of patterns of differentiation as an important dimension of change, then agency in the construction of the liberal international order looks very different. As explained above, the
key agents in the universalization of the sovereign states were not
great powers. In fact, as previous chapters have demonstrated, such
powers have often been vigorous opponents of systemic expansion,
not least after 1945, when the liberal hegemon, the United States,
joined other Western powers in opposing colonial peoples' right to
self-determination. It was subject peoples, rather, who were the principal agents in the globalization of the system of sovereign states,
the structural core of the liberal international order. Yet their agency
contributed still further to the liberal institutional architecture of the
present order. Ikenberry argues that the institutional rules and practices of the liberal international order embody a number of liberal
commitments, including open markets, economic security, multilateralism, cooperative security, democratic solidarity, and human rights
and progressive change.[20] Great powers played crucial roles in the
areas of market liberalism, multilateralism, and cooperative security;
indeed, this is one of the arguments advanced in *Moral Purpose*. The
same cannot be said, however, for human rights. Ikenberry has little to
say on this subject, but what he does say attributes almost sole agency
to the United States.[21] But as Chapter 5 explained, newly independent
postcolonial states were key actors in the negotiation of the Universal
Declaration and the two international covenants, consistently prioritizing civil and political rights, leading on enforcement issues such
the individual's right to petition, and successfully opposing Western
efforts to undermine the universal reach of the new human rights norms
through the insertion of 'colonial' and 'federal' states clauses.

---

[20] Ikenberry, *Liberal Leviathan*, pp. 169–93.
[21] Only two pages of *Liberal Leviathan* are devoted to human rights and
progressive change. See pp. 190–1.

What does this mean for the future of the liberal international order? Space prevents an extended meditation on this question, but one observation is worth making. When considering the ongoing viability of the liberal international order, commentators place considerable emphasis on the robustness of American power. The assumption is that America's hegemonic leadership was crucial in constructing the order, that core liberal institutions have been sustained by American power, and that any decline in the relative capabilities of the United States may weaken the order's foundations. Nothing here questions the crucial role played by the United States in constructing and undergirding the liberal order, or that the order's future contours will be affected by patterns of American engagement. However, as the preceding discussion shows, the liberal international order was built by diverse hands. Scholars have long pointed to the key role other Western powers played in shaping post-1945 economic institutions, but with another institutional pillar of the liberal order – the human rights regime – crucial agents came from the postcolonial world. The order thus had multiple inputs, and some came from quarters commonly ignored or denied. Of course, not all actors who contributed to the liberal order's institutional architecture remained committed – the United States turned its back on several of its institutional creations (most famously the International Labour Organization in 1975 and UNESCO in 1984), just as authoritarian regimes in the postcolonial world have denied playing any role in the construction of the human rights regime. Yet the institutions of the liberal order have engaged and empowered a variety of new actors, some state, others non-state. China, India, and Brazil are deeply enmeshed in the global trading regime, and transnational advocacy networks mobilize international human rights norms. In addition to the varied agents implicated in the construction of the liberal order, therefore, diverse actors are now invested in its institutional rules and practices. Any reasonable assessment of the order's sustainability needs to take this complex web of commitments into account.

## The cultural politics of international human rights

The codification and mobilization of international human rights norms have been accompanied by a strong universalist discourse. Individuals have human rights simply because they are human, and given this, all individuals, as human beings, hold them equally and without exception. This reasoning has been challenged on numerous fronts, but most vigorously by those who see the idea of human rights as a distinctly Western construct. According to this 'cultural particularist' thesis, ideas and practices of human rights are not universal, they emerged first in Western cultures and societies. And even there, the skeptics argue, they were not deeply constitutive values that produced or generated these societies. In Chris Brown's words, 'they were a product of a particular kind of society, one in which the "state" operates constitutionally under the rule of law, is separated from "civil society" and the "family", and in which private and public realms are, in principle, clearly demarcated.'[22] Given these culturally specific origins, ideas and practices of human rights are not easily transplanted to other cultures and societies. It 'is implausible', Brown argues, 'to think that rights can be extracted from liberal polities, decontextualized and applied as a package worldwide'.[23] Views such as these have themselves been roundly contested. Some have reasserted natural law accounts of universal human rights, and others have argued that cognate ideas to human rights can be found in all of the world's great cultural traditions. A more common approach, however, stresses the actual consensus that now surrounds the core norms of the international human rights regime. Donnelly, as noted earlier, adopts precisely this position. Presenting what I shall term a 'negotiated universalist' argument, he claims that an 'overlapping consensus' now exists, in which 'most leading elements in almost all contemporary societies endorse the idea that every human being has certain equal and inalienable rights and is thus entitled to equal concern and respect from the state'.[24]

Both the cultural particularist and negotiated universalist positions catch elements of the evolving cultural politics of international human rights. The former is correct that ideas about human rights have Western roots and that the global order is characterized by great cultural diversity. The latter, however, is correct in emphasizing the origins of contemporary human rights norms in protracted international negotiations, much of which was explicitly and deliberately intercultural.[25]

---

[22] Chris Brown, *Practical Judgement in International Political Theory: Selected Essays* (New York: Routledge, 2010), p. 68.
[23] Ibid., p. 60.     [24] Donnelly, *Universal Human Rights*, 2nd edn., p. 51.
[25] See, for example, Mary Ann Glendon's account of the negotiation of the Universal Declaration in *A World Made New: Eleanor Roosevelt and the Universal Declaration of Human Rights* (New York: Random House, 2001).

Yet neither of these perspectives captures the full complexity of the cultural politics surrounding the globalization of human rights. The cultural particularist position rests on a static billiard ball understanding of world cultures, in which cultures are imagined as discrete, atomistic entities that stand in relations of relative power and mutual miscomprehension. In the negotiated universalist position, by contrast, culture is stripped down, reduced to a thin global veneer of negotiated norms. More importantly, both accounts generate anemic and distorted understandings of the culturally embedded politics that generated the present international human rights regime. For the cultural particularists it is reduced to hegemonic imposition and cultural domination; for the negotiated universalists, to the post-1945 negotiation of the principal international human rights instruments. Neither approach grasps the five-century-long relationship between general individual rights and revolutionary social and political change within the emerging global system, a process of which the international human rights regime is a part.

A more illuminating perspective was anticipated by John Vincent in his classic work *Human Rights in International Relations*. Ideas about human rights did emerge first in the West, he accepts, but their globalization was the result of protracted processes of international and transnational political and cultural engagement, and the outcomes of these processes are not easily reduced to either simple negotiation or hegemonic imposition:

> if the modernization which was associated at its outset with westernization continues, even in circumstances of relative western decline we may call it a universal social process in which it is difficult to identify the particular contribution of this or that culture. In this regard, the international law of human rights may be an expression of this global process, and not merely of the American law of human rights writ large.[26]

Vincent did little with this observation, but work in sociology on the development of 'multiple modernities', recently taken up by a number of International Relations scholars,[27] enables us to take it several steps further, connecting it with insights from previous chapters.

Since the fifteenth century, it is argued, a 'global ecumene' has developed that encompasses multiple and varied forms of modernity.

[26] Vincent, *Human Rights and International Relations*, p. 108.
[27] See, in particular, Peter J. Katzenstein (ed.), *Civilizations in World Politics* (New York: Routledge, 2009).

Modernity originated in the Judeo-Christian West, where a series of interconnected philosophical, economic, and artistic revolutions led to new ways of thinking about the nature of individuals, their relationship to the natural and social universes, and to the implications of all of this for the nature and constitution of legitimate political authority. These ideas did not globalize through simple processes of imposition or diffusion, however. The mechanisms of transmission were certainly European military and economic imperialism. Yet, as Eisenstadt explains, the modernity of the West was not a single or coherent whole: 'it was from its beginnings beset by internal antinomies and contradictions, giving rise to continual critical discourse and political contestations.'[28] And when non-Western peoples encountered this internally variegated modernity, they interpreted its constituent ideas and practices through their own cultural lenses, leading to 'the continuous selection, reinterpretation, and reformulation of these imported ideas. These brought about continual innovation, with new cultural patterns and political programs emerging, exhibiting novel ideologies and institutional patterns.'[29] Over a period of five centuries, this produced a dynamic, global ecumenical space, characterized by multiple forms of modernity, produced through centuries of interaction between Western cultural ideas and practices and those of other civilizational complexes.[30]

Individual rights, and the struggles they animated, have been at the core of this evolving global ecumene. To begin with, the idea of general individual rights, especially those we are said to hold simply by virtue of our humanity, is closely bound up with the rise of modern conceptions of the individual. As we saw in Chapter 3, for example, the idea that individuals have a right to liberty of religious conscience flowed directly from the Protestant reimagining of the individual as a particular kind of moral being, one capable of salvation through the autonomous exercise of faith alone. In addition to this, ideas about individual rights emerged, and received each of their important reformulations, within arguments about, and struggles over, legitimate political authority.

We have already seen how struggles over individual rights helped drive configurative changes in the organization of political authority within the evolving global ecumene – from empire within heteronomy,

---

[28] S. N. Eisenstadt, 'Multiple modernities', *Daedalus*, 129.1 (2000), 7.
[29] Ibid., 15.    [30] Katzenstein, *Civilizations in World Politics*, pp. 1–40.

through sovereignty conjoined to empire, to universal sovereignty. Yet these struggles took place within a complex field of global cultural engagement that conditioned not only the nature of the struggles, but also how we think about individual rights. The first of these effects is clearly apparent in the case of Spanish America. In the decades preceding the Napoleonic usurpation, French Enlightenment ideas about individual rights and legitimate political authority spread throughout Spanish America. But in the wake of the usurpation, it was an amalgam of old and new ideas that animated the struggle for imperial reform and then independence. New ideas about individual rights informed how Spanish Americans approached questions of political representation, but older Spanish understandings of sovereignty, and longstanding views about the Americas' separate relationship with the Spanish crown, brought these questions to the fore. Old ideas set the stage for new ones.

The second effect, concerning how we think about individual rights, is evident in the way in which struggles by subject peoples gradually expanded the zone of application of such rights. Over the past five centuries, struggles for the recognition of individual rights have been waged by many human beings, on many fronts. And each time, this has involved expanding the community of individuals deemed worthy of the desired rights. But as previous chapters have shown, this pushing and shoving at the boundaries of inclusion and exclusion has changed the meaning of rights. Nowhere is this more apparent than in the post-1945 case. Between 1945 and 1960, newly independent postcolonial states of diverse cultural backgrounds successfully rehabilitated the collective right of self-determination by casting it as a necessary prerequisite for the recognition of human rights. But in doing so they played a key role in the negotiation of the major international human rights instruments. This was more than simple codification, however. In opposing colonial peoples' right to self-determination, and in trying to insert a colonial exclusion into the international covenants, leading Western states sought to exclude colonial peoples from the zone of application of emerging human rights norms. But by establishing self-determination as a right of all colonial peoples, and by preventing the construction of formal zones of imperial exclusion, newly independent postcolonial states universalized general individual rights, bringing all human beings within the zone of application. This was more than expanding the tent, though. Meanings changed; the centuries old conjunction between level of civilization and moral and political entitlement was broken. General individual rights were 'human'ized.

## On the threshold of liberty

On the cover of this book is reproduced René Magritte's surrealist work *On the Threshold of Liberty*. Magritte is renowned for his poetic approach to imagery, for cultivating a sense of mystery by placing familiar objects in unfamiliar places, disparate images on a single canvas. He denied any symbolic significance for his works; their meaning was meant to be puzzling. Yet when I first saw this work in the Art Institute of Chicago, it seemed laden with meaning. The very title resonated with a central concern of this book – the repeated historical struggles for the recognition of individual rights – and the conjoined images of the female body and a cannon, ordered among snippets of nature, urbanity, blue sky, and exercises in abstraction, conveyed, to me at least, the precarious relationship between the integrity and security of the human person and institutions of political power.

It is on this precarious and unstable relationship that I want to conclude. I argued in Chapter 2 that individual rights are institutionally dependent; they require enabling political institutions for their recognition and protection. Without such institutions, they are forever vulnerable. The Westphalian, Spanish-American, and post-1945 cases are all stories of institutional failure; of the inability of imperial institutions to accommodate new claims for the recognition of general individual rights. In all three cases, subject peoples struggled first for imperial reform – for rights within empire – but when this failed, they turned to the sovereign state as the institutional alternative. The sovereign state promised a protective yet demarcated institutional realm, one characterized by a general regime of law in which all rights bearers would stand equally, but one that was insulated from transnational authorities. This escape from empire into the arms of the sovereign state led in time to the globalization of the system of sovereign states, culminating only in the last forty years.

Many sovereign states have proven less than optimal protectors of individual rights, though. From institutionalized forms of sexual discrimination and the unequal treatment of refugees, through the suspension of civil and political liberties in the name of national security, to tyrannical forms of authoritarian rule and massive violations of human rights, the promise of the sovereign state rings hollow in many quarters. As Barry Buzan observed in his classic work *Peoples, States, and Fear*, the sovereign state stands as both the principal guarantor of individual security and the principal threat.[31] It is because of this that after World War II, in a process entwined with the globalization of the system of sovereign states, diverse actors pushed for the development of international human rights institutions beyond the state, an example of what Ruggie termed the 'unbundling of territoriality'.[32] Considerable research now focuses on this process of international institutional development, and on its impact on state practices. But as this study has shown, this is but the second half of a much longer story. Before struggles for rights encouraged the unbundling of sovereign authority, they were deeply implicated in the development of the system of sovereign states itself. Their impact has been both order constitutive and order qualifying. Such is the generative paradox of rights and states.[33]

[31] Barry Buzan, *People, States and Fear: The National Security Problem in International Relations* (Chapel Hill: University of North Carolina Press, 1983).
[32] Ruggie, 'Territoriality and beyond', p. 171.
[33] For a long discussion of this paradox, see Reus-Smit, 'On rights and institutions'.

# Bibliography

Adas, Michael, *Machines as the Measure of Men: Science, Technology, and Ideologies of Western Domination* (Ithaca, NY: Cornell University Press, 1989).

Adelman, Jeremy, *Sovereignty and Revolution in the Iberian Atlantic* (Princeton University Press, 2006).

Afshari, Reza, 'On the historiography of human rights: reflections on Paul Gordon Lauren's *The Evolution of International Human Rights: Visions Seen*', *Human Rights Quarterly*, 29.1 (2007), 1–67.

Anderson, Benedict, *Imagined Communities*, 2nd edn. (London: Verso, 1991).

Anderson, Perry, *Lineages of the Absolutist State* (London: Verso, 1974).

Andrews, George Reid, 'Spanish American independence: a structural analysis', *Latin American Perspectives*, 12.1 (1985), 105–32.

Anna, Timothy, *Spain and the Loss of America* (Lincoln: University of Nebraska Press, 1983).

Archibugi, Daniele, 'A critical analysis of the self-determination of peoples: a cosmopolitan perspective', *Constellations*, 10.4 (2003), 488–505.

Arendt, Hannah, *Imperialism* (New York: Harvest, 1968).

Armitage, David, *The Declaration of Independence: A Global History* (Cambridge, MA: Harvard University Press, 2007).

Asad, Talal, *Formations of the Secular: Christianity, Islam, and Modernity* (Stanford University Press, 2003).

Asuto, Philip L., 'A Latin American spokesman in Napoleonic Spain: José Mejia Lequerica', *The Americas*, 24.4 (1968), 354–77.

'Atlantic Charter', 14 August 1941. At http://avalon.law.yale.edu/wwii/atlantic.asp (accessed 3 Oct. 2012).

'Augsburg Confession' (1530). At www.reformed.org/documents/index.html (accessed 13 June 2012).

Baker, Ray Stannard, *Woodrow Wilson and World Settlement*, vol. III (London: Heinemann, 1923).

Barnett, Michael and Duvall, Raymond, 'Power in global governance', in Barnett and Duvall (eds.), *Power in Global Governance*, pp. 1–23.

Barnett, Michael and Duvall, Raymond, 'Power in international politics', *International Organization*, 59.1 (2005), 39–75.

Barnett, Michael and Duvall, Raymond (eds.), *Power in Global Governance* (Cambridge University Press, 2005).

Barraclough, Geoffrey, *An Introduction to Contemporary History* (Harmondsworth: Penguin, 1967).

Beitz, Charles R. and Goodin, Robert E. (eds.), *Global Basic Rights* (Oxford University Press, 2009).

Belaunde, Víctor Andrés, *Bolivar and the Political Thought of the Spanish American Revolution* (Baltimore: Johns Hopkins Press, 1938).

Beller, Elmer Adolph, 'The Thirty Years War', in Cooper (ed.), *The New Cambridge Modern History*, vol. IV, pp. 311–12.

Bethell, Leslie (ed.), *Colonial Spanish America* (Cambridge University Press, 1987).

Bethell, Leslie (ed.), *The Cambridge History of Latin America*, vol. III: *From Independence to 1870* (Cambridge University Press, 1985).

Blair, Emma Helen and Robertson, James Alexander (eds.), *The Philippine Islands 1493–1803*, vol. I (Cleveland, OH: Arthur H. Clark, 1903). At www.gutenberg.org/files/13255/13255.txt (accessed 10 Oct. 2012).

Bodin, Jean, *Six Books of the Commonwealth* (Oxford: Basil Blackwell, 1967).

Boswell, Terry, 'Colonial empires and the capitalist world economy: a time-series analysis of colonialization, 1640–1960', *American Sociological Review*, 54 (1989), 180–96.

Boucher, David, *The Limits of Ethics in International Relations: Natural Law, Natural Rights, and Human Rights in Transition* (Oxford University Press, 2009).

Bouyer, Louis, *The Spirit and Forms of Protestantism* (London: Harvill Press, 1956).

Brading, David A., 'Bourbon Spain and its American empire', in Bethell (ed.), *Colonial Spanish America*, pp. 112–62.

Breuilly, John, *Nationalism and the State* (Manchester University Press, 1993).

Brown, Chris, *Practical Judgement in International Political Theory: Selected Essays* (New York: Routledge, 2010).

Bukovansky, Mlada, Clark, Ian, Eckersley, Robyn, Price, Richard, Reus-Smit, Christian and Wheeler, Nicholas J., *Special Responsibilities: Global Problems and American Power* (Cambridge University Press, 2012).

Bull, Hedley, *The Anarchical Society: A Study of Order in World Politics* (London: Macmillan, 1977).

Bull, Hedley, 'The emergence of a universal international society', in Bull and Watson (eds.), *The Expansion of International Society*, pp. 117–26.

Bull, Hedley, 'The revolt against the West', in Bull and Watson (eds.), *The Expansion of International Society*, pp. 217–29.

Bull, Hedley and Watson, Adam, 'Introduction', in Bull and Watson (eds.), *The Expansion of International Society*, pp. 1–9.

Bull, Hedley and Watson, Adam (eds.), *The Expansion of International Society* (Oxford: Clarendon Press, 1984).

Burke, Roland, *Decolonization and the Evolution of International Human Rights* (Philadelphia: University of Pennsylvania Press, 2010).

Burkholder, Mark A. and Johnson, Lyman L., *Colonial Latin America* (Oxford University Press, 1990).

Bushnell, David, 'The independence of Spanish South America', in Bethell (ed.), *The Cambridge History of Latin America*, vol. III: *From Independence to 1870*, pp. 95–156.

Buzan, Barry, 'From international system to international society: structural realism and regime theory meet the English School', *International Organization*, 47.3 (1993), 327–52.

Buzan, Barry, *From International to World Society? English School Theory and the Social Structure of Globalisation* (Cambridge University Press, 2004).

Buzan, Barry, *People, States and Fear: The National Security Problem in International Relations* (Chapel Hill: University of North Carolina Press, 1983).

Calhoun, Craig, 'Nationalism and cultures of democracy', *Public Culture*, 19.1 (2007), 151–73.

Cameron, Euan, *The European Reformation* (Oxford: Clarendon, 1991).

Central Intelligence Agency, 'The breakup of the colonial empires and its implications for US security', 3 September 1948. At www.foia.cia.gov/ sites/default/files/document_conversions/89801/DOC_0001166383.pdf (accessed 25 Sept. 2012).

Chase-Dunn, Christopher and Rubinson, Richard, 'Toward a structural perspective on the world-system', *Politics and Society*, 7.4 (1979), 453–76.

Chiaramonte, José Carlos, 'The principle of consent in Latin and Anglo-American independence', *Journal of Latin American Studies*, 36.3 (2004), 563–86.

Church, William F. (ed.), *The Impact of Absolutism in France: National Experience under Richelieu, Mazarin, and Louis XIV* (New York: John Wiley & Sons, 1969).

Cobban, Alfred, *The Nation State and Self-Determination* (London: Collins, 1969).

Cooper, John Phillips (ed.), *The New Cambridge Modern History*, vol. IV: *The Decline of Spain and the Thirty Years War 1609–48/59* (Cambridge University Press, 1970).

'Covenant of the League of Nations' (1919). At www.unhcr.org/ refworld/pdfid/3dd8b9854.pdf (accessed 3 Oct. 2012).

Cox, Robert, 'Social forces, states, and world orders: beyond international relations theory', in Keohane (ed.), *Neorealism and Its Critics*, pp. 204–54.

Crawford, Beverley, 'Explaining defection from international cooperation: Germany's unilateral recognition of Croatia', *World Politics*, 48.4 (1996), 482–521.

Crawford, Neta C., *Argument and Change in World Politics: Ethics, Decolonization, and Humanitarian Intervention* (Cambridge University Press, 2002).

Crawley, C. W., 'French and English influences in the Cortes of Cadiz, 1810–1814', *Cambridge Historical Journal*, 6.2 (1939), 176–208.

Darwin, John, *Britain and Decolonization: The Retreat from Empire in the Post-war World* (London: Macmillan, 1988).

Darwin, John, *The End of the British Empire: The Historical Debate* (Oxford: Basil Blackwell, 1991).

Diaz-Plaja, Fernando (ed.), *La historia de Espana en sus documentos, el siglo XIX* (Madrid: Instituto de Estudios Politicos, 1954).

Dillenberger, John (ed.), *Martin Luther: Selections from His Writings* (New York: Anchor Books, 1961).

Domat, Jean, *Le Droit Public* (1697), reprinted in Church (ed.), *The Impact of Absolutism in France*, pp. 79–80.

Dominguez, Jorge I., *Insurrection or Loyalty: The Breakdown of the Spanish American Empire* (Cambridge, MA: Harvard University Press, 1980).

Donnelly, Jack, 'Human rights: a new standard of civilization?', *International Affairs*, 47.1 (1998), 1–23.

Donnelly, Jack, *Universal Human Rights in Theory and Practice*, 1st edn. (Ithaca, NY: Cornell University Press, 1989).

Donnelly, Jack, *Universal Human Rights in Theory and Practice*, 2nd edn. (Ithaca, NY: Cornell University Press, 2002).

Doyle, Michael, *Empires* (Ithaca, NY: Cornell University Press, 1986).

Dugard, John, *Recognition and the United Nations* (Cambridge: Grotius, 1987).

Dworkin, Ronald, *Taking Rights Seriously* (Cambridge, MA: Harvard University Press, 1978).

Eckel, Jan, 'Human rights and decolonization: new perspectives and open questions', *Humanity: An International Journal of Human Rights, Humanitarianism, and Development*, 1.1 (2010), 111–35.

Eckert, Andreas, 'African nationalists and human rights, 1940s and 1970s', in Hoffmann (ed.), *Human Rights in the Twentieth Century*, pp. 283–300.

Eisenstadt, Shmuel Noah, 'Multiple modernities', *Daedalus*, 129.1 (2000), 1–29.

Elliot, John H., *Empires of the Atlantic World: Britain and Spain in America 1492–1830* (New Haven: Yale University Press, 2007).

Elliott, John H., *Imperial Spain 1469–1716* (London: Edward Arnold, 1963).

Elliott, John H., 'Spain and America before 1700' in Bethell (ed.), *Colonial Spanish America*, pp. 59–111.

Emerson, Rupert, 'Self-determination', *American Journal of International Law*, 65.31 (1971), 459–75.

Evans, Peter B., Rueschemeyer, Dietrich, and Skocpol, Theda (eds.), *Bringing the State Back In* (Cambridge University Press, 1985).

Fazal, Tanisha, *State Death. The Politics and Geography of Conquest, Occupation, and Annexation* (Princeton University Press, 2007).

Fazal, Tanisha, 'State death in the international system', *International Organization*, 58.2 (2004), 311–43.

Feinberg, Joel, *Rights, Justice, and the Bounds of Liberty* (Princeton University Press, 1980).

Fisher, John, *Trade, War, and Revolution: Exports from Spain to Spanish America, 1791–1820* (Liverpool: Institute of Latin American Studies, 1992).

Forment, Carlos A., *Democracy in Latin America, 1760–1900*, vol. I (University of Chicago Press, 2003).

Forsythe, David, *Human Rights in International Relations*, 3rd edn. (Cambridge University Press, 2012).

Fraser, Nancy and Honneth, Axel, *Redistribution or Recognition?* (London: Verso, 2003).

Friedman, Rebekka, Oskanian, Kevork, and Pacheco-Pardo, Ramon (eds.), *After Liberalism* (London: Palgrave, 2013).

Fuentes, Carlos, *The Buried Mirror: Reflections on Spain and the New World* (Boston: Houghton Mifflin, 1992).

Gallagher, John, *The Decline, Revival and Fall of the British Empire* (Cambridge University Press, 1982).

Gann, Lewis H. and Duignan, Peter, *Burden of Empire: An Appraisal of Western Colonialism in Africa South of the Sahara* (New York: Praeger, 1967).

Gargarella, Roberto, 'The constitution of inequality: constitutionalism in the Americas, 1776–1860', *International Journal of Constitutional Law*, 3.1 (2005), 1–23.

Gautam, Om, 'Human rights in India', in Schwab and Pollis (eds.), *Toward a Human Rights Framework*, pp. 173–4.

Gellner, Ernest, *Nations and Nationalism* (Oxford: Blackwell, 1983).

'General Act of the Berlin Conference on West Africa', 26 February 1885. At http://africanhistory.about.com/od/eracolonialism/l/bl-BerlinAct1885. htm (accessed 21 Sept. 2012).

George, Matthew, 'Human rights in India', *Howard Law Journal*, 11.2 (1965), 286–94.

Gibson, Charles, 'Conquest, capitulation, and Indian treaties', *American Historical Review*, 83.1 (1978), 1–15.

Gilpin, Robert, *War and Change in World Politics* (Cambridge University Press, 1981).

Glendon, Mary Ann, *A World Made New: Eleanor Roosevelt and the Universal Declaration of Human Rights* (New York: Random House, 2001).

Goldsmith, Jack L. and Posner, Eric A. *The Limits of International Law* (Oxford University Press, 2005).

Gong, Gerrit, 'China's entry into international society', in Bull and Watson (eds.), *The Expansion of International Society*, pp. 171–84.

Graham, Richard, 'Review: Jorge I. Dominguez, *Insurrection or Loyalty: The Breakdown of the Spanish American Empire*', *American Political Science Review*, 76.1 (1982), 164.

Green, Vivian Hubert Howard, *Renaissance and Reformation* (London: Edward Arnold, 1969).

Greenfeld, Liah, *Nationalism: Five Roads to Modernity* (Cambridge, MA: Harvard University Press, 1992).

Greengrass, Mark (ed.), *Conquest and Coalescence: The Shaping of the State in Early Modern Europe* (London: Edward Arnold, 1991).

Griffin, James, *On Human Rights* (Oxford University Press, 2008).

Guerra, François-Xavier, 'The Spanish-American tradition of representation and its European roots', *Journal of Latin American Studies*, 26.1 (1994), 1–35.

Hager, Robert P. and Lake, David A., 'Balancing empires: competitive decolonization in international politics', *Security Studies*, 9.3 (2000), 108–48.

Hall, Rodney Bruce, *National Collective Identity: Social Constructs and International Systems* (New York: Columbia University Press, 1999).

Harris, Ronald Walter, *Absolutism and Enlightenment: 1660–1789* (London: Blandford Press, 1967).

Hart, H. L. A., 'Are there any natural rights?' in Waldron (ed.), *Theories of Rights*, pp. 77–90.

Heer, Friedrich, *The Holy Roman Empire* (London: Weidenfeld & Nicolson, 1968).

Heeren, Arnold Hermann Ludwig, *A Manual of the History of the Political System of Europe and Its Colonies* (London: Henry G. Bohn, 1846).

Heller, Agnes, *Beyond Justice* (Oxford: Basil Blackwell, 1987).

Herr, Richard, *The Eighteenth Century Revolution in Spain* (Princeton University Press, 1958).

Hinsley, Francis Harry, *Power and the Pursuit of Peace: Theory and Practice in the History of Relations between States* (Cambridge University Press, 1867).

Hirschman, Albert, *Exit, Voice, and Loyalty: Responses to Decline in Firms, Organizations, and States* (Cambridge, MA: Harvard University Press, 1970).

Hobbes, Thomas, *Leviathan* (Cambridge University Press, 1991).

Hobsbawm, Eric J., *Nations and Nationalism since 1780* (Cambridge University Press, 1990).

Hoffmann, Stefan-Ludwig (ed.), *Human Rights in the Twentieth Century* (Cambridge University Press, 2011).

Holland, Roy Fraser, *European Decolonization, 1918–1981* (London: Macmillan, 1985).

Holsti, Kalevi J., *Peace and War: Armed Conflicts and International Order 1648–1989* (Cambridge University Press, 1991).

Honneth, Axel, 'Redistribution as recognition: a response to Nancy Fraser', in Fraser and Honneth, *Redistribution or Recognition*, pp. 110–97.

Honneth, Axel, *The Struggle for Recognition: The Moral Grammar of Social Conflicts* (Cambridge, MA: MIT Press, 1995).

Hurd, Elizabeth Shakman, *The Politics of Secularism in International Relations* (Princeton University Press, 2008).

Ibhawoh, Bonny, *Imperialism and Human Rights* (Albany: State University of New York Press, 2007).

Ikenberry, John G., *After Victory* (Princeton University Press, 2001).

Ikenberry, John G., *Liberal Leviathan: The Origins, Crisis, and Transformation of the American World Order* (Princeton University Press, 2011).

'International Covenant on Civil and Political Rights', 16 December 1966. At http://untreaty.un.org/cod/avl/ha/iccpr/iccpr.html (accessed 8 Nov. 2012).

'International Covenant on Economic, Social and Cultural Rights', 16 December 1966. At http://treaties.un.org/Pages/ViewDetails.aspx?chapter=4&lang=en&mtdsg_no=IV-3&src=TREATY (accessed 8 Nov. 2012).

Ishay, Micheline, *The History of Human Rights: From Ancient Times to the Globalization Era*, 2nd edn. (Berkeley: University of California Press, 2008).

Jackson, Robert H., *The Global Covenant: Human Conduct in World Politics* (Oxford University Press, 2000).

Jackson, Robert H., *Quasi-States: Sovereignty, International Relations, and the Third World* (Cambridge University Press, 1990).

Jha, Munmun, 'Nehru and civil liberties in India', *International Journal of Human Rights*, 7.3 (2003), 103–15.

Katzenstein, Peter J. (ed.), *Civilizations in World Politics* (New York: Routledge, 2009).

Keal, Paul, *European Conquest and the Rights of Indigenous Peoples* (Cambridge University Press, 2003).

Keck, Margaret and Sikkink, Kathryn, *Activists beyond Borders* (Ithaca, NY: Cornell University Press, 1998).

Keene, Edward, *Beyond the Anarchical Society: Grotius, Colonialism and Order in World Politics* (Cambridge University Press, 2002).

Keith, Arthur Berriedale, *The Constitution, Administration, and Laws of the Empire* (London: W. Collins & Sons, 1924).

Keohane, Robert O. (ed.), *Neorealism and Its Critics* (New York: Columbia University Press, 1986).

King, James F., 'The colored castes and American representation in the Cortes of Cadiz', *Hispanic American Historical Review*, 33.1 (1953), 33–64.

Knop, Karen, *Diversity and Self-Determination in International Law* (Cambridge University Press, 2002).

Koggel, Christine M. (ed.), *Moral and Political Theory*, vol. I of *Moral Issues in Global Perspective*, 2nd edn. (Peterborough: Broadview Press, 2006).

Krasner, Stephen D., *Sovereignty: Organized Hypocrisy* (Princeton University Press, 1999).

Kupchan, Charles, *The Vulnerability of Empire* (Ithaca, NY: Cornell University Press, 1996).

Lake, David A., *Hierarchy in International Relations* (Ithaca, NY: Cornell University Press, 2009).

'Las Capitulaciones de Santa Fe', 17 April 1492. At http://webs.advance. com.ar/pfernando/DocsIglLA/CapsSantaFe.htm (accessed 10 Oct. 2012).

Lauren, Paul Gordon, *The Evolution of International Human Rights: Visions Seen*, 3rd edn. (Philadelphia: University of Pennsylvania Press, 2011).

Lecler, Joseph, *Toleration and the Reformation*, vol. I (New York: Association Press, 1960).

Lenin, Vladimir I., *Collected Works*, vol. XX (Moscow: Progress Publishers, 1964).

Lenin, Vladimir I., 'The right of nations to self-determination', in Lenin, *Collected Works*, vol. XX, p. 387.

Liss, Peggy, *Atlantic Empires: The Network of Trade and Revolution, 1713–1826* (Baltimore: Johns Hopkins University Press, 1982).

Locke, John, *Two Treatises of Government* (Cambridge University Press, 1988).

Louis, William Roger and Robinson, Ronald, 'The Imperialism of Decolonization', *Journal of Imperial and Commonwealth History*, 22.3 (1994), 462–511.

Low, Donald Anthony, *Eclipse of Empire* (Cambridge University Press, 1993).

Luther, Martin, 'Address to the nobility of the German nation' (1520). At www.fordham.edu/halsall/mod/luther-nobility.asp (accessed 13 June 2012).

Luther, Martin, 'Secular authority: to what extent should it be obeyed' (1523), reprinted in Dillenberger (ed.), *Martin Luther: Selections*, pp. 363–402.

Lynch, John, *Bourbon Spain: 1700–1808* (Oxford: Basil Blackwell, 1989).

Lynch, John, *Spain under the Habsburgs*, vol. II: *Spain and America 1598–1700* (Oxford: Basil Blackwell, 1969).

Lynch, John, *The Spanish American Revolutions: 1808–1826*, 2nd edn. (New York: Norton, 1986).

Martin, Cheryl English, 'Reform, trade, and insurrection in the Spanish Empire', *Latin American Research Review*, 19.3 (1984), 199–200.

Mayall, James, *World Politics: Progress and Its Limits* (Cambridge: Polity Press, 2000).

Mehta, Uday Singh, *Liberalism and Empire: A Study in Nineteenth-Century British Liberal Thought* (University of Chicago Press, 1999).

Meyer, John W., Boli, John, and Thomas, George M., 'Ontology and rationalization in the Western account', in Thomas et al. (eds.), *Institutional Structure*, pp. 12–37.

Meyer, John W., Boli, John, Thomas, George M., and Ramirez, Francisco O., 'World society and the nation-state', *American Journal of Sociology*, 103.1 (1997), 144–81.

Mill, John Stuart, 'A few words on non-intervention' (1859). At www.libertarian.co.uk/lapubs/forep/forep008.pdf (accessed 23 Sept. 2012).

Moeller, Bernd, *Imperial Cities and the Reformation: Three Essays* (Philadelphia: Fortress Press, 1972).

Morner, Magnus, *The Expulsion of the Jesuits from Latin America* (New York: Alfred A. Knopf, 1965).

Morner, Magnus, 'The expulsion of the Jesuits from Spain and Spanish America in 1767 in the light of eighteenth century regalism', *The Americas*, 23.2 (1966), 156–64.

Mose, Erik and Opsahl, Torkel, 'The Optional Protocol to the International Covenant on Civil and Political Rights', *Santa Clara Law Review*, 21.1 (1981), 271–332.

Moyn, Samuel, *The Last Utopia: Human Rights in History* (Cambridge, MA: Harvard University Press, 2010).

Muthu, Sankar, *Enlightenment against Empire* (Princeton University Press, 2003).

Nehru, Jawaharlal, *Glimpses of World History* (Bombay: Asia Publishing House, 1961).

Nexon, Daniel H., *The Struggle for Power in Early Modern Europe: Religious Conflict, Dynastic Empires, and International Change* (Princeton University Press, 2009).

Nexon, Daniel H. and Wright, Thomas, 'What's at stake in the American empire debate', *American Political Science Review*, 101.2 (2007), 253–71.

Normand, Roger and Zaidi, Sarah, *Human Rights at the UN: The Political History of Universal Justice* (Bloomington: Indiana University Press, 2008).

North, Douglass C., *Understanding the Process of Economic Change* (Princeton University Press, 2005).

North, Douglass C. and Thomas, Robert P., *The Rise of the Western World* (Cambridge University Press, 1973).

Nugent, Donald, *Ecumenism in the Age of Reformation: The Colloquy of Poissy* (Cambridge, MA: Harvard University Press, 1974).

Osiander, Andreas, 'Sovereignty, international relations, and the Westphalian myth', *International Organization*, 55.2 (2001), 251–87.

Parry, Clive (ed.), *Consolidated Treaty Series*, vol. I (New York: Dobbs Ferry, 1969).

'Peace of Münster of 30 January 1648 between Spain and the United Provinces', reprinted in Parry (ed.), *Consolidated Treaty Series*, vol. I, pp. 7–118.

Peterson, M. J., 'Political use of recognition: the influence of the international system', *World Politics*, 34.3 (1982), 324–52.

Phelan, John Leddy, *The People and the King* (Madison: University of Wisconsin Press, 1978).

Philpott, Daniel, *Revolutions in Sovereignty* (Princeton University Press, 2001).

Pitts, Jennifer, *A Turn to Empire: The Rise of Imperial Liberalism in Britain and France* (Princeton University Press, 2005).

Poggi, Gianfranco, *The Development of the Modern State* (Stanford University Press, 1978).

'Political Constitution of the Spanish Monarchy: promulgated in Cádiz, the nineteenth day of March 1812'. At www.cervantesvirtual.com/FichaObra.html?Ref=10794&portal=56 (accessed 1 Feb. 2008).

Pollis, Adamantia and Schwab, Peter, 'Human rights: a Western construct with limited applicability', in Koggel (ed.), *Moral and Political Theory*, pp. 60–71.

Pope Alexander VI, 'Inter caetera', 4 May 1493. Papal bull reprinted in Blair and Robertson (eds.), *The Philippine Islands 1493–1803*, vol. I, pp. 97–111. English translation by Thomas Cooke Middleton. At www.gutenberg.org/files/13255/13255.txt (accessed 10 Oct. 2012).

Rae, Heather, *State Identities and the Homogenization of Peoples* (Cambridge University Press, 2002).

Raz, Joseph, 'On the nature of rights', *Mind*, 93.370 (1984), 194–214.

Reus-Smit, Christian, 'Human rights in a global ecumene', *International Affairs*, 87.5 (2011), 1205–18.

Reus-Smit, Christian, 'Human rights and the social construction of sovereignty', *Review of International Studies*, 27.4 (2001), 519–38.

Reus-Smit, Christian, 'International crises of legitimacy', *International Politics*, 44.2–3 (2007), 157–74.

Reus-Smit, Christian, 'The liberal international order reconsidered', in Friedman, Oskanian, and Pacheco-Pardo (eds.), *After Liberalism* (London: Palgrave, 2013).

Reus-Smit, Christian, *The Moral Purpose of the State* (Princeton University Press, 1999).

Reus-Smit, Christian, 'On rights and institutions', in Beitz and Goodin (eds.), *Global Basic Rights*, pp. 25–48.

Reus-Smit, Christian, 'Struggles of individual rights and the expansion of the international system', *International Organization*, 65.2 (2011), 207–42.

Ringmar, Eric, *Identity, Interests and Action: A Cultural Explanation of Sweden's Intervention in the Thirty Years War* (Cambridge University Press, 2002).

Risse, Thomas, Ropp, Stephen, and Sikkink, Kathryn (eds.), *The Persistent Power of Human Rights* (Cambridge University Press, 2013).

Risse, Thomas, Ropp, Stephen, and Sikkink, Kathryn (eds.), *The Power of Human Rights* (Cambridge University Press, 1999).

Roeder, Philip G., *Where Nation-States Come From: Institutional Change in the Age of Nationalism* (Princeton University Press, 2007).

Ruggie, John Gerard, 'Continuity and transformation in the world polity: toward a neorealist synthesis', *World Politics*, 35.2 (1983), 261–85.

Ruggie, John Gerard, 'Territoriality and beyond: problematizing modernity in international relations', *International Organization*, 47.1 (1993), 150–1.

Sabato, Hilda, 'On political citizenship in nineteenth century Latin America', *American Historical Review*, 106.4 (2001), 1290–315.

Sassen, Saskia, *Territory, Authority, Rights: From Medieval to Global Assemblages* (Princeton University Press, 2006).

Schwab, Peter and Pollis, Adamantia (eds.), *Toward a Human Rights Framework* (New York: Praeger, 1982).

Schwarzenberger, George, *International Law*, vol. II: *The Law of Armed Conflict* (London: Stevens & Sons, 1968).

Seton-Watson, Hugh, *Nations and States: An Inquiry into the Origins of Nations and the Politics of Nationalism* (London: Methuen, 1977).

Shue, Henry, *Basic Rights: Subsistence, Affluence, and US Foreign Policy*, 2nd edn. (Princeton University Press, 1996).

Sikkink, Kathryn, *The Justice Cascade: How Human Rights Prosecutions Are Changing World Politics* (New York: Norton, 2011).

Sikkink, Kathryn, *Mixed Signals: US Human Rights Policy in Latin America* (Ithaca, NY: Cornell University Press, 2004).

Simmons, Beth A., *Mobilizing for Human Rights: International Law in Domestic Politics* (Cambridge, MA: Harvard University Press, 2009).

Simpson, A. W. Brian, *Human Rights and the End of Empire: Britain and the Genesis of the European Convention* (Oxford University Press, 2001).

Skinner, Quentin, *Liberty before Liberalism* (Cambridge University Press, 1997).

Skinner, Quentin, *Visions of Politics*, vol. I: *Regarding Method* (Cambridge University Press, 2002).

Spruyt, Hendrik, *Ending Empire: Contested Sovereignty and Territorial Partition* (Ithaca, NY: Cornell University Press, 2005).

Spruyt, Hendrik, *The Sovereign State and Its Competitors* (Princeton University Press, 1994).

Sripati, Vijayyashri, 'Human rights in India – fifty years after independence', *Denver Journal of International Law and Policy*, 26.1 (1997–8), 93–136.

Stoetzer, Carlos O., *The Scholastic Roots of the Spanish American Revolution* (New York: Fordham University Press, 1979).

Strang, David, 'From dependency to sovereignty: an event history analysis of decolonization, 1870–1987', *American Sociological Review*, 55.6 (1990), 846–60.

Strang, David, 'Global patterns of decolonization, 1500–1987', *International Studies Quarterly*, 35.4 (1991), 429–54.

Strayer, Joseph, *On the Medieval Origins of the Modern State* (Princeton University Press, 1970).

Suárez, Francisco, *Selections from Three Works of Francisco Suárez, S.J.* (Oxford: Clarendon Press, 1944).

Suárez, Francisco, 'A treatise on laws and God the Lawgiver' (1612), in Suárez, *Selections from Three Works*.

Suchman, Mark C., 'Managing legitimacy: strategic and institutional approaches', *Academy of Management Review*, 20.3 (1995), 571–610.

Tarling, Nicholas, *The Fall of Imperial Britain in South-East Asia* (Singapore: Oxford University Press, 1993).

Thomas, George M., Meyer, John W., Ramirez, Francesco, and Boli, John (eds.), *Institutional Structure: Constraining State, Society, and the Individual* (London: Sage, 1987).

Tilly, Charles, *Coercion, Capital, and European States: AD 990–1992* (Oxford: Blackwell, 1992).

Tilly, Charles, 'War-making and state-making as organized crime', in Evans, Rueschemeyer, and Skocpol (eds.), *Bringing the State Back In*, pp. 169–91.

Tilly, Charles and Tarrow, Sidney, *Contentious Politics* (Boulder, CO: Paradigm, 2006).

'Treaty of Münster of 24 October 1648' (Instrumentum Pacis Monasteriensis, IPM), reprinted in Parry (ed.), *Consolidated Treaty Series*, vol. I, pp. 319–56.

'Treaty of Osnabrück of 24 October 1648' (Instrumentum Pacis Osnabrugensis, IPO), reprinted in Parry (ed.), *Consolidated Treaty Series*, vol. I, pp. 198–269.

Trevelyan, George O., *George the Third and Charles Fox: The Concluding Part of the American Revolution* (New York: Longmans Green, 1912).

United Nations, *Yearbook of the United Nations 1948–49* (New York: UN Office of Public Information, 1949).

United Nations, *Yearbook of the United Nations 1950* (New York: UN Office of Public Information, 1950).

United Nations, *Yearbook of the United Nations 1951* (New York: UN Office of Public Information, 1951).

United Nations, *Yearbook of the United Nations 1952* (New York: UN Office of Public Information, 1952).

United Nations, *Yearbook of the United Nations 1953* (New York: UN Office of Public Information, 1953).

United Nations, *Yearbook of the United Nations 1954* (New York: UN Office of Public Information, 1954).

United Nations, *Yearbook of the United Nations 1957* (New York: UN Office of Public Information, 1957).

United Nations, *Yearbook of the United Nations 1958* (New York: UN Office of Public Information, 1958).

'United States Constitution'. At www.usconstitution.net/const.html (accessed 10 Oct. 2012).

Uribe, Victor M., 'The enigma of Latin American independence', *Latin American Research Review*, 32.1 (1997), 236–55.

'Venezuelan Declaration of Independence of 5 July 1811', reprinted in Armitage, *The Declaration of Independence*, pp. 199–207.

Vincent, R. John, *Human Rights and International Relations* (Cambridge University Press, 1986).

Waddell, David A. G., 'British neutrality and Spanish-American independence: the problem of foreign enlistment 1', *Journal of Latin American Studies*, 19.1 (1987), 1–18.

Waldron, Jeremy, *The Right to Private Property* (Oxford: Clarendon Press, 1988).

Waldron, Jeremy (ed.), *Theories of Rights* (Oxford University Press, 1984).

Wallerstein, Immanuel, *The Modern World-System*, vol. II (New York: Academic Press, 1980).

Waltz, Kenneth, 'The emerging structure of international politics', *International Security*, 18.2 (1993), 44–79.

Waltz, Susan, 'Universalizing human rights: the role of small states in the construction of the Universal Declaration of Human Rights', *Human Rights Quarterly*, 23.1 (2001), 44–72.

Watson, Adam, *The Evolution of International Society* (London: Routledge, 1992).

Watson, Adam, 'New states in the Americas', in Bull and Watson (eds.), *The Expansion of International Society*, pp. 127–42.

Weber, Max, *The Theory of Social and Economic Organization* (New York: Free Press, 1947).

Webster, Charles K., *Britain and the Independence of Latin America 1812–1830* (London: Octagon Books, 1970).

Weeks, Gregory, 'Almost Jeffersonian: US recognition policy toward Latin America', *Presidential Studies Quarterly*, 31.3 (2001), 490–504.

Wendt, Alexander, 'Collective identity formation and the international state', *American Political Science Review*, 88.2 (1992), 384–95.

Wheeler, Nicholas J., *Saving Strangers: Humanitarian Intervention in International Society* (Oxford University Press, 2003).

Whitaker, Arthur P., 'The dual role of Latin America in the Enlightenment', in Whitaker (ed.), *Latin America and the Enlightenment*, pp. 3–22.

Whitaker, Arthur P. (ed.), *Latin America and the Enlightenment*, 2nd edn. (Ithaca, NY: Cornell University Press, 1961).

Wight, Martin, *Systems of States* (Leicester University Press, 1977).

Wilson, Woodrow, 'Address to a Joint Session of Congress on the Conditions of Peace', 8 January 1918. At wwi.lib.byu.edu/index.php/President_Wilson%27s_Fourteen_Points (accessed 3 Oct. 2012).

# Index

Adelman, Jeremy, 145, 147
Afghanistan, 188
Afshari, Reza, 165
agency, change and, 198–201
Alexander VI, Pope, 117–18, 119, 133
Algeria, 157
Anabaptists, 96
ancient Greece, 13, 15, 76
Aquinas, Thomas, 119, 122
Archibugi, Daniele, 187
Arendt, Hannah, 173
Argentina, 110, 148
Argüelles, Agustin de, 139
Armitage, David, 2
atheists, 6
Atlantic Charter (1941), 153, 174, 180–1
Augsburg, Peace of (1555)
    on church unity, 82
    *cuis regio, eius religio,* 7–8, 69, 93, 94, 98, 101
    failure, 78, 90
    flaws, 98
    overview, 93–5
    pluralism, 10
Australia, 156, 183, 184, 185, 191
Austria, 110
Austro-Hungarian Empire, 161, 171

Barbados, 157
Belgium, 185, 191
Berlin Conference (1885), 154, 155, 156
Bohemia, 96–7
Bolivar, Simón, 110, 115
Bolivia, 20, 110, 148
Bonaparte, Joseph, King of Spain, 107, 114, 122, 130–1, 132
Brazil, 110, 185, 205

Britain
    *See also* United Kingdom
    Atlantic Charter (1941), 153, 174, 180
    empire, 26
        American colonies, 33
        Canadian colonies, 110
        collapse, 161, 162–3, 164
        Nigerian independence struggle, 179–81, 197
        response to anti-colonial movements, 197
    hegemony, 204
    Latin American independence and, 26, 29, 149
    United Nations and
        human rights covenants, 185–6
        self-determination, 190
        UN General Assembly Resolution 637, 191
Brown, Chris, 206
Bull, Hedley, 16, 17, 18, 31, 66, 67, 197, 202
Burkina Faso (Upper Volta), 157, 159
Burma, 188
Bushnell, David, 117
Buzan, Barry, 211
Byzantium, 79, 81

Calhoun, Craig, 52
Calvin, John, 84, 85, 88, 89, 92
Campillo y Cossio, José del, 126
Canada, 110, 183, 184, 185
Catholic Church
    *See also* Papacy
    Counter-Reformation, 8, 95–6
    crisis of Latin Christendom, 77
    heteronomy and special rights, 78–81
    Diets of Regensburg and, 7

# Index

235

For EU product safety concerns, contact us at Calle de José Abascal, 56–1°,
28003 Madrid, Spain or eugpsr@cambridge.org.